范存忠

1903—1987

字雪桥、雪樵，上海市崇明县人。1926年毕业于国立东南大学外语系；1931年获哈佛大学哲学博士学位后回国；1944—1945年在牛津大学讲学；1931—1949年间，历任原中央大学外国语言文学系教授、系主任，文学院院长等职；1956年后，曾任南京大学副校长、图书馆馆长、中国英国史研究会名誉会长等职。主要著作有《英美史纲》、《英国文学史纲》、《英国文学论集》、《中国文化在英国》、《中西文化散论》等。

《英国文学史纲》分十二章展现各个时期的文学代表人物和作品。作者从“英国文学史是英国人民的文学史”这个观点出发，站在哲学、历史及社会学的高度，讲述英国文学的历史发展，重点讨论剖析社会现实，反映人民情感、思想和意愿，而对社会起到进步作用的伟大作家与卓越作品，从而说明这些文学遗产在社会发展中的作用及一定的局限性。

英国文学史纲

A Brief History of English Literature

范存忠 著

译林出版社

图书在版编目(CIP)数据

英国文学史纲 = A Brief History of English Literature: 英汉对照 / 范存忠著. —南京: 译林出版社, 2015.11
(范存忠文集)
ISBN 978-7-5447-5712-6

Ⅰ. ①英… Ⅱ. ①范… Ⅲ. ①英国文学-文学史-英汉 Ⅳ. ①I561.09

中国版本图书馆CIP数据核字(2015)第192290号

书　　名	**英国文学史纲**
作　　者	范存忠
责任编辑	许　昆
出版发行	凤凰出版传媒股份有限公司 译林出版社
出版社地址	南京市湖南路1号A楼, 邮编: 210009
电子邮箱	yilin@yilin.com
出版社网址	http://www.yilin.com
经　　销	凤凰出版传媒股份有限公司
印　　刷	南京爱德印刷有限公司
开　　本	718毫米×1000毫米 1/16
印　　张	25.5
插　　页	4
字　　数	260千
版　　次	2015年11月第1版 2015年11月第1次印刷
书　　号	ISBN 978-7-5447-5712-6
定　　价	59.00元

译林版图书若有印装错误可向出版社调换
(电话: 025-83658316)

再版序言

《英国文学史纲》原是范存忠先生在1954年至1955年期间,在南京大学为英国语言文学专业英国文学课程撰写的英文讲授提纲。这部教材在英语界影响很大,同行们一致认为是一部简明扼要并具有特色的好教材,有些兄弟院校还将其翻印作为教材。为了使更多的英语爱好者受益,1981年,范先生采纳了同行们的建议,着手将这本教学提纲整理为英文专著,于1983年由四川人民出版社正式出版。为了便于更多的读者阅读,对范先生的英文版本添加了中文翻译。

范先生这本专著的一个特点就是把英国各个时期的代表作家和代表作品,放在其特定的历史和社会条件下进行考察,站在哲学、历史和社会学的高度来剖析;不只是讨论作家的文学成就,而是进而指出他们在当时的社会意义和历史局限性。这对英语专业的学生和英国文学爱好者去深入了解作家的创作背景,以及去分析和理解文学作品有着很大的帮助。正如范先生自己所指出的那样:“英国文学史是英国人民的文学史,这个课程就从这个观点来讲述它的发展,重点讨论揭露社会现实,反映人民群众的情感、思想和意愿,而对社会起进步作用的大作家与大作品，从而说明这份文学遗产在社会发展中的作用及其一定的局限性。”

范先生这本专著的另一个特点就是它别具一格的文体。英国文学的发展，从英国古诗《贝尔武甫》到萧伯纳的戏剧，纵横几千年的历史，范先生提纲挈领，在短短的12章里，将每个时期的文学代表人物和作品、其文学贡献，及在各自时期的历史和社会意义，剖析得清清楚楚。他的语言不仅简明扼要、深入浅出，而且生动有趣、引人入胜。

在译林出版社的努力下，范先生这本《英国文学史纲》重新再版了，作为范存忠先生的家属，我们感到由衷的高兴。我们衷心希望范存忠先生的这本专著，能对更多的英语专业学生和英国文学爱好者，有所裨益。

范家宁　王英

2014年7月

Contents

CHAPTER I

ENGLISH LITERATURE TO THE TIME OF CHAUCER

I Old English Poetry: *Beowulf*

1. Literature, Oral and Written The earliest literature of the English people, like that of any other people, was not written, but oral. Stories and legends passed from mouth to mouth and were enlarged and improved with each telling. The people participated in the making of this literature.

Naturally, such stories or legends were retold by those who could tell them best—and so each group came to have its own special story-teller called a scôp, which meant a Shaper or Maker of Songs. For it was in song, in a sort of chant, that these stories were told; any good story seemed the better for being sung or chanted. The scôp (i.e. poet) and also the gleeman (i.e. reciter) occupied honoured places in tribal and feudal society.

In early Saxon England, the scôps sang songs of the heroic deeds of their people. They improved on the stories with each telling, and sometimes weaved several different stories into a long narrative. Passed on for generations by word of mouth from one scôp to another, these stories came at last to be written down. But only a fraction of what had been produced was written down, and only a fraction of what was written down has been preserved. The longest and finest of extant Old English poems is "Beowulf", which has been called the national epic of the English people.

2. Story of *Beowulf* *Beowulf* is a tale of adventure, a tale of marvels. Beowulf, the hero, is a Geat, in the southern part of Sweden. He is a champion, a slayer of monsters. He hears that the people of Denmark have suffered from the attacks of a monster by the name of Grendel, who visits night after night the king's hall and carries away the sleeping warriors. With fourteen companions, he sets out for Denmark and offers to fight Grendel. In a terrible hand-to-hand struggle at night, Beowulf tears off an arm of the monster, who is mortally wounded and flees to his den beneath the sea.

This is the end of Grendel; but Grendel's mother comes to avenge her son. She renews attacks on the hall. Beowulf runs after her and follows her to a cave underneath the rushing waters of a dusty lake. There he meets her in combat. With a magic sword left by the giants of olden times, he hews off the monster's head. There, too, he finds the body of Grendel himself, and cuts off his head as well. He goes back to the Danish hall with the two hairy heads as trophies. The triumph is celebrated in feasting and song.

Beowulf goes home. He becomes king and reigns over his people for fifty years. Then it comes to pass that a fire dragon, stirred up from his long sleep, sets out to burn with his flaming fire everything that lies in his path. Beowulf, an old man now, fights the dragon single-handed. The dragon is killed, but Beowulf is mortally wounded in the combat. The poem ends with the funeral of the old hero and the lament of the people:

> So they mourned — the Geat people —
> His hearth comrades, bewailing their lords;
> Declared that he was of all kings on earth
> The mildest of men, and aye the gentlest,
> Kind to his people, craving most a good name.

3. Life and Manners Reflected in *Beowulf* The matter of *Beowulf* is a folk legend brought to England by the Teutonic tribes from their continental homes. The poem as we have it was composed between 700 and 800 by an English poet. It reflects the life and manners of many centuries from tribalism to early feudalism.

The main stories — the fights with Grendel, with Grendel's mother, and with the dragon — are evidently folk legends of primitive Teutonic tribes. Such tribes, as we have learned, lived along the northeastern coast of Europe from the mouth of the Rhine to the peninsula of Jutland. Back of their little settlements were almost impenetrable forests. In front of them was the stormy North Sea. They had to fight against the beasts. They had to struggle against the forces of nature, which remained mysterious and unknown. When they returned from their exploits and voyages, the warriors would tell stories of strange monsters that lived beneath the sea, or in the marshes and dark forests inland. They were brave; but they were terror-haunted. Such is the background of the marvellous stories.

But *Beowulf* is by no means a poem that reflects only primitive ages. It was written down in England when Christianity had been introduced—when English society was well on its way to feudalism. It reflects, too, the spirit of English life of the 7th and 8th centuries, presenting a blending of old folk ways with new, a welding of tribal heroism with feudal ideals. The ideal of gentleness is united to strength, and valour ennobled by virtue. The favourite theme of *Beowulf* poet is the loyalty of the thane to the lord. The thanes live in close relation to their lord. The lord leads and protects them among unneighbourly neighbours, and they fight and die for him. Feud and treachery, murder of kindred and usurpation are condemned as they were condemned in Saxon England of the 8th century.

Beowulf is a tale of tribal society retold in the dawn of feudalism. Beowulf the hero is more than a tribal chief; he is the embodiment of knighthood.

4. Language and Poetic Form The Old English language differs in many ways from Modern English. It is a language of strong stresses and many consonants. It is highly inflectional. Like Modern German or Modern Russian, it depends for its meaning on the endings of words rather than on the positions of words. Moreover, Old English is rich in synonyms, most of them being compound words of the kind that are met with in Modern German. There are, for instance, numerous terms for the sea or ocean; e.g. "seal-bath", "whale-path", "swan-road".

The basis of Old English verse is alliteration — i. e. the use of words beginning with the same consonant. Normally, each line contains four stresses, with a pause between the second and the third, thus dividing the line into two parts. Usually the first three stresses, or often two, of which one is always the third, are alliterative; e.g.

> Steap stanhlitho — stige nearwe.
> (Steep stone-slopes — paths narrow.)
> Tha com of more under mist-hleothum
> Grendel gongan; godes yrre bar.
> (There came from the moor under the mist-clouds
> Grendel going; God's ire he bore.)

The verse seems to us harsh and monotonous, but probably it was not. We cannot recall the sound of the original recital by the singer (scôp or gleeman) of the early days, as it fell on the ears of the young warriors in their lord's banquet hall.

II Old English Prose: Bede and Alfred

1. Bede and His *Ecclesiastical History* Bede (673—735) was reared in the monastery at Jarrow. He learned all that could be learned as a scholar, and had forty works, all in Latin, to his credit. His most well-known work is *Ecclesiastical History of the English People*, written in Latin and later translated into English.

Ecclesiastical History tells us more about early English life than any other work. It reviews the first conquests and settlements, the struggles of the little kingdoms, pagan and Christian, the coming of the Roman mission, the founding of the monasteries and the new culture. It aboundes in impossible miracles and marvels of the credulous, but it contains as well charming pictures of the life and manners of his age. Among the most often quoted passages is the account about the poet Caedmon.

Caedmon was a cowherd, an untutored man. He was well on in his humble life, and at merry gatherings was unable to sing and play like everyone else. Often he had slunk home in shame. One night he took refuge in a familiar stable. He fell asleep, when there appeared to him a stranger, saying:

> "Caedmon, sing me something."
>
> "I don't know how," answered Caedmon, "and that is just why I left the table and came out here — because I couldn't sing."
>
> Quick the answer, "Nay, but for me you have a song."
>
> "What am I to sing?"
>
> "Sing the beginning of all creatures."

And upon the word Caedmon all of himself began to sing verses in praise of God the Creator which he had never heard before. And so Caedmon became a poet. People said, "Heavenly grace had been conferred upon him by the Lord."

This vision of the cowherd is a characteristic attempt in early ages to explain the source of poetic inspiration. Similar legends occur in many lands and many literatures.

2. King Alfred and *Old English Chronicle* Alfred (849—899) was a good soldier and a remarkable scholar. For seven years he offered resistance to the Danes and succeeded in consolidating the kingdom of Wessex. For the education of his people, he had a number of Latin works translated into English. He prepared English versions of Bede's *Ecclesiastical History*, that his people might know their own past. To the same end he renewed and set going *Old English Chronicle* — a memorandum year by year of English events up to 1154 by later scholars.

The early part of *Chronicle* has no historical perspective: eclipses, comets, earthquakes and poor harvests rank as of equal importance with social and political events. But after 755 the *Chronicle* begins to convey a better sense of reality. Especially remarkable are the records of Alfred's resistance to the Danes. A few short specimens are given below:

> A. D. 875. That summer King Alfred went out to sea with a fleet, and fought against the forces of seven ships, and one of them he took, and put the rest to flight.

> A. D. 897. ... King Alfred commanded long ships to be built to oppose the "ashes" (Danish ships). They were full twice as long as the others; some had sixty oars, and some had more; they were both swifter and steadier, and also higher than the others. They were shaped neither like the Frisian nor the Danish, but so as it seemed to him they would be most efficient.

> A. D. 901. This year died Alfred ... He was king over the whole English nation, except that part which was under the dominion of the Danes, and he held the kingdom one year and a half less than thirty years. And then Edward, his son, succeeded to the kingdom.

The style of *Old English Chronicle* is simple, primitive, often repetitious and awkward, but at times it exhibits an elemental vigour. In the works of Alfred, we mark the beginning of English prose literature.

III Chivalry and Romance

1. Feudalism, Chivalry and Romance Feudalism, which had begun in late Saxon England, was strengthened and became more elaborate after the Norman Conquest. A new social hierarchy came into being: the feudal lords with the king at the top; the knights; the vassals; and at the bottom the villeins or serfs.

The knights were central figures in that society. They were pledged to do military service for their lords. In time of war, they would come riding in their armour and with their swords and lances, and with vassals, their bowmen, following them. In time of peace, they would arrange tournaments, in which they would compete with each other. This was known as knighthood.

But the knight should not only be loyal to his lord, and brave in combat, but also be exalted in sentiments and devoted to a lady. The love-cult originated in Italy and France as a revolt against monastic asceticism. The alliance of the knighthood of the north with the love-cult of the south produced an institution known as chivalry.

The institution of chivalry gave rise to an immense body of literature known as metrical romance, which arose in France in the course of the 12th century. French romance had two themes — prowess in arms and fantastic love. Much of it was written in England under the patronage of Norman queens and the Anglo-Norman aristocracy. Later, romance came to be written in English, but nearly all English romances were derived from French sources.

Of the romantic stories, some are about Greek and Roman warriors (e.g. Alexander the Great), some about the French king Charlemagne and his followers, some about ancient Britain. The best of all romantic stories are those associated with the name of Arthur, a legendary king of ancient Britain. They are known as Arthurian romances.

2. Language and Poetic Form During the two hundred years after the Norman Conquest, the English language underwent tremendous changes. The old inflections — alterations in the forms of words to show their relation to the rest of the sentence — began to die away. A synthetic language gradually became analytic. In vocabulary, it assimilated thousands of French words, colourful and sonorous. The bone and joints of the language, the frame and structure, remained English; but the loan-words gave it fullness, diversity and the grace of French song.

Under the French influence, a new verse form came into vogue. The alliterative metre of Anglo-Saxon verse gradually gave way to intricate patterns of rhyme and assonance. The regular form of verse, especially in the romances, was the eight-syllable or four-stressed rhymed couplet — the common metre of Old French poetry. As to alliteration, it ceased to be regular, though a few romances continued to be written in that measure. But it was different from the old metre, because the language had changed.

In general, the literary medium of the 13th and 14th centuries is almost a new language with new tunes.

The finest of English romances is *Sir Gawain and the Green Knight*, written down in about 1370 in the northwest of England — Cheshire or Lancashire.

3. *Sir Gawain and the Green Knight* King Arthur and his knights and ladies are feasting at the New Year, when there rides into the hall a huge green knight, gorgeously clad with a green axe, on a green horse. "Who will chop off my head with this green axe, and let me chop off his, at the Green Chapel, a year hence?" Young Gawain accepts the challenge, and swings a great blow. Across the floor leaps the head. The Green Knight picks up his head, gets on his saddle and rides away.

In November Gawain starts his journey — long, lonely and cheerless — among the wild mountains of North Wales. On Christmas Eve he comes upon a fair castle, where he finds a hearty welcome and luxurious comfort. The Lord of the Castle offers to direct him to the Green Knight, but prevails on him to stay in the castle until the New Year. In jest, they agree that for the following days each will give the other whatever he may obtain.

Each day the Lord is out hunting, and Gawain rests in his room. Each day the Lady of the Castle visits Gawain, encourages him to make love to her — and kisses him. Each night Gawain gives the host hearty kisses in exchange for the deer, the boar, the fox that the host brought back. But the third day he is weak enough to accept the Lady's silken girdle which is supposed to have the power to protect from wounds.

On New Year's Day, Gawain is taken to a desolate snow-filled hollow among the cliffs. Out rushes the Green Knight, axe in hand; the blow falls and wounds Gawain slightly. Gawain springs to defence. But the Green Knight coolly explains that he was no other than the Lord of the Castle, who had set his wife to tempt Gawain, and that Gawain's error in accepting the Lady's protecting girdle had cost him the little wound. Gawain, with mingled shame and high relief, makes his long, lonely way back to Arthur's court.

The story is shaped with a sense of narrative unity not often found in Arthurian romances. It contains all the traditional elements of metrical romance — marvellous adventure, courtly life and fantastic love-making. It depicts the knightly society, not as what it was, but as what it might be. Like other romances, it shows almost complete detachment from the life of man.

But the poem contains admirable descriptions of the scenery through which Sir Gawain wanders — the landscape not bred of fancy, but characteristic of Arthur's own Britain. The hunting of the deer, the boar and the fox is, too, depicted from reality.

IV Folk Tales and Folk Songs

1. Folk Tales While the metrical romances were primarily composed for the knights and ladies of the court and the castle, the folk tales were based upon folk lore and meant for popular consumption. They are much shorter than the romances. They run from beast fables to rather unsavoury incidents of bourgeois life — dull husbands tricked by clever wives, or greedy men gulled by jesting rogues.

Of the beast fables, *The Owl and the Nightingale* written not far from 1200, may be taken as an illustrative example. It is a long debate between the two birds. The owl, says the nightingale, is a bird of darkness, blind with raucous song, like a hen lost in the snow; but she, the nightingale, sings sweetly, usefully, and is beloved of men. The owl retorts that the nightingale is wanton, useless, chattering like a priest, local and provincial, while she, the owl, sings cheerfully, prophesying, advising, and edifying mankind. Even after death she is useful as a scarecrow! All night they debate. The nightingale claims the victory just as dawn breaks, and all about little songbirds burst into chorus in the nightingale's favour. But the wise wren calls for the verdict, and they all fly off to find a good judge.

> But how they sped, and what the doom,
> When they to Portisham had come,
> I know not, so I cannot tell;
> Here ends the tale, and so — farewell.

The general question is a familiar one — youth versus age, pleasure versus sobriety, the world versus the cloister. Humour is mixed with satire. The poem is an epitome of many motives in early medieval literature.

2. Folk Songs English songs had existed long before the Norman Conquest, but recorded songs are scanty. The reason is that folk songs are not learned by rote; they flit from ear to ear, anonymously, for a good song belongs not to the composer but to the people.

The song tradition continued after the Norman Conquest. We hear of a 12th-century priest who was kept awake all night while the villagers were singing and dancing in the churchyard. Next morning at service he would have begun, "Dominus vobiscum" (i. e. "The Lord be with you"), as usual, but to the scandal of the whole diocese he repeated what he had heard the previous night, "Sweet Heart, have pity!"

Among the scanty relics of the 13th century is *Cuckoo Song*, which kept in its cadence a measure of homely vigour and simplicity:

Summer is y — comen in!
    Loud sing cuckoo!
Groweth seed and bloweth mead,
    And springeth the wood now,
    Sing cuckoo! ...

And there were carols and rounds that sprang from folk dances; there were work-songs, especially of women spinning and sewing; there were "aubes", the parting dialogue-songs of lovers interrupted by the watchman's cry at dawn; there were songs of the ill-married, still questing wife; songs of spring; "chanson d'aventure", of the general formula:

I went walking the other day,
And saw a fair maid by the way...

The influence of Provençal poetry must be mentioned. For it was in Provence that such lyrics arose, and it was from Provence that such lyrics passed to northern France and Norman England. Of the Provençal nation, Engels remarks, "It was the first of the newly formed nations to have a cultured language. Its poetry served as an unrivalled model to all the romance peoples, and even to the Germans and the English."

CHAPTER II

CHAUCER AND THE 15TH CENTURY

I Langland, Wycliffe and the Lollards

1. Langland and *Piers Plowman* The 14th century, the age of the Black Death and the Peasant Rising, is well reflected in its literature. *Vision of Piers Plowman*, a notable poem of the age, has come down to us in three versions written in about 1363, 1377 and 1393 respectively. Authorship is uncertain, but it is commonly ascribed to one William Langland. The verse is alliterative, and the language—from the West of England.

The poem is a series of dreams — the dream being a popular device of medieval literature. The personages that appear in the dreams are largely personifications of abstract conceptions; e.g. Truth, Mead (Graft), False, Reason and Gluttony. But these figures are made real, and the scenes in which they move are indelibly vivid.

The poem is a satire, incise and bitter, upon the social vices of the day; e.g. the idleness of the noble, the profligacy of the rich monks and friars, the parasitism of the merchants. It also gives pictures of the lives of the poor peasants, fighting for their bare existence;

... the poor in the cottage
Charged with a crew of children and with a
  landlord's rent.
What they win by their spinning to make their
  porridge with
Milk and meal, to satisfy the babes —
The babes that continually cry for food —
This they must spend on the rent of their houses,
Aye and themselves suffer with hunger,
With woe in winter rising a-nights,
In the narrow room to rock the cradle,
Carding, combing, clouting, washing, rubbing,
  winding, peeling rushes.
Pitiful it is to read the cottage woman's woe,
Aye and many another that puts a good face on it,
Ashamed to beg, ashamed to let neighbours know
All that they need, noontide and evening.
Many the children, and nought but a man's hands
To clothe and feed them; and few pennies come in,
And many mouths to eat the pennies up...

The author had no intention of upsetting the social order, but he exalted the poor and oppressed and considered the toilsome peasant to be the nearest to divine truth and to salvation. The poem was extremely popular among the "lower" classes, and the name of Piers Plowman became a catchword during the Peasant Rising of 1381.

2. John Wycliffe and Anti-Clericalism John Wycliffe

(c. 1320—1384) came from the sturdy Yorkshire stock and was educated at Oxford, where he became Master and Professor. He had a belief in the common man, and wrote and worked against the oppressors of the common man. Everywhere he saw the abuses of the church — Popes, prelates, monks and friars, degenerate and unworthy with wealth and ease. He attacked the monastic ownership of lands, which in proper use should support the people at large. He also questioned the old doctrine of the church, and had the Bible translated into English, so that ordinary men could read and interpret and think for themselves.

Loud on every side rose the yell of "heretic". Wycliffe and his followers fled from Oxford, but he continued to preach and write and inspired an immense following known as Lollards, who went in barefoot poverty throughout the land, preaching and doing good to the common man. His doctrines were the doctrines of Protestantism before the Reformation.

Wycliffe's service to literature is great. Aside from learned works, he wrote two volumes of sermons — "plain sermons for the people". His prose is like him — straightforward, unadorned, solid in texture and in argument, and unusually vigorous. A few short specimens may be given:

> Lord, where is fredom of Christ, whenne men ben casten in siche bondage?
> (Lord, where is freedom of Christ, when men are cast in such bondage?)

> Therefore flee hypocrisye, and be scholere of treuthe; and outher seems that thou art, or be that thou semes.
> (Therefore, flee from hypocrisy and be learned of truth; and either seem

what you are, or be what you seem.)

3. John Ball and the Rising of 1381 John Ball was one of Wycliffe's "poor priests", preaching against the corruption of the noble and rich, and calling on the peasants to end this corruption. The essence of his preaching has been preserved in Froissart's *Chronicles*:

> My good friends, matters cannot go well in England until all things shall be in common; when there shall be neither vassals nor lords; when the lords shall be no more masters than ourselves. How ill they behave to us! For what reason do they thus hold us in bondage? Are we not all descended from the same parents, Adam and Eve? And what can they show, or what reason can they give, why they should be more masters than ourselves? They are clothed in velvet and rich stuffs, ornamented with ermine and other furs, while we are forced to wear poor clothing. They have wines, spices and fine bread, while we have only rye, and the refuse of the straw; and when we drink, it must be water. They have handsome seats and manors, while we must brave the wind and rain in our labours in the field; and it is by our labour that they have wherewith to support their pomp. We are called slaves, and if we do not perform our service we are beaten, and we have no sovereign to whom we can complain or who would be willing to hear us. Let us go to the King and remonstrate with him; he is young, and from him we may obtain a favourable answer, and if not we must ourselves seek to amend our condition.

This was not an appeal to the oppressors to mend their ways, but a call to action directed to the oppressed.

Ball had been thrown into Maidstone jail, from which he sent out secret messages, usually in rhyming couplets, calling for an armed rising of the people. In 1381 he was set free "by 20,000 men". Together with Watt Tyler and Jack Straw, he placed himself at the head of the peasants and started for London. At Blackheath he preached a sermon, giving as his text the old rhyme:

> When Adam delved and Eve span,
> Who was then the gentleman?

The gist of his sermon was the idea of equality before God, and partly equality of property. When the rising was crushed, Ball was arrested and hanged.

II Chaucer and His *Canterbury Tales*

1. Chaucer's Life and His Early Works The son of a wine merchant who had connections with the court, Geoffrey Chaucer (c. 1340—1400) began life as a page to a prince's wife. He saw military service in France during the Hundred Years' War and was a prisoner for a year. Before 1366 he married; his wife also had connections with the court. He served on various embassies in the seventies, including two to Italy. Later he held various posts, was an M. P., became Master of Works to the King, yet he experienced some years of poverty. He died in 1400, and was buried in Westminster Abbey, in what is now known as the Poets' Corner.

Several portraits of Chaucer have survived. He was rather short in stature, with a thoughtful face and downcast eyes — a shy, silent man, but shrewdly observant. He was a man of books as well as a man of affairs. After office hours, he would retire to his library of sixty volumes — a large library for the times — to read and write till all hours. With a good knowledge of Latin, French and Italian, he was acquainted with French and Italian masters, including Petrarch, Boccaccio and Dante, some of whose works he translated and adapted. These include romances of chivalry, love visions, folk tales, of which the most remarkable is *Troilus and Criseyde*, based upon Boccaccio's *Il Filostrato* (*The Love-stricken*). But his best known work is *Canterbury Tales*, with which he busied himself in the last dozen years of his life.

2. Plan of *Canterbury Tales* It was springtime, and people began to move about. One evening, thirty pilgrims stopped at Tabard Inn in Southwark (London) and were ready for a journey of sixty miles on horseback to the shrine of St. Thomas the Martyr at Canterbary. It was an odd assortment of people — high, humble, good, bad, lively, dull — and all classes were represented except the royalty and the poorest peasant. It was also a colourful company. Some were dressed in long gowns and plain hoods; some in short coats and tight-fitting "hosen", blazing with colour; men "wore their estates on their backs". Youth was "expressed in fancy". Both men and women of fashion wore enormous head-dresses of fantastic shape, like horns, turbans, or towers.

When supper was over, the Host of the inn proposed that, to beguile the journey, each of the pilgrims tell two stories on the way out, and two on the way back; that the Host himself act as manager and call on each in turn; and that the best story-teller be given a dinner paid by the rest of them. The Proposal was accepted, and story-telling was to start on the morrow.

Such, as outlined in the Prologue, is the plan of *Canterbury Tales* — a gigantic plan. Only a quarter of the tales were finished, together with a Prologue and some ten fragments. But these tales are sufficient to give a picture of English society in the 14th century.

3. The Canterbury Pilgrims Here is a list of the pilgrims, divided into four groups:

(1) Gentry

(a) Knight. A great warrior, a man of chivalry. ("And of his port as meke as is a mayde.")

(b) Squire. Handsome, well-dressed, educated in arms, poetry, drawing and etiquette.

(c) Franklin. An important land-owner, white-bearded, fond of good living. ("Ful ofte tyme he was knight of the shire.")

(d) Prioress. Young, of noble birth, fond of pretty clothes and dogs. (She may also be listed under Clergy.)

(2) Clergy

(a) Monk. A great hunter, fond of good living. ("A fat swan loved he best of any roost.")

(b) Friar. A merry rascal, familiar with women and taverns.

(c) Summoner. A drunken and scoundrelly official of the church court, who summoned people before the court for moral offences, but could be bribed to let them go.

(d) Parson. Poor but generous to the poor. ("He was a shepherde and no mercenarie.")

(e) Prioress's Nun and three Priests.

(f) Pardoner. A quack, yellow-haired, with falsetto voice.

(3) Liberal Professions

(a) Doctor of Physic. A humbug, grounded in astrology, making money out of the plagues.

(b) Sergeant of the Law. Knowing all the statutes by heart.

(c) Clerk of Oxford. Poor, lean, but learned, fond of books. ("And gladly wolde he lerne, and gladly teche.")

(d) Chaucer. Not mentioned in the Prologue.

(4) Tradesmen and Craftsmen

(a) Merchant. Prosperous-looking, with a long forked beard.

(b) Wife of Bath. A great cloth-maker, overdressed with a broad-rimmed hat and red stockings, who had married and buried five husbands.

(c) Haberdasher, Carpenter, Webber, Dyer and Tapicer. Prosperous townsmen. ("Wel semed ech of hem a fair burgess.")

(d) Cook. A good judge of ale. ("He coude roste, and sethe, and broille, and frye.")

(e) Shipman. A sunburned mariner, a smuggler. ("Of nyce conscience too he no keep.")

(f) Miller. Thick, heavy, hard-headed, red-bearded with a wart on his nose. ("Wel coude he stelen corn, and tollen thryes.")

(g) Plowman. Hard-worker, generous to the poor, though far from rich himself.

(h) Reeve. Manager of an estate.

(i) Yeoman. Brown, round-headed, a skilled archer.

(j) Harry Bailey, the Host. Large, jolly, who acts as guide and manager of the journey. ("Bolde of his speche, and wys, and wel y-taught.")

(k) Manciple. Steward to a college of lawyers, who was clever enough to trick them all.

4. Types and Forms of the Tales *Canterbury Tales* contains practically all the major types of medieval literature — romances of knights and ladies; folk tales, moral and merry; fabliaux, etc. Some are exalted or full of fun, others plain and tiresome, still others coarse and vulgar. They are all old — in the sense that they had been told before. And Chaucer was fond of old things:

> For out of olde feldes, as men seith,
> Cometh al this newe corn fro yere to yere
> And out of olde bokes, in good feith,
> Cometh al this newe science that men lere.

Sometimes, the Pilgrims tell stories against each other; e.g. the Miller and the Reeve, the Friar and the Summoner. Sometimes, stories form a series. Most notable is what has been known as the "marriage group". At first, the Wife of Bath describes her own experience of matrimony and maintains that happiness in marriage depends upon the acceptance of the wife's mastery. Then the Clerk tells how a woman submitted to her husband and was rewarded by happiness. Finally, the Franklin shows by his own story that domestic life should be governed by mutual tolerance and forbearance as well as confidence and love.

Chaucer's language is Modern English — and yet not quite modern. He wrote in the language from which Modern English is descended. He raised the language to a higher literary level by writing in it with polish and ease.

Chaucer's contribution to English versification is great. He established the heroic line — five stressed iambic — which has become the surpassing vehicle of English poetry. He was a master of the heroic couplet.

5. Chaucer as a Master of Realism *Canterbury Tales* is more than a collection of stories: it is a pageant of 14th century English life, a human comedy, in which a group of thirty people of various classes act their parts in such a way as to reveal themselves — their private lives and habits, their qualities good and bad. Much of this life is revealed not by the stories they tell but by their behaviour along the road.

Chaucer's portraits are life-like. It is likely that he had singled out of his wide world certain picturesque originals to start with. There was an actual Tabard Inn in Southwark, and an actual well-known innkeeper named Harry Bailey. There were a rascally reeve and a piratical shipman whom Chaucer knew ... But Chaucer's portraits are not only individuals sharply defined, but also "typical characters under typical circumstances" — a typical inn-keeper, a typical shipman, etc. As Gorky has pointed out, Chaucer was the founder of English realism.

In outlook, Chaucer represented the nobility, the rich merchants and the successful "civil servants". He was no Lollard. But no one laid bare more than he did in *Canterbury Tales* the corruption and all sorts of lawlessness of the clerics, particularly the summoner and the pardoner. And no one exposed more skillfully the greed, selfishness and faithlessness of the rising bourgeoisie — tradesmen, craftsmen, and men of liberal professions. The only members of the Canterbury group who come well out of the Prologue are the Knight, the poor Oxford scholar, the Parson and the Plowman. It is significant that with the last two characters Chaucer expressed unusual sympathy.

III The Popular Ballad

1. The Popular Ballad: Themes and Form The origin of the popular ballad has been a subject of controversy. Some hold that the popular ballads were composed at dances and other folk gatherings, not by any one author but by members of the group, each contributing a few lines, while others believe that the popular ballads, like all other poems, were made by individual authors. But whether we adopt the folk or the individual theory of authorship, the popular ballad remains folk literature, for the individual was but the mouthpiece of the many, and most of the ballads were not written down until they had passed through centuries of life on the lips of the people.

The English popular ballads flourished from the 12th to the 15th century. In this period, while the nobility were amusing themselves with romances of chivalry, the people were expressing their interests and ideals in poetry much simpler in form and more genuine in sentiment. The popular ballad reflects the life of the age as the people saw it.

All ballad themes are of popular interest: (1) Heroic deeds; e. g. *Sir Patrick Spens*. (2) Love tragedy in high life; e.g. *Bonny Barbara Allen*, *Lord Rondel*. (3) Domestic tragedy; e.g. murder of a father, as in *Edward*, or of a sister, as in *The Two Sisters*. (4) Folklore, in which fairies, ghosts, or monstrous creatures play a role. (5) Humourous ballads, which deal especially with the universal victim of the satirist, the henpecked husband.

The popular ballad is dramatic. The action moves breathlessly and vigorously from one picturesque or stirring episode to another. Dialogue is much used; many ballads are nothing but dialogues. Emotional effects are also secured by the liberal use of suspense and climax.

The popular ballad was almost always written in simple four-stressed stanzas (quatrains), often called "ballad metre":

> Come listen to me, you gallants so free,
> All you that loves mirth for to hear.
> And I will you tell of a bold outlaw,
> That lived in Nottinghamshire.

2. Robin Hood Ballads Most remarkable are the Robin Hood ballads, which took shape before 1400 and were popular in the 15th century. Robin Hood is a popular hero. Gathered around him is a band of outlawed yeomen — e.g. the freeborn among the peasantry. They rob the rich in order to give to the poor and to keep themselves alive. Their particular enemies are the upper ranks of the nobility — earls, barons, archbishops, bishops and abbots, and the royal officials. On the other hand, the outlaws show unusual tenderness for the peasants — their own folk. Thus says Robin to Little John:

... But look ye do no husband harm
   That tilleth with the plough
No more ye shall no gode yeoman
   That walketh by greenwood shaw [i. e. thicket]

The historical origin of Robin Hood and his band is to be found in the conditions of the perpetual struggles of the oppressed against their oppressors — the peasants against their manorial lords, against the local officials of the Crown, and against the royal judges in whose courts they could be placed outside the law.

There are some peculiar aspects in the Robin Hood ideology. One is Robin Hood's attitude towards religion. He appears to be devout and orthodox. He holds the Virgin Mary in great reverence and for her sake exempts all women from robbery on the road. But this does not prevent him from despoiling the men of religion, especially the abbots.

Another peculiar aspect is the attitude towards the King. In *Gest of Robin Hood*, the finest of Robin Hood ballads, the King appears as if he were an intermediary between the outlaws and his officials and judges — as if he were the outlaws' eventual benefactor. The King is conceived as above the contending classes of society. This was the prevailing illusion among the peasants of the day.

IV Forms of Early Drama

1. The Miracle Play (or Mystery) From the 13th to the 15th century, the miracle plays were enacted in some 125 towns and villages. They had for their subjects stories from the Bible; e. g. creation of the world, Noah and the flood, birth of Christ. They were usually produced on feast days such as Christmas, Easter, Corpus Christi Day. The production was under the charge of the local city government, which assigned the plays among the various trade and craft guilds of the town. On the feast days stages on wheels moved forth to their stations through the city, and people could pass from one to another and see as much of the plays as they liked. The performances often lasted for three days. Stage devices were crude, but costuming and make-up were matters of concern.

The miracle plays are not all religious. The stories from the Bible were usually adapted and dramatized by the common people and for the common people. The supernatural is often skilfully blended with the homeliest realism.

In the play entitled *The Shepherds*, originally performed by the crafts of Wakefield, there are significant touches of real life. It is night, on a bare hill side. Shepherds are lying on the ground. "Lord, how cold it is!" says one, "I am half frozen, stiff as can be, I have slept too long. And this rain, will it never stop? 'Tis a hard life, what with the taxes and the way the gentry use us. The other day came one of them to borrow my waggon and my plow. What could I do? I were better be hanged Than once say him nay." Another shepherd takes up the tale, saying that the weather is beastly and life is hard. And he says, "While we are out in this, and half starved, the rich have good food and comfortable beds."

This play, written in the latter part of the 14th century, reflects the condition of the age, when the peasants were ground down by special taxes and by the oppression of the gentry.

2. The Morality The morality appeared in about 1400 as an offshoot of the miracle play. Instead of biblical characters — Adam, Eve, Noah, Abraham, or Judas Iscariot — the writers of moralities gave such names to their characters as Mercy, Mischief, Conscience, Folly, Strength, Knowledge, Good Deeds. Naturally, Mercy used to say and do good things, Folly foolish things. And they contend for the possession of one's soul. In *Everyman*, the finest of moralities, Everyman is summoned by Death to make his journey to the grave. He appeals in vain to his worldly friends — Kindred, Beauty, Five Wits, Strength and Knowledge. He finds at last that only Good Deeds will accompany him.

It seems that the morality was a step backward in the evolution of the drama. While the miracle plays attempt to reveal character through speech and action (and that is the very essence of the drama), the morality contains little actual story and is but an endless speech-making on the part of each character and an endless sermonizing. Nevertheless, the morality is significant. Its motive is an old motive in literature, called the *psychomachia* (soul-fight). Being a struggle it contains high dramatic possibilities. The tragedies of Shakespeare and a lot of modern drama are essentially of this sort.

Besides, in the moralities the biblical stuff is thrown off, and the playwright will find his way to free invention.

CHAPTER III
THE RENAISSANCE

I Humanism in England

1. Engels on the Renaissance The Renaissance, which began in the 13th and 14th centuries, was a great cultural movement in Europe. It was brought about by the growth of productive forces in the wombs of feudal society, by the development of new forms of social relations. It signified the beginning of the disruption of feudalism.

In the Introduction to *Dialectics of Nature*, Engels has given the classical treatment of the epoch of the Renaissance:

> It was the greatest progressive revolution that mankind has so far experienced, a time which called for giants and produced giants — giants in power of thought, passion and character, in universality and learning. The men who founded the modern rule of the bourgeoisie had anything but bourgeois limitations. On the contrary, the adventurous character of the time inspired them to a greater or less degree. There was hardly any man of importance then living who had not travelled extensively, who did not command four or five languages, who did not shine in a number of fields ... The heroes of that time had not yet come under the servitude of the division of labour, the restricting effects of which, with its production of one-sidedness, we so often notice in their successors. But what is especially characteristic of them is that they almost all pursue their lives and activities in the midst of the contemporary movements, in

the practical struggle; they take sides and join in the fight, one by speaking and writing, another with the sword, many with both. Hence the fullness and force of character that makes them complete men.

2. The Humanists in England The Renaissance began in Italy. In the 13th and 14th centuries there arose progressive thinkers — Dante, Petrarch, Boccaccio, etc. They interpreted the master minds of ancient Greece and Rome — Homer, Socrates, Plato, Cicero — and brought them back to life. With their knowledge of the classics, they fought against the inertness and ignorance of the time, and against the religious fanaticism that hindered the free development of man. They worked for freedom and enlightenment. They were called "humanists".

In the 15th century several Englishmen got to Italy, caught what they could of the New Learning, and came back with their packs full of books. In the early years of the 16th century there appeared a group of humanists known as "Oxford Reformers" — William Grocyn, Greek scholar; Thomas Linacre, physician; John Colet, Dean of St. Paul's. All of them knew Greek, and through them new knowledge and new ideas from the ancient world and from Italy and France were diffused in Tudor England. Erasmus, the Dutch humanist, came and went, teaching Greek at Cambridge. He was the scholar of the age. His *The Praise of Folly* is a satire directed against the corruption and ignorance of the clergy.

The finest of the English humanists was Sir Thomas More (1478—1535), a close friend of Erasmus. Scholar, lawyer, M. P. and an eminent statesman, he was the only member of the Oxford Group who had the creative gift. His *Utopia*, which has become a world classic, may be regarded as a true prologue of the English Renaissance.

3. Thomas More's *Utopia* *Utopia* (1515—1516) was written in Latin and circulated throughout Europe. Its first English translation was made by Ralph Robinson in 1551. It consists of two books, which are consciously contrasted, and artfully play the old world against the new.

In Book I Hithloday the humanist-voyager tells us about the conditions in England. Among the social evils, he mentions the savagery of the laws (e, g. hanging for theft), the inordinate greed (e. g. enclosure and eviction of peasants), nationalistic ambition, selfish war, unjust taxation, and the unequal distribution of property. No particular remedies are suggested, but the underlying cause is given. That cause is the rule of private property, the private ownership of goods. "As long as private property remains, the largest and far the best part of mankind will be oppressed with an inescapable load of cares and anxieties." These remarks at the end of Book I are the focal point of the whole work.

In Book II we have a description of Utopia, an ideal commonwealth in some unknown ocean of the New World. All land in Utopia is in public possession. There is no private property, and no evils that private property brings with it. Labour is organized by the state, and so are production, consumption, trade and commerce. Nobody is idle, yet the working day is but six hours long, and "a great multitude of every sort of people, both men and women, go to hear lectures". And there exists complete religious liberty. More's conclusion is ironic: he cannot agree to all the things told by Hythloday, and he must confess that many things that exist in Utopia are rather wished for than hoped for in England.

4. More and Utopian Socialism *Utopia* is a great social document of the age of primitive accumulation. The author gives an analysis of the Tudor society, which he speaks of as "a conspiracy of the rich against the poor". He supports his assertion by facts based upon his own observation of the social developments in the world around him — the enclosures of land, the eviction of small tenants, the lessened demand for workers on the land, the impoverishment and misery of the masses. "Even a beast's life," he remarks, "seems enviable" as compared with that of the labourer.

More was a man of exceptionally wide intellectual vision. He was acquainted with Plato's *Republic*, about an imaginary commonwealth. He knew contemporary writings about the life of the American and West-Indian natives, who held their land and dwellings in common and made no distinctions between "mine" and "thine". At the same time he was deeply affected by the misery of the masses around him. He could not discover a force capable of removing the social contradictions he noted and condemned — the bourgeois order was just coming into being. He could only evolve out of his brain an imaginary commonwealth of social equality and community. His *Utopia* is a work amazing in its depth and discernment.

More has been acknowledged the father of utopian socialism and one of its greatest exponents. The very words "Utopia" and "utopian" come from his little classic.

It must not be thought, however, that More was completely modern; he was medieval in many respects. He applauded religious toleration in his *Utopia* and disapproved of asceticism, yet he himself was a submissive Catholic, who wore a hair shirt and who as Henry VIII's Lord Chancellor prosecuted the first protestants in England. When the Church of England was separated from Rome, he refused to conform and died a martyr to his faith.

II Non-dramatic Poetry

1. Songs and Sonnets The early English song tradition was re-enforced in the Renaissance. Medieval asceticism being out of mode, cultivation and enjoyment of sensuous earthly beauty found fuller expression in music and poetry. The second half of the 16th century, commonly known as the Elizabethan age, was an age of song — an age of notable musicians and composers of music (e. g. William Byrd, John Dowland, Thomas Campion); an age in which love of music and singing was more general, more widely diffused, than it had been in England at any other time before.

Elizabethan plays are studded with songs, many of which are often sung today, sometimes to the old airs to which they were written, sometimes to music written by modern composers; e.g. "Who Is Silvia" (from *Two Gentlemen of Verona*), "Where the Bee Sucks" (from *Tempest*), "Hark, Hark the Lark" (from *Cymbeline*).

The sonnet, an exacting form of verse in fourteen lines of iambic pentameter intricately rhymed, was perfected by the Italian poet Petrarch, and was introduced into English poetry by 1557. For the next half a century it was one of the most popular forms of verse. It was the custom for poets to compose "sequences" of sonnets — each sonnet complete within itself, but the whole series of sonnets more or less related in theme — dedicated to a beauty, bewitching and yet unfair or unresponsive.

Many are the moods in which the Elizabethan lyrics were written; but two are particularly characteristic of the age. One is a sense of the shortness of life and the yearning to catch the fleeting moment of happiness — Live today, for tomorrow we die! The other is the mood of escape — the dream of a simple country life (e. g. Marlowe's *The Passionate Shepherd to His Love*). These moods were inherited from Greek and Latin poets. But at the same time they reflected the spirit of the age — of the intensity and recklessness which marked the period of enterprisers and adventurers, and of escape from all sorts of turmoil characteristic of the age.

2. Spenser's *Faerie Queene* The longest non-dramatic poem of the Elizabethan period is Edmund Spenser's *Faerie Queene* (1590—1596) in six books, which everybody knows something about but very few have read through. The general purpose of the poem, as Spenser himself explains, "is to fashion a gentleman or noble person in virtuous and gentle discipline". The poem was dedicated to Queen Elizabeth, "the most excellent and glorious person".

The theme is developed in a curious way. Spenser gives no rules or precepts. He does not say that the gentleman or noble person ought to do this or ought not to do that. Instead, he takes us into a sort of dreamland where anything may happen and the most extraordinary things do happen. There are a series of knights, each of whom embodies in his adventures a virtue, a principle of right living. One represents Holiness; another, Temperance; still another, Chastity, etc. The knights in glittering armour often fight against scaly monsters and magicians — very much like what happens in metrical romance.

But the ideology of *Faerie Queene* is bourgeois rather than feudal. The knights as a whole represent England or the Church of England, and the evil figures and the difficulties and dangers that the knights encounter stand for Philip of Spain, Mary Queen of Scotland, or the Church of Rome. And the knights themselves are not so much adventurers of metrical romance as courtiers under Elizabeth.

The poem is remarkable for a soft haunting music that fits the life of the fairyland. The nine-line stanza with an intricate rhyme scheme (ababbcbcc) and a long last line, has since been known as the Spenserian stanza. It is the verse form of Byron's *Childe Harold's Pilgrimage*.

III Tudor Prose

1. Elizabethan Translations The Elizabethan age was an age of translations, through which the culture of the ancients, of Italy and France, entered into the growth of English literature. The list is long, but mention must be made of Tindale and Coverdale's versions of the Bible and Sir Thomas North's translation of *Lives of Noble Grecians and Romans* by Plutarch.

The English Bible was an ideological weapon of the Protestant Reformation. Like Wycliffe and the Lollards, the Reformers insisted that the Bible should not remain in Medieval Latin and monopolized by the

Pope and prelates, but must be made accessible in the language that the people understood.

In 1525 William Tindale (d. 1536) published his translation of the New Testament at Cologne. "If God spare me life," he said, "ere many years I will cause the boy that driveth the plow to know more of the Scriptures" than the theologians. His work was completed by Miles Coverdale, who published his translation of the Old Testament in 1537. Many other versions appeared in the next half the century. But the work of Tindale and Coverdale was to become the determining basis of the English version to this day. Written in a language exalted and yet easy to understand, it has entered into the bone and fibre of English prose and poetry.

Plutarch was a Greek writer of the first century. His *Lives* is a pageant of the Greek and Roman world. The great figures of the ancient times (e. g. Julius Caesar, Cleopatra, Mark Antony) are made life-like with a wealth of anecdotes. Sir Thomas North, whose version of "Lives" appeared in 1579, was not a mere translator: he recreated Plutarch in a language vigorous, lively and colloquial. It is extraordinary good reading — certainly the Elizabethans thought so. Many stories, many characters, and many a casual phrase in Shakespeare's Roman plays can be traced back to North's Plutarch.

2. Elizabethan Voyages of Discovery The Elizabethan age was the age of great geographical discoveries. English voyagers like Frobisher, Hawkins, Gilbert, Drake, and Sir Walter Raleigh brought back wonderful tales of strange lands, which became topics of excited talk in tavern, street, hall, cottage, or theatre.

In 1589 Richard Hakluyt, though he had never travelled, published his great collection of *Principal Navigations, Voyages and Discoveries*, which was later reissued and enlarged. It contains more than one hundred narratives of great voyages of discovery, English and foreign. The collection is uneven in quality: some show exceeding skill, others are crude and unfinished. But the romance of action runs through even the most pedestrian accounts of perils and profits. Hakluyt's aim was not so much to record deeds as to inspire them, to urge his countrymen to explore and colonize unknown countries, and to encourage trade with the distant parts of the earth. Michael Drayton, one of the poets, roused by the accounts of the voyagers, wrote:

> Thy Voyages attend,
> Industrious Hakluyt!
> Whose reading shall inflame
> Men to seek fame;
> And much commend
> To after times thy wit.

3. Elizabethan Prose Fiction Elizabethan fiction can be grouped into two categories: (1) romances for the "gentle reader" and (2) plain tales of bourgeois life. To the first category belongs John Lyly's *Euphues* (1579—1580). Euphues is an Athenian youth who goes to Naples, falls in love and is jilted, and then finds his way to England. There isn't much story in it, but there are endless speeches on love and manners. *Euphues* was written in a peculiar style known as "euphuism", which consists in the use of balanced sentences, alliteration, and figures of speech. Here are two specimens:

> Let my rude birth excuse my bold request.

> Although I have shrined thee in my heart for a trusty friend, I will shun thee hereafter as a trothless foe.

Akin to *Euphues* is Sir Philip Sidney's *Arcadia* (1580). Two princes, finding their way to Arcadia, encounter in the forest two princesses. They fall in love with them — and of course ultimately marry them. But there are disguises, mistaken identities, and knightly battles, which make a very long book. The style is a bit euphuistic. A maiden's blushing cheeks are described as "a little smiling, like roses, when their leaves are with a little breath stirred." Like *Euphues*, *Arcadia* was written as if the form were more important than the story.

More remarkable is the other category — tales of the unvarnished realities of life. One of such tales is Thomas Nash's *Jack Wilton* (1594), the story of a page, who follows his master from city to city of Europe and "sees life". This novelette started the fashion of carrying an adventurer through a succession of experiences all of which are real; involving him with all sorts of people, all of whom are true to life; and thus making a broad, truthful picture of the life of the times. Later novelists like Defoe, Fielding and Thackeray wrote in that tradition.

Equally interesting is a little book entitled *The Gentle Craft* (1597) by Thomas Deloney, a Norwich weaver. The book consists of three stories, one of which tells us "how Simon Eyre, being at first a shoemaker, became in the end Mayor of London". That simple, artless story is the first of a long line of novels, which depend for their interest upon the truthfulness of their studies of ordinary people and of their pictures of everyday life.

IV Predecessors of Shakespeare

1. Medley of Dramatic Forms The Tudor drama assumed various forms. Miracle plays continued to be popular until the Reformation, and Moralities lingered on well into the middle of the 16th century. Side by side with the late moralities, there arose another type of play called "interludes", of which the characters are social types rather than virtues or vices.

A typical interlude is John Heywood's playlet called *The Four P's* (c. 1530), in which a Palmer, a Pardoner, a Pedlar and a 'Potecary (apothecary) fall to arguing which can tell the biggest lie. The Pedlar acts as a judge. It is the Palmer who wins — for he solemnly states that in all his varied experience with the sex he has never seen a woman out of patience!

Meanwhile, through the revival of classical literature, the playwrights came into contact with Greek and Latin drama. From it they learned all important lessons in structure and style, more exact conceptions of comedy and tragedy, and from it they found an inexhaustible store of matter. They were taught the orderly division into five acts. They were taught the use of such stock characters as the rascally servant, the smart lover, the grumpy father, and the strutting military man. And they were shown the effective use of ghosts, the "chorus", and a kind of noisy rhetoric. Tragedies and comedies on Latin models abounded in the middle of the 16th century.

Miracle plays, moralities, interludes, classical plays, and popular mixtures of various sorts — such were the forms of drama in the early years of Elizabeth. Out of this medley, the drama of Marlowe and Shakespeare takes form.

2. Theatres, Actors and Audience In early days plays were enacted in the courtyard of the inns, where temporary stages were set up for that purpose. Certain old London inns housed performances so habitually as to become essentially playhouses.

The regular playhouses appeared in about 1576. They were of two types: private and public. The private playhouses, of which the Blackfriars was the first, were roofed, charging high prices, and having companies of boys for actors. The public playhouses — the Theatre, the Curtain, etc. — were regarded as centres of scandal. They were kept out of town, first to the north, afterwards south of the Thames. But their growth was rapid. By the end of the century there were eight of them — a surprising number for a town of hardly 200,000 inhabitants. It was a proof of the popularity of dramatic performances. The famous Globe—Shakespeare's theatre — rose in 1599.

The stage was almost bare. The curtain was put towards the back, not in the front as on the modern stage. Doors on either side gave access, but movable scenery was little used till the Restoration.

On this almost naked stage the actor's part had an unusual importance. His art was therefore carried to a high pitch. There were no actresses: women's parts were played by boys. Although they were almost outcasts from society, the actors not only enjoyed popularity with the people at large, but were patronized by the nobility. Some of them rose to great fame: the Burbages, father and son; Edward Alleyn, who created the leading parts in Marlowe's plays.

The audiences who crowded into the Elizabethan theatres represented every class and every trade. The "ordinary people" usually stood in the pit, the rich citizens and lords sat in galleries, and the mannerless coxcombs got on the stage, cracking nuts. The great mass of the audience was, however, made up of simple folk — curious, imaginative, and easily-moved.

3. Marlowe and the Renaissance Of the many dramatists before Shakespeare, the most gifted was Christopher Marlowe (1564—1593). Born as the son of a Canterbury shoemaker, Marlowe was trained at Cambridge, where he received the Master's degree, in 1587 he got to London, and for the next seven years he wrote seven plays and various poems. On a May day in 1593, he was mixed up in a tavern brawl and was stabbed to death. His life was brief but sensational.

Marlowe was a scholar, one of the truest of his time. He knew the classics, which he put to good use in his dramatic works. He had the Renaissance scholar's passion for truth, for fair play in intellectual disputes. He raised his voice in defence of alien races and alien creeds. Better a true Turk, he says, or a consistent Jew, than a faithless Christian.

It was for opinions like this that the bigots stigmatized him as "libertine" and "atheist".

Marlowe was the Renaissance incarnate — the embodiment of the sense of the infinite possibilities of mankind. Thus he says in the mouth of Tamburlaine:

> Nature that framed us of four elements,
> Warring within our breasts for regiment,
> Doth teach us all to have aspiring minds:
> Our souls, whose faculties can comprehend
> The Wondrous architecture of the world,
> And measure every wandering planet's course,
> Still climbing after knowledge infinite,
> And always moving as the restless spheres,
> Will us to wear ourselves and never rest,
> Until we reach the ripest fruit of all ...

Marlowe is known, among other things, for his "mighty line". Few poets have equaled the ability that he possessed of condensing much in little. Blank verse — rhymeless iambic pentameter — had been written before him, but in his hands it became the most expressive and the grandest of English metres.

4. Marlowe's Representative Works Of his seven plays, three stand out prominently: *Tamburlaine* (1587), *Dr. Faustus* (1588), and *The Jew of Malta* (1589), each reflecting the Renaissance spirit of endless search and extreme individualism. *Tamburlaine* is a gorgeous pageant, in two parts or ten acts, of the Tartar conqueror's triumphs over the weaker nations of Europe and Asia. Its theme is lust for infinite power — conquest of the world:

> We mean to travel to the antarctic pole,
> Conquering the people underneath our feet,
> And be renowned as never emperors were.

The Jew of Malta gives the picture of a greedy, intriguing and treacherous man of property (Barabas). Its theme is lust for gold in the budding age of capitalism. His most famous play is *Dr. Faustus*, which has for its theme lust for infinite knowledge and the power which knowledge and magic give to mankind.

Young, brilliant and inquisitive Faustus finds himself bored with the ease of attainment. He has dreams of superhuman power; he wants to know, to understand, and in that sense to possess, the kingdoms of the earths:

> All things that move between the quiet poles
> Shall be at my command. Emperors and kings
> Are but obeyed in their several provinces.
> Nor can they raise the wind or rend the clouds;
> But his dominion that exceeds in this
> Stretcheth as far as doth the mind of man.

In order to gain all that he longs for, he sells his soul to the Devil for twenty-four years of magical power. Once in possession of that power, he scorns all tradition and sets his heart on knowledge for its own sake or as a means for wealth, on political and military power, on enjoyment of life. He has mental conflicts and is bored, tired, disillusioned and at times worried, yet he goes on with his endless striving for what is not yet attained — until he is carried away by the Devil.

The story is based upon a popular German legend (Faust-book). But in Marlowe's hands it becomes a reflection of the yearnings and aspirations of the age — an assertive individualism, scepticism, and a sense of the infinite possibilities of mankind.

CHAPTER IV

WILLIAM SHAKESPEARE

I Shakespeare and the Renaissance

1. Facts about Shakespeare's Life Shakespeare was born in April 1564 (the 23rd of April is celebrated as his birthday) at Stratford-on-Avon, a prosperous little town with a population of about two thousand. His father, John Shakespeare, was a well-to-do dealer in wool and leather and once held the office of chief alderman. Young Shakespeare attended Stratford Grammar School and had a good training in Latin. At eighteen he married Anne Hathaway, a farmer's daughter, eight years his senior.

Probably in 1585, Shakespeare got to London, and into the theatrical life. Little is known of his activities in London until 1592. Tradition has it that he was once a horse-holder and call-boy at the theatres. By 1592 he had attained so much success as playwright and actor as to draw the scorn of an elder dramatist Robert Greene. He was called "an upstart crow, beautified with our feathers".

The next twenty years were spent as an actor, and as a reviser and a writer of plays. As an actor he does not seem to have distinguished himself; but his genius as a playwright won quick recognition. He prospered, became part owner of the famous Globe Theatre, made occasional visits to Stratford, bought a considerable house there, and in about 1613 gave up his work in London and retired to spend his declining years in his native place. He died on 23rd April (4th May of our calendar), and was buried in Stratford Church, which has become a shrine of literary pilgrimage.

Shakespeare was "a handsome, well-shaped man, very good company, and of a very ready and pleasant smooth wit". Ben Jonson criticized his art, but with all his faults Shakespeare was to Jonson the greatest of dramatists.

In 1623 appeared the first collected edition of Shakespeare's works, known as the First Folio. The complete works of Shakespeare consist of 2 poems, 154 sonnets and 37 plays.

2. Shakespeare and Renaissance Culture During his first years in London, Shakespeare must have come into contact with the student circles of the day. One of his early plays, *Comedy of Errors* (1592) was written in the tradition of "school drama", i. e. dramas written and performed in schools and universities. A notice has been preserved of the amateurish performance of the play in the law institutes, the Inns of Court, in London. And this contact with the student circles was continued. The university students provided the milieu that helped Shakespeare in his mastery of thc progressive culture of the time, without which his creative works would be unthinkable.

Again, before 1592 Shakespeare was admitted to the house of the Earl of Southampton, a patron of theatrical performances, to whom Shakespeare dedicated his poems *Venus and Adonis* (1593) and

Lucrece (1594). In the court circles he must have come into contact with the productions of Renaissance art: Italian painting and Italian music. Numerous passages in his works testify to his love for painting, especially for music. Nor was his knowledge confined to matters of Italy; he was acquainted with the French and the ancients as well. Again and again he drew upon Italian, French and classical stories for his dramas. And North's Plutarch, mentioned in the previous chapter, was one of his major source books for dramatic composition.

But alien culture mingled in the poet and dramatist with a rich native element. Shakespeare brought with him from his youth in the country a substantial treasure; namely, folklore and folk songs, the usage and manners of the people with whom he had lived. His early experiences and acquaintances were to be represented in his plays: town constables, schoolmasters, parsons, "mechanical" tradesmen, villagers, country squires, etc.

3. Shakespeare "Unlocked His Heart" It is unfortunate that Shakespeare never wrote about his life. Biographical details about him are singularly scanty. Perhaps, something can be gathered from his sonnets, with which (as Wordsworth remarks) he "unlocked his heart".

In writing sonnets, Shakespeare was following the fashion of the time; most Renaissance poets tried their hands at sonneteering, professing devotion to a beloved and complaining of her unresponsiveness and unfairness. But in many of his sonnets the veritable Shakespeare speaks. Some reveal the struggle between the sense of his own intellectual greatness and the consciousness of his lowliness in social life (e. g. Sonnet 29), others enumerate the articles of social injustice of the day.

Here are a few lines (Sonnet 110) about the irksomeness of his profession as an actor and dramatist:

> Alas! 'tis true I have gone here and there,
> And made myself a motley to the view,
> Gored mine own thoughts, sold cheap what is most dear,
> Made old offences of affections new.

And here is the well-known Sonnet 66, about social injustice in general:

> Tired with all these, for restful death I cry
> As, to behold desert a beggar born,
> And needy nothing trimmed in jollity,
> And purest faith unhappily forsworn,
> And gilded honour shamefully misplaced,
> And maiden virtue rudely strumpeted,
> And right perfection wrongfully disgraced,
> And strength by limping sway disabled,
> And art made tongue-tied by authority,
> And folly (doctor-like) controlling skill,
> And simple truth miscalled simplicity,
> And captive good attending captain ill:
> Tired with all these, from these would I be gone,
> Save that, to die, I leave my love alone.

The sonnets were the work of a man still young, touching the most intimate personal life, though they remained unpublished until seven years before his death, when he was a successful and distinguished citizen.

II Early Tragedies and Comedies

1. *Romeo and Juliet* As a dramatist, Shakespeare began with prentice work. Not a few of his early works are revisions of old plays, and they are by no means all masterpieces. It was through failures and half-successes that he learned the art of dramatic composition.

Romeo and Juliet (1595—1596) is his earliest success in tragedy. The story is Italian in origin, and the scene is laid in Verona. The tragedy is an exposure of the old feudal world with its endless internal strife and its unnatural human relations.

The pair of lovers, Romeo and Juliet, belong to two hostile families, Montague and Capulet. Each is devoted to the other, but union is impossible. Romeo kills a Capulet and is banished; Juliet is intended for somebody else for whom she has no affection. Juliet consults Friar Laurence, who suggests a daring intrigue to relieve her from the forced marriage and to give an opportunity for Romeo to take her away. She takes a drug and appears dead for forty-two hours. She is taken to the tomb. Romeo, informed of Juliet's funeral, hastens back, goes to the tomb, and kills himself just before Juliet wakes. Finally Juliet wakes, only to find Romeo dead, and she kills herself.

Romeo and Juliet are images of true love, symbols of faithfulness — one of Shakespeare's favourite themes in his poems and plays. They are children of the Renaissance presented against the drab background of feudal families, with bigoted parents and feudal usages of love and marriage.

Romeo and Juliet, a tragedy with poetry and romance, was a favourite play with young Englishmen and remained so down to the outbreak of the English Revolution. The text in the Oxford copy of the First Folio was almost thumbed to pieces by eager students of the 17th century.

2. *The Merchant of Venice* One of the popular comedies of Shakespeare is *The Merchant of Venice* (1596—1597). The story is, again, Italian in origin, and the scene is laid in Venice. A young Venetian adventurer named Bassanio is making preparations to court Portia, a celebrated beauty at Belmont (wherever it may be). He is in need of money and appeals to Antonio, a merchant, for help. But Antonio's money is invested in ships, now at sea. To fit out Bassanio for his wooing, he borrows of Shylock the Jewish usurer. Shylock, who has suffered in the hands of the Christians, agrees to lend the required sum on condition that if the amount were not repaid by a certain date, he should cut a pound of flesh from Antonio's body. Bassanio gets to Belmont and is wedded to Portia. But Antonio stands in danger: the Jew demands the pound of flesh.

At this critical moment a doctor of law arrives at Venice. The case is tried before him, and the Jew is justified of his bond. But the learned doctor warns the Jew, upon forfeit of his life, that he must fulfil the very letter of his bond, taking no more and no less, and spilling no drop of blood. Seeing himself thwarted by impossible conditions, the enraged Jew tears up the bond and leaves the court. The learned doctor is no other than Portia in disguise! The play ends with romance and song.

The comedy gives a picture of feudal-bourgeois society with its typical characters: the merchant-prince (Antonio), the usurer (Shylock), the fortune-hunters (Bassanio and others). It exposes the evils of that society: greed, malice, racial prejudice, money-worship, injustice, and cruelty. The drab conditions are, however, lit up by the bright image of Portia, a woman of the Renaissance — beautiful, prudent, cultured, courteous, and capable of rising to an emergency. She is one of Shakespeare's ideal women.

3. Shylock the Jew The most remarkable character in *The Merchant of Venice* is Shylock the Jew. Shakespeare shows us everything of Shylock's meanness, cunning and cruelty, and yet his portrayal of the Jew enlists our sympathy. The Jew is not at all a monster.

A few years before *The Merchant of Venice* was produced, a certain Dr. Lopez, the royal physician and a Portuguese Jew, was put on trial on the charge of attempting to poison Queen Elizabeth. There was no strong evidence that Lopez was guilty and the Queen apparently believed him innocent. But the anti-Semitic feeling was high, and he was hanged, drawn and quartered.

Shakespeare's *The Merchant of Venice* is not an anti-Semitic propaganda. On the contrary, much is said for the persecuted Jewish race. Shylock has all the sins of the usurer, but he is "more sinned against than sinning". He has reasons for his grudge against the Christian merchant:

> Hath not a Jew eyes? Hath not a Jew hands, organs, dimensions, senses, affections, passions? fed with the same food, hurt with the same weapons, subject to the same diseases, healed by the same means, warmed and cooled

by the same winter and summer, as a Christian is? If you prick us, do we not bleed? If you tickle us, do we not laugh? If you poison us, do we not die? and if you wrong us, shall we not revenge? If we are like you in the rest, we will resemble you in that. If a Jew wrong a Christian, what is his humility? Revenge. If a Christian wrong a Jew, what should his sufferance be by Christian example? Why, revenge. (3, 1, 62ff)

Such are the words of Shylock — or rather the words of Shakespeare put into the mouth of Shylock, a man under persecution. It is Shakespeare that compels us to cry out, upon the Jew's exit, "By Heaven, the man is wronged!"

III Historical Plays

1. Shakespeare and Historical Drama When Shakespeare began his apprenticeship, the English people were still exultant over the defeat of the Armada. Historical subjects appealed to their pride and were often dramatized on the stage. But such performances, known as chronicle plays, are but successions of scenes from the reign of this king or that — rambling pageantries, lacking in form and finish.

Shakespeare wrote a number of such plays between 1590 and 1599: *King John* and a long series of plays from Richard II to Richard III (i.e. *Richard II*, *Henry IV* in two parts, *Henry V*, *Henry VI* in three parts, *Richard III*) — a long series about the struggles between the Houses of

York and Lancaster.

Shakespeare's early historical dramas are but little better than the old chronicle plays. But his later ones show remarkable improvements. He pruned away superfluous scenes, transposed and even altered the events narrated in chronicles so that there would be a real dramatic development of the story. Moreover, he introduced all sorts of everyday people, with their familiar habits and manners and even absurdities, and weaved their doings into the great events of court and battlefield. So, in Shakespeare's hands, the old chronicle play became the historical drama, laying bare the hearts of real men.

2. *Henry IV*, Part I Among the most remarkable historical plays of Shakespeare is *Henry IV* (1597—1598), which gives the picture of a troubled reign. Henry IV takes the crown from Richard II, but he never feels easy on the throne. His rebellious subjects give him no rest. The great barons rise in the north, and the nobles like the Percy family and the Welshmen league against the king. It is Henry's young son, Prince Hal, the future Henry V, who leads the army to victory over the rebels. All these Shakespeare takes from *Chronicles* of Holinshed and from an old play, but he adds life to the old chronicle. Here we have a king, weary, timid and suspicious; Henry Percy, "a very valiant rebel"; Prince Hal, a wild and reckless youth who mends his ways.

In this play Shakespeare gives us a picture of the struggle between the two opposing principles of feudalism and monarchy. And, like the Elizabethan bourgeoisie, he stands for the monarchy and order. In the great first scene of Act III, he presents with wit and humour the rebels' design to parcel out the kingdom among themselves; this part for me, that for you, and a tiny portion for the titular king of England. Here, he seems to say, is what a feudal baron would do if he had the power. And this can hardly have failed to appeal to the audience of Shakespeare's time.

3. Sir John Falstaff, Knight Most memorable is the character of an old fat knight, Sir John Falstaff, one of the boon companions of Prince Hal. He is gross, old, ugly, guilty of many sins, selfish, treacherous, too lazy to be brave, yet at times he exhibits agility, lightness, and vivacity of mind. He is a bundle of incongruities, and innumerable volumes have been written on him.

When war is declared and Prince Hal takes his proper place at the head of the forces, Falstaff leads a rugged company, with "but a shirt and a half" among them, to take part in the battle. When one of the rebel leaders attacks him, he falls down and "plays dead". When Henry Percy is slain by Prince Hal, Falstaff jumps up and pretends to have slain Percy himself. And all the while he is so genial in his rascality, so carefree and witty that decidedly he has a charm of his own.

Sir John Falstaff is one of Shakespeare's great creations. He appears not only in the second part of *Henry IV* but also in a comedy of laughter — *The Merry Wives of Windsor*, in which he becomes a source of great fun.

In a letter to Lassalle, Engels wrote: "What a variety of quaintly characteristic character sketches are to be found at this period of dissolution of a feudal ties in the penniless ruling kings, poverty-stricken freelancers and adventurers of all sorts." Falstaff is one of such characteristic characters. He is a feudal knight, when feudal ties are being dissolved. And he looks like a capitalist too. With a belly oozing with fat, he moves about, eating, drinking and doing nothing. He is a social parasite. Marx regards him as a capitalist in the period of primitive accumulation — as Capital, personified at the dawn of capitalism.

IV Great Tragedies

1. The Tragic Gloom So far we have been dealing with the representative works of Shakespeare up to about 1600. Works of this period are pervaded with a spirit of youth, bright and cheerful. Even the tragedy of *Romeo and Juliet* is lit up by the spring and sunshine of the South. Toward 1600, however, storm-clouds gathered, so to speak, over the creative activities of Shakespeare. He began to observe life with penetration, to disclose rudely and expose mercilessly the contradictions of Elizabethan society. This was the period of great tragedies: *Hamlet* (1601), *Othello* (1604), *King Lear* (1605), and *Macbeth* (1605).

The tragic gloom of Shakespeare was also that of his fellow-dramatists at the turn of the century. There appeared on the stage heroes and heroines, victims of injustice, bitterly denouncing the order of the day and appealing for vengeance. Even comedies became dark and gloomy.

The tragic gloom is but a reflection of the economic and social crisis which began at the end of the reign of Elizabeth and continued up to the English Revolution. The co-operation of the Crown and the bourgeoisie, which was the basis of the Elizabethan order, was now over.

The Crown tended to be absolutist, and the bourgeoisie struggled for free development. There were protests in Parliament against the economic policy of the government. There were plots against Elizabeth. In February 1601 the Earl of Essex, a former favourite of Elizabeth, started a rising, which cost him his head. And there rose the undermasters in London, who were being converted into wage labourers under capitalist exploitation. It was in the atmosphere of a general social unrest that Shakespeare created the great tragedies.

2. *The Tragedy of Hamlet* The story of *Hamlet* — the vengeance of a son upon the murderer of his father — comes from an Old Danish legend of the 13th century. A play had been written (probably by Thomas Kyd) on the subject before 1599, and Shakespeare must have seen it. It was a tragedy of "thunder and blood". Shakespeare's *Hamlet*, written between 1601 and 1602, retains some traces of the old play, but it is no longer a mere revenge play.

The play opens amid agitation and gloom. Young Prince Hamlet is brooding over his father's sudden death and his mother's hasty marriage to his uncle. From his father's ghost he gets the story of a foul murder. He pretends to be mad, endeavouring to find proof for the murder. His uncle becomes suspicious and sends one courtier after another to find out the cause of his madness. For a time Hamlet and his uncle seem to have equal advantage. Hamlet thinks a lot, imagines a lot, is ready for action, but seems unable to take prompt action. Finally, in a fencing match, arranged by his uncle, Hamlet is poisoned, but before his death he effects the revenge.

Such is the bald outline of the play. The tragic greatness of the central character trying to resolve conflicts internal as well as external, the luminous insight into human motives and passions, and the terrible sweep of forces ruthlessly crushing the innocent with the guilty — all these give *Hamlet* a place among the world's greatest dramas.

3. The Problem of Hamlet A great deal has been written about the character of Hamlet, "to pluck out the heart of his mystery". Why is Hamlet unable to take prompt action? Is it because he thinks too much? Is he a weak man by nature? ...

Hamlet may be regarded as a humanist of Shakespeare's age. Like other humanists, he sees the ugly reality, dreams of healthful human relations, and yet is unable to realize his dream. And the brighter the dream, the more gloomy becomes for him the surrounding reality, and the more acute are his mental conflicts.

> To be, or not to be — that is the question:
> Whether 'tis nobler in the mind to suffer
> The slings and arrows of outrageous fortune,
> Or to take arms against a sea of troubles,
> And by opposing end them ... (3.1.56ff)

The tragedy is a reflection of the contradictions of the age in which Shakespeare lived and worked.

In a significant passage, *Hamlet* echoes Thomas More's *Utopia*. "All the world is a prison," wrote More. Shakespeare's Hamlet repeats exactly the same words: "Denmark's prison", and again: "A goodly one; in which there are many confines, wards, and dungeons, Denmark being one of the worst".

Hamlet can effect his personal vengeance by killing his uncle-king. But the great task, which he only vaguely realizes — i. e. reconstruction of the world — is beyond his power, He does not see the road to the reconstruction; nor does Shakespeare, nor does any of his contemporaries. The reason lies not in their subjective incapability, but in historical limitations of the consciousness of the men of the age. They could only dream about healthful human relations.

4. *The Tragedy of King Lear* The legend of King Lear and his daughters originated in ancient Britain, probably before the invasion of the Romans. It had been retold more than once in verse and prose before Shakespeare took it up about 1605.

Old Lear, King of ancient Britain, is a self-willed despot with three daughters. He divides his kingdom between his two elder daughters, Regan and Goneril, with whom he plans to live in turn, and he disowns the youngest daughter, who had angered him by untactful honesty. Soon the king of imperious temper comes into contact with the self-willed Regan and Goneril. He is driven from their homes and becomes insane in the violence of a storm. His youngest daughter Cordelia, who has been married to the King of France, comes back with an army, is defeated, and dies in prison.

There is a sub-plot. Gloucester, one of Lear's courtiers, is deceived by an illegitimate younger son as to the character of his elder son, who in consequence has to flee for his life and adopt the disguise of a crazy beggar. Gloucester, because of his kindness to Lear, is cruelly blinded by one of Lear's sons-in-law.

The theme is not simply filial ingratitude. The play depicts a great social upheaval. In the miseries of Lear, as in the miseries of Gloucester, is disclosed the essence of a corrupt society, in which each is ready to nullify the other. No images are more frequently met with in the text than the images of lower animals; e.g. the dog, the horse, the cow, the sheep, the hog, the lion, the bear, the wolf, the fox, the monkey, the rat, the frog, the worm. *King Lear* is one of the bitterest among the tragedies of Shakespeare.

5. Lear and "Houseless Poverty" The age of Shakespeare was the age of primitive accumulation — an age marked by monstrous impoverishment of the masses. This is presented with poignancy and power in the Storm Scene of the tragedy.

At the outset of the play, Lear is depicted as so self-willed a despot as to be absolutely regardless of others. He is detached from the reality. Every action of his excites our indignation, but once he is driven away from the homes of his daughters, when he is wandering on the gloomy heath and sees with his own eyes how the poorest of his subjects live, he begins to have compassion for what he calls "houseless poverty".

> Poor naked wretches, whereso'er you are,
> That bide the pelting of this pitiless storm,
> How shall your houseless heads and unfed sides,
> Your loop'd and window'd raggedness, defend you
> From seasons such as these? O, I have ta'en
> Too little care of this! Take physic, pomp;
> Expose thyself to feel what wretches feel,
> That thou mayst shake the superflux to them,
> And show the heavens more just. (3, 4, 28ff)

Here Lear is changed, and so are our feelings about him. Thus remarks Dobrolyubov:

> On looking at him [Lear] we at first feel hatred for this wanton tyrant. But as we watch the drama unfold we become more and more reconciled to him as a man, and we end with being filled with indignation and burning anger *not against him, but for his sake* and for the sake of the whole world; we feel anger against the savage inhuman conditions which can make even men like Lear such wanton tyrants.

The "poor naked wretches" are not of ancient Britain, but of late Elizabethan England.

V The Art of Shakespeare

1. Shakespeare as a Realist In *Hamlet* (3, 2, 24—28) Shakespeare remarks on dramatic performance. The purpose of playing, he says, is "to hold, as 'twere, the mirror up to nature; to show virtue her own feature, scorn her own image, and the very age and body of the time his form and pressure". This principle of dramatic performance is the principle of his dramatic composition. It is, in essence, the principle of realism.

Shakespeare knew his age and its contradictions. What Thomas More calls "the conspiracy of the rich against the poor" is reflected in numerous passages of his plays. In *Pericles* (in late 1607 or early 1608), one fisherman asks another fisherman, "How the fishes live in the sea?" The other fisherman answers thus:

> Why, as men do a-land — the great ones eat up the little ones; I can compare our rich misers to nothing so fitly as to a whale; a' plays and tumbles, driving the poor fry before him, and at last devours them all at a mouthful. Such whales have I heard on o' the land, who never leave gaping till they've swallowed the whole parish, church, steeple, bells, and all. (2, 1, 31ff)

Shakespeare, too, reflects fully the all-revolutionizing power of money in the age of growing capitalism. *The Timon of Athens* (1606) contains the well-known passage on the corrupting influence of gold:

> Gold! Yellow, glittering, precious gold!
>
> ...
>
> Thus much of this will make black white, foul fair,
>
> Wrong right, base noble, old young, coward valiant.
>
> ...
>
> This yellow slave
>
> Will knit and break religions; bless the accursed;
>
> Make the hoar leprosy adored...
>
> Come, damned earth,
>
> Thou common whore of mankind, that put'st odds
>
> Among the rout of nations; (4, 3, 25ff)

Citing the monologue of Timon, Marx wrote, "How excellently Shakespeare describes the essence of money!"

2. Shakespeare as a Creator of Characters The stories of Shakespeare's plays do not always originate in England and his characters are often clothed in foreign dresses — Italian, French, Danish, Celtic, Roman, etc. — but the thoughts and feelings of the characters, their attitudes towards life and towards each other belong to the age of Shakespeare. Shakespeare wrote about his own people and for his own people.

Shakespeare's principal characters are created in typical real situations: the feudal castle, the medieval city, the king's court with its courtly atmosphere, etc. Their fundamental traits are revealed in their conflicts with their surroundings, in their relations with their fellowmen (e. g. the development of the character of Lear, the tragedy of Hamlet, etc.). Each of them is disclosed as an upholder of a certain social-historical tendency, as a representative of a whole group of men, in whose manners are embodied to a great extent their typical traits (e. g. Hamlet the humanist, Shylock the usurer, Falstaff the relic of chivalry, etc.). Yet they are not "mere mouthpieces of the spirit of the time" (Engels). They are given characteristic individual traits that make them wonderfully life-like. Thus Shylock is a usurer, yet not a usurer in general; Falstaff is a sort of Don Quixote, yet not quite like Don Quixote, etc. Shakespeare never overlooked the realistic because of the intellectual elements. This is what Marx calls "Shakespearizing".

Shakespeare was the favourite author of Marx and Engels, whose works contain numerous references to the episodes and characters of Shakespeare. Paul Lafargue tells how much Marx was fond of Shakespeare:

> He had made an exhaustible study of Shakespeare, for whom he had an unbounded admiration, and whose most insignificant characters, even, were familiar to him. There was a veritable Shakespeare cult in the Marx family, and the three daughters knew much of Shakespeare by heart.

For the last three centuries many actors and actresses have established their reputations by taking Shakespearian parts; e.g. Garrick in the 18th century and Kean and Irving in the 19th. And the popularity of Shakespeare is not confined to England. He is a great wrier of world renown.

3. Dramatic Form and Language The dramatic form fits perfectly the content of the Shakespearian play. The action is developed freely, without being hindered by the rules of the classical unities (place and time). It moves from city to city, from country to country, or from the royal chamber to the battlefield; it covers several days, several weeks, or even many years. All depends on the character of the action, on the nature of the theme. Sometimes, a single play may contain more than one theme: the main plot and the sub-plot exist side by side. Thus the form and structure of the drama is subject to the requirements of the theme and the content.

Shakespeare's attempt to reproduce the manifold image of life, its contrasts and contradictions, results in a peculiar combination characteristic of his drama — a combination of the majestic and the funny, of the high and the lowly, of the poetic and the prosaic. This wealth of humanity has commanded the admiration of Marx, Engels,

Pushkin and many other critics.

Shakespeare was a great master of the English language at all its levels. The language of each of his heroes fits his status in society and discloses the peculiarities of his character. Thus in the language of Hamlet is revealed the high culture of the humanist, the many-sidedness of his interests, his gifts, his intellectual depth.

Shakespeare commanded a vocabulary larger than that of any other English writer. He used 16,000 words (of course he knew much more). He loved to play with words, to jingle them, to make puns with them. He often ran to excesses, and became obscure or too subtle for understanding. But he has enriched the English language with new words, new turns of expressions. A few instances from *Hamlet*: "Brevity is the soul of wit"; "more matter, with less art"; "caviare to the general"; "cudgel one's brains"; "to be or not to be"; "sicklied o'er with the pale cast of thought"; "to speak by card".

Shakespeare was a master of many poetic forms: the song, the sonnet, the couplet, the quatrain, the blank verse. He was especially at home with the blank verse, which adapts itself in his plays to the changing emotions of every speaker, "from merely colloquial dialogue to strains of impassioned soliloquy, from comic repartee to tragic eloquence, from terse epigrams to elaborate description".

A word must be said about prose, of which Shakespeare was a master too. His prose is varied, from the plain and matter-of-fact (e. g. "Who's there") to the impassioned and ornate (e. g. "What a piece of work is man!" *Hamlet*, 2, 2).

The best writer of prose in the age of Shakespeare was Shakespeare himself.

CHAPTER V

THE EARLY 17TH CENTURY

I Francis Bacon

1. Bacon and Modern Materialism Francis Bacon (1561—1626) was Shakespeare's exact contemporary. Born of a family associated with the court, he was from twelve to fourteen a student at Cambridge, at fifteen a professional student of law, at twenty-three in Parliament, and for thirty years the most learned statesman and jurist of the time. At fifty-seven he was made Lord Chancellor. Three years later he was convicted of having received bribes from suitors and was deprived of all his offices. He died at sixty-five, in aged disgrace.

Bacon was the founder of modern science. His lifelong object was to reorganize the various fields of knowledge and to work out better methods of study and investigation in these fields. In every branch of learning, he said, people were inclined to take too much for granted: they accepted the principles or theories handed down from the ancients and tried to make facts fit such principles or theories. Bacon worked the other way around. He would keep his eyes open, accept nothing that was not proved, and develop theories to fit the facts — this, he maintained, was the only method to get at the truth. In 1605 he published *The Advancement of Learning*, in which he disposed of the fallacies and errors of traditional scholars. In 1620 he published the Latin treatise *Novum Organum* (*New Instrument*), which gave an exposition of the inductive method.

Marx and Engels wrote:

> The real progenitor of English materialism is Bacon. To him natural philosophy is the only true philosophy, and physics based upon the experience of the senses is the chiefest part of natural philosophy ... According to him the senses are infallible and the source of all knowledge. All science is based on experience, and consists in subjecting the data furnished by the senses to a rational method of investigation. Induction, analysis, comparison, observation, experiment, are the principal forms of such a rational method.

2. Bacon and English Prose Bacon was a gifted speaker. "He was full of gravity in his speaking," says Ben Jonson, "No man ever spoke more neatly, more (com) pressedly, more weightily, or suffered less emptiness, less idleness in what he uttered. No member of his speech but consisted in his own graces."

Bacon wrote as he spoke. The neatness, the compressedness (i. e. compactness, brevity), the gravity, the weightiness are likewise the essential qualities of his writing. Most of his contemporaries wrote a kind of prose involved, decorated and sonorous. Bacon preferred the plain and direct manner of writing. He was straightforward, but not without grace. It is especially so in his *Essays*, which he wrote as "brief notes" and finally collected in 1625. *Essays* covers a wide variety of topics —

marriage, love, high position or great place, friendship, gardens, reading, honour, and "The Vicissitude of Things".

A number of Bacon's pithy remarks have become wise old saws. About books and reading, for instance, he wrote in *Of Studies*:

> Some books are to be tasted, others to be swallowed, and some few to be chewed and digested. That is, some books are to be read only in parts; others to be read but not curiously; and some few to be read wholly, and with diligence and attention ... Reading maketh a full man; conference a ready man; and writing an exact man.

Bacon was also the author of a fragmentary utopian book called *New Atlantis*, written probably early in the migrations to New England. The most remarkable thing about his utopia, which he put in the Pacific Ocean, is a college or society, called Solomon's House, a sort of scientific society. *New Atlantis* is known to have inspired scientific societies that came into being, in England and on the Continent in the course of the 17th century.

II Ben Jonson and John Donne

1. Jonson and Satirical Comedy Of the many contemporaries and successors of Shakespeare, the most well-known was Ben Jonson (1572—1637). Once a brick-layer, Jonson rose, still in his thirties, to be one of the leading dramatists of the day. Tradition has it that he and Shakespeare had many a "wit combat" at the Mermaid Tavern, assailing each other "like a Spanish great galleon and an English man-of-war". Shakespeare was the greater genius, but Jonson knew more of the classics.

Like Shakespeare, Jonson was a realist — with this difference: whereas Shakespeare laid his scenes anywhere on earth — Venice, Verona, the Forest of Arden, the Coast of Bohemia, or a desert island — Jonson concerned himself most with the world about him, i.e. London at the turn of the century. The street cries, the shops, the scamps, the hurlyburly, households of gentry or of solid trading bourgeoisie, fairs, freaks, pedants — all mingle to make up the picture of Jonson's restless and noisy London in his comedies, of which the most remarkable are *Everyman in His Humour* (1598) and *The Alchemist* (1610).

Among the targets of attack in Jonson's comedies are: aristocratic and bourgeois characters; the affected courtier, who "wears clothes well, practices by his glass how to salute, and speaks good remnants"; the court lady, who "does observe as pure a phrase, and use as choice figures in her ordinary conversation as any that be in the Arcadia"; and Sir Epicure Mammon who wants limitless luxury.

> My meat shall all come in, in Indian shells,
> Dishes of agate set in gold, and studded
> With emeralds, sapphires, hyacinths, and rubies.

Jonson also wrote masques for performance at court and tragedies on classical models.

2. Jonson as a Poet and Critic Jonson had the mental capacity and memory of a great scholar, but he also had the prolific genius of a poet. He was the author of a number of lovely lyrics (e. g. *To Celia*). But unlike most of the Elizabethans, he was impatient of sentimentality and romantic extravagances. He aimed at a better art, or "composition" as he called it — i. e. the careful planning of the whole poem, the fitting together of every link, the definite coming to a stop when the poem had said what it had to say. He strove for sharper, more clear cut images, less flow and more precision. The following lines may illustrate his neatness and simplicity:

> Give me a look, give me a face
> That makes simplicity a grace.
> Robes loosely flowing, hair as free;
> Such sweet neglect more taketh me
> Than all the adulteries of art;
> They strike mine eyes, but not my heart.

Jonson was first and last a conscious artist in poetry.

Around Jonson in his ripe years gathered the poets who loved to sit at his feet in London taverns and were proud to call themselves "Sons of Ben". Among them was Robert Herrick, author of such lyrics as *Gather Ye Rose-Buds While Ye May* and *Corinna Going A-Maying*.

Jonson was also a good critic. His *Timber, or Discoveries* (1641) contains a number of memorable passages. About Shakespeare he wrote, "I remember, the players have often mentioned it as an honour to Shakespeare that in his writing (whatever he penned) he never blotted out a line. My answer hath been 'Would he had blotted a thousand' ..." His prose style is lucid and terse — very much like that of Francis Bacon.

3. Donne and "Metaphysical" Poetry John Donne (1573—1631), the son of a wealthy London merchant, was a prodigy. He entered Oxford at eleven and Cambridge at fifteen. He studied law, served as a soldier, and wrote satires. After a period of adventure or misadventure, he took the Holy Orders and died Dean of St. Paul's Cathedral.

Donne wrote a sort of learned poetry. His desire would seem to be to say what never had been said before, and he said it in a language loaded with elaborate metaphors and conceits, sometimes fresh and original, and sometimes far-fetched and distracting. He can involve himself in the most grotesque metaphors — as this, when he imagines two lovers looking in each other's eyes:

> Our eye-beams twisted, and did thread
> Our eyes upon one double string.

But when he likes, he can hammer out lovely lyrics; e. g. *Break of Day*:

> Stay, O sweet, and do not rise:
> That light that shines comes from thine eyes;
> The day breaks not, it is my heart,
> Because that you and I must part.
>   Stay, or else my joys will die
>   And perish in their infancy.

Donne had his followers — Richard Crashaw, George Herbert, and Abraham Cowley — who wrote in his manner. They belong to the so-called "metaphysical" school of poetry, of which Donne was the founder.

Metaphysical poetry is poetry of the library, poetry for the few. Under the Stuarts, it seems, poets turned from the court and public life to the libraries, and their poetry smells of the library where it was produced.

III Milton and the English Revolution

1. Parentage, Education and Early Poems John Milton (1608—1674) was born and bred in the heart of London. His father was a Protestant. A successful scrivener (i. e. small bank-lawyer) by profession, a musician and composer of madrigals by avocation, the elder Milton encouraged his son to study languages — Latin, Greek, French, Italian, Hebrew — and to love beautiful things.

From private tuition at home and a few years at St. Paul's school, Milton proceeded to Cambridge, where he spent seven years. He was not altogether happy in the assigned tasks, but he came into contact with the philosophical works of Francis Bacon. In 1631, having finished his course at Cambridge, he retired to his father's country-place at Horton, about twenty miles from London, for further study. There he wrote his important early poems — *L'allegro*, *Il Penseroso*, *Comus* and *Lycidas*.

L'allegro and *Il Penseroso* are companion pieces, being graceful studies of two contrasted moods: the joyous one and the pensive one. *Lycidas* (1637) was occasioned by the death of Edward King, a fellow student of Milton's at Cambridge. But it is more than a conventional elegy: it reflects Milton's views as to what was wrong in the state of the Church of England. He was anticipating the war between Parliament and Crown when he wrote:

> But that two-handed engine at the door
> Stands ready to smite once, and smite no more

By the "two-handed engine", as critics have pointed out, Milton meant the two Houses of Parliament.

2. Defence of the Free Press: *Areopagitica* The English Revolution began with the summoning of the Long Parliament in 1640. In 1642 began the Civil War which was to result in the defeat of the king's forces, the beheading of Charles I (1649), and the rule of Oliver Cromwell as Protector.

Milton's part in the struggle was with the pen rather than with the sword. He turned out a vast number of pamphlets, of which the most well-known is *Areopagitica* (1644) — a plea for freedom of thought and freedom of the press.

The Royalists had used the Star Chamber to suppress freedom of thought. In 1640, when the Long Parliament was convened, the Star Chamber was abolished and every man was free to think and print what he pleased. In 1643, however, the Presbyterians in Parliament passed an act that no book or pamphlet should be printed until it had been read and licensed by an official censor. Milton addressed his pamphlet to the "Lords and Commons", the court of final authority in England, just as the Assembly of the Areopagus was the court of final authority in ancient Athens. Hence the title *Areopagitica*.

The gist of Milton's argument is this: No censorship could decide what was truth and what was error, for truth could only be decided by free discussion. He says:

> He that can apprehend and consider vice with all her baits and seeming pleasures, and yet abstain, and yet distinguish, and yet prefer that which is truly better, he is the true warfaring Christian. I cannot praise a fugitive and cloistered virtue, unexercised and unbreathed, that never salliest out and sees her adversary, but slinks out of the race, where that immortal garland is to be run for, not without dust and heat ... And though all the winds of doctrine were let loose to play upon the earth, so Truth be in the field, we do injuriously by licensing and prohibiting to misdoubt her strength. Let her and Falsehood grapple; who ever knew Truth put to the worse in a free and open encounter?

3. Milton and the Commonwealth In 1649, Charles I was executed, and reactionary Europe was shocked. Within two weeks of Charles's death, Milton published his *Tenure of Kings and Magistrates*. The gist of his argument is: (1) that government is by the consent of the governed, and (2) subjects are not bound to endure an unjust rule. This was the theory of the bourgeois revolution which John Locke was to elaborate in his *Treatise of Government*.

The value of Milton's *Tenure of Kings and Magistrates* the Commonwealth government was quick to appreciate. Milton was appointed Secretary for Foreign Tongues to the Council of State. His duties were: (1) to translate official communications from foreign countries, (2) to put into Latin official communications from the Council of State to foreign countries, and (3) to answer the attacks made upon the Commonwealth by enemies abroad. This last involved Milton in many violent and protracted controversies on political and religious subjects.

Of the many papers that Milton wrote as Latin Secretary, the most remarkable are *The Defence of the English People* (1651) and *The Second Defence of the English People* (1654), in answer to foreign attacks upon the Commonwealth. The latter of these two pamphlets contains a famous passage in which Milton visualized the mightest audience he was addressing as a revolutionist:

> I seem to survey, as from a towering height, the far extended tracts of sea and land, and innumerable crowds of spectators, betraying in their looks the liveliest interest, and sensations the most congenial with my own. Here I behold the stout and manly prowess of the Germans disdaining servitude; there the generous and lively impetuosity of the French; on this side, the calm and stately valour of the Spaniard; on that, the composed and wary magnanimity of the Italian. Of all the lovers of liberty and virtue, the magnanimous and the wise, in whatever quarter they may be found, some secretly favour, others, who had long been proof against conviction, at last yield themselves captive to the force of truth. Surrounded by congregated multitudes, I now imagine that, from the columns of Hercules to the Indian Ocean, I behold the nations of the earth recovering that liberty which they so long had lost...

4. Milton and the Sonnet During the years of the Revolution,

Milton wrote no verse except a handful of sonnets. Milton's sonnets are not love poems, nor do they form a sequence: they are occasional poems, polished to perfection. The best ones are on political subjects and for the cause of liberty. He wrote against the Presbyterians in Parliament whom he called "new forcers of conscience", and he summed up his attacks in the famous line: "New Presbyter is but old Priest writ large."

He wrote against the persecution of Protestants in Piedmont (*On the Late Massacre in Piedmont*). He also wrote on Cromwell and exhorted the great generals of the Commonwealth. And in each of these he struck a new note of lofty dignity. Wordsworth remarked:

> In his hands
> The Thing became a trumpet; whence he blew
> Soul-animating strains — alas, too few!

There are also a few personal sonnets, of which the one on his blindness is the noblest. During the tenure of his Latin secretaryship, he bent himself to the labour and overtaxed his eyes. In 1654 he worked against warning on *The Second Defence of the English People*, and he rose from it blind — when he was only forty-five. In a sonnet he tells us how he felt about it.

Milton's sonnets, though few, are important in the history of English poetry. They were to become models with the Romantic poets—Wordsworth, Byron and Shelley.

IV *Paradise Lost* and *Samson Agonistes*

1. *Paradise Lost*: Theme and Style In 1655 Milton's official duties as Latin Secretary were lightened. With great leisure and with the greater concentration of mind induced by his blindness, he began to meditate a poem to be entitled *Paradise Lost*. In 1658 he started to write — or rather dictate to his secretary. At the Restoration, he lost his Latin Secretaryship; he lost his fortunes; but somehow he escaped hanging and was allowed to return to private life. For the space of five years the poem grew. It was completed in twelve books in 1663 and published in 1667.

The stories of the poem were drawn from the Bible and from various elaborators of the Bible. They are: the creation, the rebellion in Heaven of Satan and his fellow-angels, their defeat and expulsion, the creation of earth and of Adam and Eve, Satan's temptation of Eve, and the departure of man from Eden. To us all this sounds like an allegory, but Milton took it with high seriousness. His purpose, as we are told at the outset of the poem, was "to justify the ways of God to man" — i.e. submission to the Almighty. But, strangely enough, he was perpetually on the side of the rebels.

The poem was written in blank verse, already made familiar by Marlowe and Shakespeare. But in Milton's hands it became a magnificent organ-music. His diction is a combination of plain English and classical Latin — stately, sonorous, and yet essentially simple. It is the "grand" style.

2. The Character of Satan According to the logic of the argument that Milton gives at the outset of *Paradise Lost*, Satan is the spirit of evil. He is a rebel, a plotter. Yet in spite of himself, Milton was in deep sympathy with Satan. Milton was a rebel too, challenging alike the authority of King and Church, "resolved not to repose upon the faith or judgment of others" and "determined to lay up as the best treasure of a good old age ... the honest liberty of free speech".

As represented in the poem, Satan does not appear to be ignominious as he ought to be. When cast down by the Almighty power, he exclaims:

> What though the field be lost?
> All is not lost — the unconquerable will,
> And study of revenge, immortal hate,
> And courage never to submit or yield:
> And what is else not to be overcome.
> That glory never shall his wrath or might
> Extort from me. To bow and sue for grace
> With suppliant knee...
> That were an ignominy and shame beneath
> This downfall! —

And Satan is the questioning spirit. When he gets to the Garden of Eden, he can see no reason why Adam and Eve should be forbidden to taste the fruit of the tree of knowledge:

> Knowledge forbidden?
> Suspicious, reasonless! Why should their Lord

> Envy them that? Can it be sin to know?
> Can it be death? And do they only stand
> By ignorance? Is that their happy state,
> The proof of their obedience and their faith?
> O fair foundation laid whereon to build
> Their ruin! —

It is as if in telling that part of Satan's story, Milton remembered his own spiritual independence, his own love of freedom and desire above all things to know, his own adherence to the revolutionary cause, though that cause was lost and he himself had "fallen on evil days".

Belinsky wrote:

> The poetry of Milton is obviously the product of his age: he himself, without suspecting the fact, depicted in the person of his proud and sombre Satan an apotheosis of rebellion against authority, though his intention had been quite different.

3. *Samson Agonistes* Of Milton's later works the most notable is *Samson Agonistes* (published in 1671), a dramatic treatment of the story of Samson "the athlete" from the *Old Testament* ("Judges", Chapters 13—16): How Samson, the strong man of the Israelites, had lost his strength and regained it; how he was betrayed by his Philistine wife Delilah, blinded by the Philistines (who ruled over the Israelites), and led into the temple to make them sport; and how he wrecked his vengeance upon the Philistines by pulling down the temple upon them and upon himself in a common ruin.

Apparently, Samson had a special appeal to Milton. Like Milton, Samson is a dedicated soul,

> a person rais'd
> With strength sufficient and command from Heaven
> To free my country.

Like Milton, he has been embittered by an unwise marriage, has suffered blindness, and yet is unconquerable. When *Samson* was written, Milton had passed from resignation to rebellion in mood, when he saw signs of the rise of Whig opposition which would overthrow the Stuart dynasty. *Samson Agonistes* is the most personal of Milton's productions, and the most passionate.

Samson Agonistes contains little of the excitement that one looks for in stage drama. It is strictly modelled on Greek tragedy, with the Chorus and Messenger and Dramatic Unities. It belongs with nothing in the Elizabethan or the Restoration stage.

CHAPTER VI

THE LATE 17TH AND THE EARLY 18TH CENTURY

I John Bunyan and John Dryden

1. Bunyan and His *Pilgrim's Progress* John Bunyan (1628—1688) was a poor tinker, and a tinker's son, with but schooling enough to read and write. During the Revolution he fought for Parliament. He was a gifted preacher to plain folks. After the Restoration, Puritans were forbidden to assemble together, but Bunyan continued his preaching. He was arrested and imprisoned in Bedford for twelve years. His masterpiece, *Pilgrim's Progress* (1678), was written in prison.

On the face of it, *Pilgrim's Progress* is but a religious allegory. It tells how Christian flies from the City of Destruction, meets with perils and temptations of the Slough of Despond, Vanity Fair, and Doubting Castle, faces and overcomes a monster, and comes to the Delectable Mountain and the Celestial City. But what makes the book valuable is the realistic picture it gives of the people in town and country: lowly cottages, back streets, muddy roads, Vanity Fair with rows of booths, rascals, light-minded men and women. It is a story written by a man who knew how his fellowmen had lived and worked.

Here is, for instance, a picture of the English jury. Christian and Faithful get to the Vanity Fair. As they refuse to buy anything but Truth, they are beaten and put in a cage, and then taken out and led in chains up and down the Fair, and at length brought before a district court. Judge Hate-Good summons three witnesses: Envy, Superstition, and Pickthank (i. e. tale-bearer), who testify against them. The case is given to the jury, composed of Mr. Blindman, Mr. No-Good, Mr. Malice, etc. Each gives a verdict against Faithful, who is presently condemned.

No one of the late 17th century has given such a faithful picture of the English bourgeoisie as we have in *Pilgrim's Progress*. And Bunyan's knack of telling the story has made it one of the most popular books in the English language.

2. Dryden and Bourgeois Journalism No one is more characteristic of the period of reaction and compromise than John Dryden (1631—1700). Born of a well-to-do Puritan family, he was educated at Cambridge. Like Bunyan, he grew to manhood during the Revolution. But unlike Bunyan, he seems never to have made up his mind about politics and religion. He honoured Cromwell in verse, sang later as a Royalist and an Anglican, and in 1685, when James II ascended the throne, became Catholic.

Dryden was a prolific dramatist. He wrote two kinds of plays — comedies in which men and women of fashion displayed obscene wit, and "heroic plays" in which men of great valour declaimed love to virtuous ladies. None but specialists now read most of his plays — and they not for mere pleasure.

Dryden was a master of satire. He was a Tory and wrote against the Whigs. Here is a satiric "character", in masterly couplets, of Buckingham:

> A man so various that he seemed to be
> Not one, but all mankind's epitome.
> Stiff in opinions, always in the wrong;
> Was everything by starts and nothing long;
> But, in the course of one revolving moon,
> Was chemist, fiddler, statesman and buffoon;
> Then all for women, painting, rhyming, drinking,
> Besides ten thousand freaks that died in thinking.
> Blest madman, who could every hour employ,
> With something new to wish or to enjoy!

Dryden was Poet-laureate. But when James II was driven from the throne, he lost the laureateship, and had to make a living for himself. The bourgeois reading public stood in need of ready aids to culture. And these Dryden endeavoured to supply in the form of translations and adaptations from the classics; e.g. Virgil, Chaucer, Boccaccio. So with the changes of the time, Dryden the court poet became a man of letters of bourgeois society.

3. Dryden and Modern Prose Dryden must be remembered as a master of modern prose. English prose before Dryden was in general elaborate in structure. Magnificent, such as Milton's at its best; but sometimes too long-winded to be clear. Such was the style of the Elizabethans and Jacobeans, with the exceptions of Bacon, Bunyan and a few others.

But during the late 17th century a change was taking place. Classical French prose, which was influential in England, taught the lessons of clearness, directness and simplicity. Meanwhile, the growing interest in science, brought with it a desire for simplification. The Royal Society, founded in 1662, made it explicit that plain talk was preferred to "fine" writing.

The best writer of the new prose was Dryden, whose style is clear, simple and plain — but never dull. Here are two illustrative passages, one about Chaucer and the other about Shakespeare:

> Some of his [i.e. Chaucer's] persons are vicious, some virtuous; some are unlearned, or (as Chaucer calls them) lewd, and some are learned. Even the ribaldry of the low characters is different; the Reeve, the Miller, and the Cook, are several men, and distinguished from each other as much as the mincing Lady Prioress, and the broad-speaking, gap-toothed Wife of Bath. But enough of this; there is such a variety of game springing up before me, that I am distracted in my choice, and know not what to follow. 'Tis sufficient to say, according to the proverb, that here's God's plenty...

> All the Images of Nature were still present to him [i.e. Shakespeare], and he drew them not laboriously, but luckily: when he describes any thing, you more than see it, you feel it too. Those who accuse him to have wanted learning give him the greater commendation: he was naturally learned; he needed not the spectacles of Books to read Nature; he looked inwards, and found her there.

This natural, simple, and yet pungent style, written as it was spoken — this was what the new world needed. It was to become the best language of clubs and coffee-houses of bourgeois society in the 18th century.

II Addison, Steele and Pope

1. Addison, Steele and Periodical Essay Joseph Addison (1672—1719), son of an English clergyman, and Richard Steele (1672—1729), son of an Irish attorney, were schoolmates in the Charterhouse and at Oxford. Addison was distinguished for his scholarship, and at thirty was marked for public service. "Dick" Steele was of another sort — affectionate and lovable, but thriftless and unpredictable. He left Oxford without a degree, fought a duel, and wrote sentimental comedies for the stage.

From 1709 to 1711 Steele ran a periodical, *The Tatler*, published three times a week. Addison was a regular contributor. In 1711, when *The Tatler* was stopped, Steele and Addison issued *The Spectator*, which rose at its peak to a circulation of 14,000 copies. It was published daily and ended in 1712.

With *The Tatler* and *The Spectator* Addison and Steele intended to make a gentleman of the parvenu — i.e. trader, manufacturer, or enterpriser. Vices and foibles of bourgeois society (e.g. gambling, duelling, party strife, snobbery, silly fashions) were ridiculed with gentle humour. At the same time, the papers offered expert instruction in manners and taste and culture in such a manner as the parvenu could accept; easy criticism of the drama and literature, which told him what was proper to think and to say if the subject came up; familiar letters, which might serve as his models; character sketches (e.g. Sir Roger de Coverley and his friends), which were figures in a mirror wherein the readers could recognize themselves as they were or would like to be. The papers aimed to give both instruction and amusement.

The papers had a subtle effect on bourgeois culture. Throughout the century they were read and re-read and imitated until they became a part of the literary tradition. And their style, particularly Addison's, was considered a model of simplicity, naturalness and colloquial ease.

2. Pope and His Poetry If Addison and Steele were the representative essayists of the bourgeois society, Alexander Pope (1688—1744) was its representative poet. He was born a delicate child of a Catholic linen draper, and suffered from being under-size. Though debarred by birth from social distinction, he attained the highest fame among the men of letters: he was the true successor to Dryden in poetry.

Pope was the spokesman of bourgeois complacency and self-satisfaction: "One truth is clear, whatever is, is Right." But Pope was a Tory, and he wrote for the Opposition during the Whig supremacy. He was afraid of no one, not even the Philistine George II, who would have no "poetry". Like Dryden, he was a master of satire, social or political. In his satires is reflected the universal corruption under the premiership of Sir Robert Walpole:

> In solider, churchman, patriot, man in power,
> 'Tis avarice all, ambition is no more!
> ...

All, all look up, with reverential awe,
At crimes that 'scape, or triumph o'er the law;
While truth, worth, wisdom, daily they decry —
"Nothing is sacred now but villainy."

For us, the most remarkable about Pope is perhaps his neat phrasing of common sense in his *Essay on Criticism* (1711) and *Essay on Man*(1733—1734). There are couplets (of which he was master) which have become familiar quotations:

A Little Learning is a dangerous thing,
Drink deep, or taste not the Pierian spring.

True Wit is Nature to advantage dressed,
What oft was thought but ne'er so well expressed.

III Daniel Defoe

1. Defoe and His Political Writings No writer of the whole century had a life more full of surprising adventures than Daniel Defoe (1661—1731). He was the son of a dissenting butcher named James Foe (Daniel added the honorific "De" when over forty years of age). He was well married, and for some years prospered as a wholesale merchant. He supported William of Orange and welcomed the Glorious Revolution. When his trade was ruined in William's war with France, he took up writing. Practically all of his works was done after he was thirty-five, and his masterpiece *Robinson Crusoe* was produced when he was sixty.

In 1701 he published his popular verse *The True-Born Englishman*, attacking such aristocrats as had attacked King William as a foreigner:

> Wealth (howsoever got) in England makes
> Lords of mechanics, gentlemen of rakes!
> Antiquity and birth are needless here.
> 'Tis impudence and money makes a peer.

In 1702 Defoe wrote a mocking pamphlet, *The Shortest Way with the Dissenters*, supposed to be an argument by an Anglican churchman that all dissenters should be hanged. He was imprisoned and put in the pillory. With characteristic audacity he wrote a *Hymn to the Pillory*, describing the persons who really deserved to be where he was. His friends rallied about him, and cheered him as a hero.

When he was released, he began a periodical, *The Review* (1704—1711), containing political essays, social gossip and witty comment on life and manners. He wrote its nine volumes single-handed — and he had other journalistic connections. A collection of his periodical writings would make a considerable library.

2. *Adventures of Robinson Crusoe* In 1711 appeared the accounts of Alexander Selkirk, a Scottish mariner, who had lived for some five years on a lonely island off Chile. Defoe took the accounts as a point of departure, transformed and developed them with his invention into a fictitious biography — *Adventures of Robinson Crusoe* (1719). It was acclaimed at once: four editions were called for within four months.

Robinson Crusoe, we are told, is shipwrecked. He fights his way out of the water and finds himself on an uninhabited island, where he is to remain for eighteen years. All alone he builds a fortified place, grows barley and rice, domesticates the goats, makes a boat, fights the cannibals, and has innumerable mishaps before he is carried home by an English ship. The long series of incidents keeps the reader's mind on the stretch to the very end.

The supreme quality in *Robinson Crusoe* is its sense of reality, its lifelikeness. And Defoe takes pains to convince his readers that what he is writing about is "real life".

> Before I set up my tent, I drew a half circle before the hollow place, which took in about ten yards in its semi-diameter from the rock, and twenty yards in its diameter, from its beginning and ending. In this half circle I pitched two rows of strong stakes, driving them into the ground till they stood very firm like piles, the biggest end being out of the ground about five foot and a half, and sharpened on the top; the two rows did not stand above six inches from one another. Then I took the pieces of cable which I had cut in the ship, and laid them in rows one upon another, within the circle, between these two rows of stakes, up to the top, placing other stakes in the inside, leaning against them, about two foot and a half high, like a spur to a post, and this fence was so strong that neither man nor beast could get into it or over it.

This is an example of Defoe's method. Lifelikeness is achieved by the insistence on detail: the size of the fence and its building materials. Defoe tells us not merely that something is done, but how it is done. The language of his prose is the ordinary language of the ordinary people — "explicit, easy, free, and very plain".

3. Significance of *Robinson Crusoe* *Adventures of Robinson Crusoe* is an expression of the bourgeois qualities of individualism and private enterprise. Robinson is a new man — a man sure of himself and sure of being able to establish himself anywhere in the world. He is a man of a new age, in which doubt and uncertainty are replaced by hope and confidence. He is what Marx calls the 18th century individual — "the joint product of the dissolution of the feudal form of society and of the new forces of production which had developed since the 16th century".

Robinson is the enterpriser of his age. He is ready to command nature, his enemy, and to found his colony beyond the seas. He is a merchant-adventurer, interested in material profits. He is the colonist, the empire builder. *Adventures of Robinson Crusoe* is an embodiment of the spirit of individual enterprise and colonial expansion of the rising bourgeoisie.

To *Adventures or Robinson Crusoe* Defoe published a sequel: *Farther Adventures of Robinson Crusoe* (1719). It may be of interest to note that in the sequel Robinson lands on the China coast with his crew, who are "gentlemen as well as merchants". And they pay visits to Nanjing and Peking.

Adventures of Robinson Crusoe expressed the epic theme of the power of the average man to preserve life and to organize economy in the face of the most unpromising environment. Throughout the 18th century it was used as the basis for lectures in political economy.

IV Jonathan Swift

1. ***A Tale of a Tub*** Jonathan Swift (1667—1745) came of an ancient English family. He was a posthumous child born into poverty in Ireland. Through the aids of his uncles, he received his early education and obtained his degree from Trinity College, Dublin. At the age of twenty-two (1689), he entered the household of the Whig diplomat Sir William Temple, a distant relative of his mother's. There, in Surrey, he spent about ten years as secretary; and there, in 1696 to 1697, he wrote *A Tale of a Tub*, an attack on the three religious organizations of his time — the Church of England, the Roman Catholic Church, and the Dissenters or Nonconformists. The phrase "a tale of a tub" was a 17th century slang for a joke, a hoax, an idle discourse.

Once upon a time, so Swift begins the tale, there was a man who had three Sons — Peter, Martin, and Jack. Upon his death-bed, he gave each of the lads a new coat and told them how to wear and manage it. He also commanded them in his will that they should live together like brothers. The "father" is meant for Christ, the coats the Christian faith and practice, the will the New Testament, the three sons the three churches — the Roman Catholic Church (Peter), the Church of England (Martin), and the Dissenters (Jack).

At first the three sons lived together like brothers and friends. Then they began to put different interpretations upon one and the same will. And finally the plain words of the will were made to mean what they did not mean. This was how the religious organizations departed from the simple faith which Christ had taught, and how they built on that simple foundation a super-structure of worldly display and intrigue and spurious doctrines and feud and hatred of one another.

The tale gave offence to all parties concerned. Queen Anne was never placated. But it was a great satire. It is said that upon re-reading this early work in the latter part of his life, Swift laid the volume down with the exclamation, "Good God, what a genius I had when I wrote that book!"

2. The Irish Pamphlets From 1699 onward Swift held several small livings in the vicinity of Dublin. In 1713 he was made Dean of St. Patrick's (Dublin). He did not like Ireland, which he described as "a wretched, dirty dog-hole", a place of "slaves and knaves and fools". But years of living among the Irish made him realize why Ireland had become what it was. He wrote pamphlet after pamphlet against the English oppressors.

In 1724 he published a series of letters in the name of a drapier (*The Drapier's Letters*) against the English attempt at debasing the Irish coinage (i.e. inflation). A patent had been issued to a William Wood to supply Ireland with an enormous sum in copper coinage, and the Irish themselves had not been consulted. In *The Drapier's Letters* Swift exposed the base injustice and stirred up the Irish to assert their rights. He won the battle in 1725, when the patent was withdrawn. The Irish adored him and kept his birthday.

The longer Swift brooded over the degradation of the Irish people, the more savagely he wrote against their oppressors. In 1729 appeared the most terrible of his satires: *A Modest Proposal for Preventing the Children of Poor People in Ireland from Being a Burden to Their Parents or Country, and for Making Them Beneficial to the Public*. In this pamphlet Swift proposes, as plainly and soberly as if he meant every word, that the children be fattened and butchered for the English market. "A young healthy child, well nursed, is at a year old a most delicious, nourishing and wholesome food, whether stewed, roasted, baked, or boiled ..." Moreover, adds Swift, it would be good economy to "flay the carcass, the skin of which, artificially dressed, will make admirable gloves for ladies, and summer-boots for fine gentlemen".

When *Modest Proposal* was published, Ireland was in a state of famine and many absentee landlords were spending their rents exacted from their tenants on luxurious living in England or elsewhere outside Ireland.

3. *Gulliver's Travels* and Its Significance *Gulliver's Travels* (1726) has become one of the most fascinating of story-books for children. Gulliver the mariner is shipwrecked and lands in Lilliput, a land of little men, each of whom one-twelfth of his size, their king being taller by the breadth of a finger-nail than any of his subjects. Among the Lilliputians, Gulliver looks like a giant. He sleeps upon a bed made up of 600 Lilliputian beds, and he consumes meat and drink sufficient to support 1728 Lilliputians. There, Gulliver has countless adventures. After leaving Lilliput, Gulliver is shipwrecked on an island of giants (Brobdingnag), beside whom he looks as tiny as the Lilliputians looked beside him. The dinner-table is "thirty feet high from the floor", and the dish of meat is twenty-four feet in diameter. There, again, Gulliver has countless adventures, no less wonderful.

But *Gulliver's Travels* is much more than a children's book. It is a satire upon England. Lilliput is England diminished into pettiness; Brobdingnag is England grotesquely magnified, and every trifle is made ridiculously big. And through the veil of satire is visible the English politician whom Swift chose for special attack. The lord high treasurer of Lilliput is named Flimnap, expert on the tight-rope. He "can cut a caper an inch higher than any other lord in the Empire". This was Sir Robert Walpole, Chancellor of the Exchequer.

So much for the first two parts of the satire. Part III, which is the least effective, ridicules pseudo-scientists and pedants. In Part IV, in the voyage to the country of the Houyhnhnms, Swift enlarges his plan to include the whole race of mankind.

Thus says William Hazlitt:

> Gulliver is an attempt to tear the mask of imposture from the world, to strip empty pride and grandeur of the imposing air which external circumstances threw around them. And nothing but imposture has a right to complain of it.

Swift's positive philosophy is difficult to determine. But *Gulliver's Travels* shows his bitter anger at what man has made of man in his own age. This anger springs from a courageous realism, an ability to look the facts of 18th-century society in the face, an unflinching sense of life. And he expresses what he felt in a style of his own — plain and hard-hitting.

CHAPTER VII

THE MID-18TH CENTURY

I Richardson, Smollett and Sterne

1. Richardson and Sentimental Fiction Samuel Richardson (1689—1761), son of a joiner in Derbyshire, rose to be a substantial printer in London. In 1740, when he had passed his 50th year, he produced a novel in the form of letters, *Pamela or Virtue Rewarded*, in four volumes.

Pamela is a poor servant-girl (the first servant-girl in fiction), to whom Mr. B., the unscrupulous son of her employers, pays unwelcome attentions. She resists, makes attempts to escape, even tries to drown herself. Realizing that her character is above reproach, Mr. B. proposes marriage, which she accepts. So virtue is rewarded with a considerable income and a higher social position. The whole affair is conveyed in letters—naive, sentimental, heart-rending. Tears were shed over the book.

Encouraged by the success of the first novel, Richardson proceeded to write the second, *Clarissa Harlowe* (1747—1748), in six volumes. Clarissa is a pure and high-minded girl of a good family. In her effort to escape from a forced marriage and her unhappy home, she falls into the trap of her dissolute lover Lovelace. She is persecuted and ruined, and dies in broken-hearted shame. Being a tragedy, *Clarissa* drew more tears from its readers. Its influence was felt on the Continent, over Diderot, Rousseau, etc.

Richardson has obvious defects as a novelist. He is repetitious and long-winded — the very length of his books has become a joke. He is always moralizing, always preaching, but not always pleasant. His idea of "virtue rewarded" — either in this world or the next — is utilitarian, bourgeois morality that demands some kind of dividend for the expenditure of righteous effort. But Richardson introduced something new into fiction; namely, sensibility. The theme of his novels is invariably virtue in distress — a pathetic theme, in the exploration of which he disclosed the intimate feelings of the individual human heart.

2. Smollett and Picaresque Fiction Tobias George Smollett (1721—1771) came from a landed family in Scotland. He had some training in physic. From nineteen to twenty-six he served as a surgeon in the West Indies. Much of his early career he has built into his first novel *Roderick Random* (1748).

Roderick, like Smollett himself, is a Scot. After some training in surgery, he wanders southward with his old school-fellow Strap, a barber's son. Extraordinary mishaps and encounters (e. g. narrow escapes from highwaymen) come one after another. At London, "the devil's drawing room", Roderick takes a situation with a French apothecary and becomes mixed up with the affairs of his mistress and her daughters. Then as surgeon's mate on a man-of-war, he sails to the West Indies. An inside view is given of the filth, the horrors, the brutality of seafaring life in the most exciting cycles of adventures. The ending of the novel is insipid and crude. Roderick gets back to England, visits London and Bath, and in the midst of despair meets his long lost father, now fabulously rich. He ends in wealth and marital joy.

Roderick Random is a picaresque or rogue novel. And picaresque are Smollett's other novels —*Peregrine Pickle* and *Humphrey Clinker*. They are plotless but fast moving strings of wild ups and downs of adventurers. Smollett wrote in the tradition of Cervantes and Le Sage, of whom he was a translator.

Though not a first-class novelist, Smollett is a good story-teller with a vigorous and incisive style. He exposes the vices and follies of various social classes and professions. His nautical chapters in *Roderick Random* are particularly remarkable: they are the first pictures of real sea life in English fiction. His influence as a realist can be traced in the works of Scott, Dickens and Thackeray.

3. Sterne and "Shandyism" Like Richardson, Sterne was a sentimentalist. But the mood differs. Richardson's sentimentalism is mixed up with morality, and the story of Pamela, or of Clarissa, moves on with solemnness. Sterne's touch is lighter: he sentimentalizes with wit and humour.

Sprung of landed gentry, Laurence Sterne (1713—1768) was educated at Cambridge, where he did much out-of-the-way reading. He was a parson at York, brilliant but unpredictable. In 1760 to 1767 appeared *The Life and Opinions of Tristram Shandy*. The very title is a piece of deliberate humour. We have the life and opinions, not of Tristram Shandy, but of Walter Shandy, Toby Shandy, Corporal Trim, etc. Tristram is only born when we are half through with the novel, and he disappears long before the end of the book.

The manner of writing is no less odd. Grammar and rhetoric are thrown overboard. Some chapters are long, some very short; some are inserted, some omitted; some seem to be mislaid and leave nothing but blank pages and dots. Everywhere are digressions, which Sterne regarded as "the life, the soul of reading".

The book is a book of endless talk. Walter Shandy, Tristram's father, talks with Mrs. Shandy and with Dr. Slop at Shandy's birth. Uncle Toby, an invalided war veteran, talks with his servant, Corporal Trim. Uncle Toby falls in love with the widow Wadman, and they talk and talk. The talk jumps from topic to topic, and can never be kept to the main line.

In *Tristram Shandy*, Sterne puts emphasis on two things. One is sentiment, or the tenderness of the heart as a protest against the indifference and brutality of the time. An ass, a fly, any object, however mean it might be, could not fail to enlist his sympathy. Next to sentimentalism is individuality (or eccentricity). Sterne gives vent to his own way of looking at life, his whims and whimsicalities.

Mention must be made of Sterne's *Sentimental Journey Through France and Italy* (1768), a book of casual adventures on the Continent — flirtations, delicate situations, tears for a poor monk, for an old man and an ass on the roadside, for some caged starlings, etc. "I laugh till I cry, and in the same tender moments cry till I laugh. I Shandy it more than ever," says Sterne.

II Henry Fielding

1. Fielding and His Early Novels Henry Fielding (1707—1754) was the son of a general who served under Marlborough. He was educated at Eton. Coming to London in the thirties, he wrote burlesques and farces, loaded with attacks on Walpole and his administration, until they were stopped by Walpole's Licensing Act in 1737. In 1740 appeared Richardson's *Pamela*. While thousands were moved to tears, a few responded with a loud guffaw. Fielding, one of the few, produced a parody, *Joseph Andrews* (1742), which enraged the serious-minded printer.

Joseph Andrews is brother to Pamela, who is now happily married to Mr. B.. A handsome foot-boy in the household of Lady Booby, Pamela's aunt-in-law, he rejects the advances of the lady with a solemn piety which burlesques Pamela's attitude towards Mr. B.. Dismissed by Lady Booby, Joseph sets out afoot to seek his sweetheart Fanny, a servant-girl. Upon the road he comes across all sorts of people — innkeepers, highwaymen, parsons good and bad, kind travellers and selfish travellers, amiable gentlemen and supercilious gentlemen. Finally it is revealed that the humble Fanny is a sister of the famous Pamela and that Joseph is the son of a gentleman (they wore mislaid in infancy!). And so they were married, to the approval of Pamela.

Joseph Andrews is more than a burlesque. It is Fielding's first attempt at what may be called humane realism. Fielding ridicules all that seems to him to be unrealistic and false in Richardson's novel — its hypocrisy and bogus morality. At the same time he presents the humble but kind people — the postillion, the common soldier, the farmer, etc. Herein lies Fielding's kinship with the people.

Fielding's next novel, *Jonathan Wild the Great* (1743), is a fictitious biography of a thief and thief-taker, who was hanged in 1725. Fielding follows Wild's "triumphant" career from childhood to the gallows, giving his background of thieves, highwaymen, card-sharpers, and the corrupt and brutal officials of Newgate jail. The grim picture of the underworld is thrown into higher relief by the introduction of a few men of simple virtue and affection — the jeweller Heartfree, his wife and children, and their apprentice Friendly. Fielding's object was to point out that success is often independent of virtue — that the same qualities which made Wild a great thief have brought other men, really no better than Wild, to prosperity, wealth and high position.

Jonathan Wild is not a great novel. The characters are made too much the mouthpieces of the ideas that underlie the novel, greatness and goodness. But it remains the best, certainly the most sustained, piece of ironical writing in the English language. Almost every aspect of bourgeois society is satirized: Whigs and Tories, the party system itself, the corruption of office, and economic exploitation.

2. *History of Tom Jones* Fielding is at his best in *Tom Jones*(1749). Tom Jones the foundling is the adopted son of the rich squire Allworthy. He is brought up together with Blifil, son of Allworthy's sister Bridget, and also Allworthy's legitimate heir. Tom and Blifil stand in precise antithesis to each other: Tom is happy-go-lucky, yet rebellious when provoked, while Blifil is hypocrisy incarnate. Both are much in company with Sophia Western, daughter of a neighbouring squire. Sophia falls in love with Tom, but her family is pressing a match with the odious Blifil.

At the instigation of Blifil, Tom is driven from squire Allworthy's home. He sets out for London to enlist. Sophia defies the convention and takes the road to London in search of him. Time and again they come near to finding each other on the way, but never meet. Will the two ever meet and become reconciled? Fielding keeps one wondering. Upon the road they come across various sorts of people — benevolent gentlemen, sharp-tongued wives and old maids, double-faced villains. Then they get to London, and town life with its gallantries and its dissolution is mirrored in the novel. Episodes are many, and digressions innumerable. Only at long last is it revealed that Tom is the son of Allworthy's sister, and that Blifil is at the root of all troubles. Tom is now recognized heir to his uncle, and the story winds up with his marriage with Sophia.

Tom Jones was one of the favourite books of Karl Marx. Franz Mehring wrote, "Marx thought highly of the English novels of the 18th century and in particular of Fielding's *Tom Jones*, which in its own way is also a mirror of its time."

To be "a mirror of its time" is the aim of Fielding's fiction. Fielding insists on calling *Tom Jones* an "history". "It is our business," he says, "to discharge the part of a faithful historian, and to describe human nature as it is, not as we would wish it to be."

3. *Amelia* — Fielding's Last Novel Fielding regarded his fiction as a "comic epic in prose " — i. e. an art form that would be to 18th century society what the epic had been in more primitive world: it was at once a realistic mirror and a critical consideration of the life of the times.

And so was his last novel, *Amelia* (1751). Here is the first sentence of the novel: "The various accidents which befell a very worthy couple after their uniting in the state of matrimony will be the subject of the following history." Fielding had been appointed Justice of the Peace for Middlesex in 1749, and was therefore able to depict what he had seen, heard and felt about London life of the day. Unlike *Tom Jones*, *Amelia* gives a grim picture. Of the "very worthy couple", the husband is Captain Booth, an erring man, but the wife (i.e. Amelia) is a courageous mother and a faithful wife. Booth tries to mend himself and earn an honest living, but he is continuously subject to all sorts of social abuses. There are prostitutes, procuresses; ruffians, male and female; tricksters and sharpers, who molest and prey upon the weak and the unfortunate. And the picture of Newgate prison is only a bit more lurid epitome of society outside, where rank has privileges and merit counts for nothing. The problem of the social injustice, which is the problem of the novel, remains unsolved. When the reader finishes the book, he must exclaim with Amelia: "Good Heavens! What are our great men made of? Are they in reality a distinct species from the rest of mankind? Are they born without hearts?" The ending is unnatural. Booth becomes a devout Christian and Amelia gets an inherited property so that the couple can leave for the country in peace. In spite of these limitations, however, the novel may be considered a forerunner of the problem drama of Diderot and the problem fiction of Godwin.

III Johnson and His Circle

1. Johnson, Lexicographer and Critic Samuel Johnson (1709—1784) was the son of a bookseller in Lichfield. His boyhood was spent in his father's bookshop, where he "looked into a great many books which were not commonly known at the universities". He had a few terms at Oxford, but took no degree. In 1737 he arrived almost penniless in London and began his life as a hack writer.

In 1747 Johnson was employed by a group of booksellers to prepare a dictionary of the English language. He counted on the patronage of Lord Chesterfield. But His Lordship was indifferent until 1754, when the work was brought to completion. Johnson wrote a letter to Chesterfield, which has become deservedly famous:

> Seven years, my Lord, have now passed since I waited in your outward rooms or was repulsed from your door; during which time I have been pushing on my work through difficulties, of which it is useless to complain, and have brought it, at last, to the verge of publication, without one act of assistance, one word of encouragement, or one smile of favour. Such treatment I did not expect, for I never had a patron before...

The letter is significant. It indicates that the age of the author under aristocratic patronage had gradually given way to the age of the author as a producer under the capitalist system. Authorship had become a profession, and literary production a commodity. The literary output that Johnson turned out was miscellaneous: two poems, one play, one novel, an edition of Shakespeare, *Lives of the English Poets* and a sheaf of periodical essays. *Dictionary*, which appeared in 1755, established his reputation, but did not increase his means; and he never ceased to struggle until he was given a pension by the government in 1762. "No one but a blockhead ever wrote except for money," remarked Johnson.

Johnson was a Tory, a Conservative. His works, including *Dictionary*, betray his Tory prejudice. In *Lives of the English Poets*, the work of his old age, he wasn't fair about Swift and Milton, whom he could not quite understand. He had no sympathy for social and political movements of the time. He opposed the American Revolution, and would have opposed the French Revolution if he had lived longer.

2. Boswell's *Life of Johnson* For later generations, Johnson lives not so much in his own writing as in Boswell's biography of him, which has been considered the greatest biography in the English language.

James Boswell (1740—1795) was of aristocratic Scotch birth, but had little or nothing of aristocratic dignity about him. He lived and practised law in Edinburgh, but law was not his forte. He was a lion-hunter and good "mixer". At the age of twenty-three, he met Johnson, who was then past fifty. He was admitted to Johnson's circle, which included Goldsmith the journalist, Reynolds the painter, Dr. Burney the composer, Garrick the actor and Sheridan the playwright. He observed and studied Johnson till he could reproduce his master's very tone and idioms and manner of speech. In 1791 appeared his epoch-making *Life of Johnson* in two volumes.

The chief merit of *Life of Johnson* lies in its lifelikeness. Boswell records the bad as well as the good, the rough as well as the smooth —

Johnson's bearishness, his bad table manners, his ferocious appetite, his unconquerable thirst for tea, his boisterous laughter, his argument for argument's sake, his "blowing out his breath like a whale" at the end of the argument, his violent prejudices and his bundle of contradictions. "I would not cut off Johnson's claws to please anybody," says Boswell. But what emerges from *Life of Johnson* is not a caricature, but a full-length portrait. "I will venture to say," says Boswell, "that he [Johnson] will be seen in this work more completely than any man who has ever lived."

Biographies had been panegyrics. "Let not his frailties be remembered; he was a very great man" — that had been the motto of biographers. Boswell thought differently: he strove for what was real and true and lifelike. His *Life of Johnson* looks like the diary of one man written by another man. It marked the dawn of modern biography.

3. Goldsmith's Verse and Prose Oliver Goldsmith (1730—1774), another member of Johnson's circle, was the son of an Irish clergyman. Amid menial poverty he picked up a sort of education at Trinity College, Dublin. Upon graduation, he spent some years of picaresque wandering on the Continent. In 1756 he turned up in London and took up the pen for a living, drudging for the slave-drivers of journalism. He established himself as an author, but what he got he spent through indiscretion. So in spite of fame and friends, his hackwork continued to the end. He really worked himself to death.

Of the works of Goldsmith, mention must be made of the following: (1) *The Vicar of Wakefield*, (2) *The Deserted Village*, and (3) *She Stoops to Conquer*. *The Vicar of Wakefield* (1766) has always been popular. The plot is slight, even absurd; but there is peculiar charm about it. No one who has read it can ever forget the Vicar, with his sermonizing, his mixture of vanity and humility, his "natural goodness", his troubles with his impossible family. The feudal-bourgeois society depicted in the novel is enveloped in idyllic fancy.

The same idyllic fancy pervades *The Deserted Village* (1770), written in heroic couplets. The poem contains some significant passages on the cruelty of enclosure and eviction, but the pictures that he gives of rural amenities — the dance, the evening out of doors and in, the tavern, the schoolmaster, the old vicar — are idealized. "Where are such charming persons and charming things?" — People asked one another, and they hunted in vain for their originals, in England or Ireland.

She Stoops to Conquer (1773) was an immediate success, and has always remained one of the half-dozen most popular comedies in English. Young and bashful Marlowe goes to court Miss Hardcastle. He mistakes her house for an inn, her father Squire Hardcastle for an innkeeper, and herself as a barmaid. And Miss Hardcastle plays the barmaid to win her bashful lover. There is a lot of fun, a lot of practical jokes. There are also charming songs. The sources of the comic are the unnatural relations of feudal-bourgeois society. But, again, there is idyllic charm.

Goldsmith was not a profound social critic. He only scratched the surface, but never cut very deep.

4. Sheridan and His *School for Scandal* Like Goldsmith, Richard Brinsley Sheridan (1751—1816) was of Irish birth. His father was by turns actor, theatre manager and elocutionist, while his mother was the author of one novel and two plays. Young Sheridan was educated at Harrow and at home. By about twenty he wrote a clever satire, which contains one couplet often quoted:

> You write with ease, to show your breeding;
> But easy writing's vile hard reading.

At twenty-four he succeeded Garrick, first as manager and then proprietor of Drury Lane Theatre, and so continued for many years.

His masterpiece, *The School for Scandal*, was produced in 1777. There are really two plots: (1) the scandal group and (2) the Sir Peter group. The scandal group, headed by Lady Sneerwell, gives the atmosphere of the play. The Sir Peter group consists of an old husband and a sprightly young wife; two brothers, one a hypocrite and the other a spendthrift; a long-absent uncle from India; and a young heiress, ward to Sir Peter. Sheridan is not a maker of good plots, but a creator of successful scenes (e. g. the Scandal Club, the auction, the screen scene).

Sheridan was a great critic of 18th-century society. He satirized young fops, fashionable ladies, sentimental girls, stupid husbands, hypocrites, bad critics, newsmonger, etc. His satire is a sword-play of wit.

Crowned with stage success before thirty, Sheridan went into politics. He became M. P. and held several government posts for short periods under the brief Whig administration. He opposed the American War; he laboured for the impeachment of Warren Hastings; and he stood for fair representation in Parliament and the freedom of the press.

IV Poetry: From Neo-Classic to Romantic

1. Changing Modes in Poetry For almost half a century, Pope set the fashion for English verse, in heroic couplets. The poetry of Pope and his group is poetry of reason rather than of sentiment or feeling, poetry of the city rather than of the country, poetry imitative of the classics rather than spontaneous. This is known as Neo-classic poetry.

In the second quarter of the century, signs of change were discernible. James Thomson (1700—1748), author of *Seasons*, turned from the "clamour of the smoky towns" to the "delightful prospects of the country", from the generalized human nature to the simple lives and daily tasks of the peasant folk. In the mid-century, William Collins wrote feelingly about evening (*Ode to Evening*), and Thomas Gray, the Cambridge scholar, sang in faultless music of the obscure dead (*Elegy Written in a Country Churchyard*).

> Let not ambition mock their useful toil,
>   Their homely joys, and destiny obscure;
> Nor grandeur hear with a disdainful smile,
>   The short and simple annals of the poor.

Meanwhile, James Macpherson produced *Ossian* (1762), a long narrative poem supposed to have been written by an ancient Gaelic poet. Thomas Percy revived old English ballads and songs. Matters of far-away and long-ago were brought to bear upon the development of poetry. Poets expressed their distaste for the unrest of the age, and yearned for "nature's simple plan". In the last quarter of the century, Goldsmith, Cowper, and Crabbe exposed the heart with which each in his own way felt the difficulties of contemporary existence. It was Cowper who declared: "God made the country, and man made the town. "

Thus poetry left the drawing-room for the simple and lowly. It was emancipated from the school of Pope, from his "straight-backed measure with stately stride". Predominance of reason was replaced by the predominance of sentiment or feeling. Such poetry, for lack of a better term, is called Romantic.

2. Burns and His Lyrics Robert Burns (1759—1796), the greatest 18th century lyric poet, was born on the banks of Doon, not far from Ayr, in the southwestern corner of Scotland. His father was a poor "renter". Young Burns knew many a weary day at the plough-tail and in harvest, but he found time for the ordinary education of the Scotch peasant. He had listened to ballads from his mother's lips. Later he pored over a collection of popular songs. "I pored over them," he said, "driving my cart, or walking to labour, song by song, verse by verse."

In 1784, the Burns family settled on a little farm of Mossgiel, in a two-room house with a garret. Burns ploughed, made love and sang. When he returned from his day's work, he used to retire to his garret and write down what he had composed in the fields. In 1786 appeared *Poems, Chiefly in the Scottish Dialect*, which made the peasant-poet known in literary circles in Scotland and England. Later he was made an excise man at Dumfries — "gauging auld wives barrels" as he called it. With a living wage and leisure, he continued his writing. He died in 1796, in his 37th year.

Burns's lyrics are based on the rich folk songs of Scotland. They are simple and unpretentious. Not that they lack art — but they spring so naturally and flow so freely from the moment's mood that they seem as artless as a bird-song.

My love is like a red, red rose
  That's newly sprung in June:
My love is like the melodie
  That's sweetly played in tune:

As fair art thou, my bonnie lass,
  So deep in love am I:
And I will love thee still, my dear,
  Till a' the seas gang dry...

Auld Lang Syne, *John Anderson, My Jo*, *Ye Banks and Braes O' Bonnie Doon*, *Highland Mary*, *Scots, Wha Hae Wi' Wallace Bled*, *O, Wert Thou in the Cauld Blast* — they are among the lasting things that came from Burns's pen.

3. Burns's Satires and Narratives As a poet Burns knew where he was and what he was about. He protested against distinctions founded on birth or rank as in *A Man's a Man for a' That*; and, on the other hand, he depicted the homely feelings and manners of the "virtuous populace" in his immortal *Cotter's Saturday Night* (The "toilworn cotter" is a portrait of his own father, the "renter"). He scorned academic learning, and protested that true inspiration was rather to be found in "ae spark o' Nature's fire".

In the eyes of "auld lichts", Burns was a rebel. He was a master of satires levelled against hypocrisy, formalism, corruption, and especially the hell-and-damnation theology. His *Holy Fair* is full of fun and laughter. Three women are walking on the road to the tent-preaching, which Burns calls "Holy Fair":

My name is Fun — your cronie dear,
 The nearest friend ye hae;
An' this is Superstition here,
 An' that's Hypocrisy.

At the Fair the Minister starts to preach and talks of hell, "where the devils dwell" —

A vast unbottomed, boundless pit,
 Filled fou o' lowin brunstane,
Whase ragin flame an' scorchin heat,
 Wad melt the hardest whun-stane!
The half-asleep start up wi' fear,
 An' think they hear it roarin,
When presently it does appear,
 'Twas but some neibor snorin,
 Asleep that day.

Burns had a strong sympathy with the French Revolution, which brought him into sharp clash with the local society. Though famed as a poet, he was almost ostracized.

CHAPTER VIII

THE ROMANTIC PERIOD (I)

I Radicalism and Romanticism

1. Price, Burke and Tom Paine In 1789, after the fall of the Bastille, Dr. Richard Price, a Nonconformist preacher, delivered a sermon to the English radicals in London. The gist of his argument is that people have the right to elect the governors and "cashier them for misconduct". To this sermon Edmund Burke, M.P., wrote an answer, *Reflections on the French Revolution* (1790). Burke saw nothing but cruelty in the Revolution, ignoring the misery, suffering, injustice of the Old Regime. His *Reflections* provoked many answers, of which Tom Paine's *Rights of Man* was the most remarkable. In Tom Paine's immortal phrase, Burke "pitied the plumage and forgot the dying bird".

Tom Paine (1737—1809), the "emancipator of the human mind and heart", was by turns a stay-maker, a sailor, and an excise officer. In 1774, at the age of thirty-seven, he went to America and became a journalist, advocating the abolition of slavery and justice for women. After the outbreak of the American War, when the colonial leaders were still hoping for a peaceful settlement, Paine published an extremely popular pamphlet *Common Sense*, proposing the formation of "The Free and Independent States of America". He rendered invaluable service to the cause of the Colonies.

Paine's *Rights of Man* appeared in 1791. Its motto is "Liberty". Paine absorbed the doctrines of political liberalism of Locke and Rousseau and breathed into them a spirit of indignation against inequality and oppression, a contempt for privileges, and a profound respect for the rights of the humblest men. It was under his influence that Thomas Hardy, a Scottish boot-maker, founded the London Corresponding Society for Parliamentary Reform. There were 30,000 members, including Tom Paine, William Blake, and William Godwin. The year 1794 marked the height of the revolutionary tide in England: in an anniversary the chief toasts were "Rights of Man" and "Liberty".

2. Godwin, Philosopher and Novelist The controversies over the French Revolution, as sketched above, were finally raised to the height of philosophy by William Godwin, author of *Political Justice* (1793).

William Godwin (1756—1820) started as a Presbyterian minister. Under the influence of French materialists, he gave up his faith and developed his revolutionary thought. In his *Political Justice* he points out that history hitherto has been the record of crimes — war, despotism, fraud, robbery, injustice, and inequality of men. This, he maintains, is due to the deficient social and political institutions, for man is necessarily conditioned by his circumstances. Man himself, however, is perfectible if the circumstances be altered and adapted to human welfare. Godwin insists on the equality of all people on the basis of reason, which is the sole guide of life, and on the abolition of artificial ranks whatever. Such doctrines contain a lot that is utopian, but they were of tremendous revolutionary significance.

Godwin also wrote several novels, of which *Caleb Williams* (1794) is the most interesting. Caleb, a youthful servant, has become possessed of the secret that his master, Squire Falkland, has committed a murder; but the social prestige of Falkland enables him to retain the mastery and to pursue his victim implacably. The novel shows the power possessed by the privileged on the one hand and the helplessness of the lowly on the other. It supplements the treatise *Political Justice* as a general indictment of the existing society.

Godwin's influence on the younger generation was tremendous. William Hazlitt wrote, "No one was more talked of, more looked up to, more sought after; and whenever liberty, truth, justice was the theme, his name was not far off." Again, "No work in our time gave such a blow to the philosophical mind of the country as the celebrated *Enquiry Concerning Political Justice*".

3. William Blake — A Precurser of Romanticism For more than a century William Blake was remembered for a few short lyrics (e. g. *The Tyger*) and some quotable lines like the following:

> To see a World in a Grain of Sand,
>   And Heaven in a Wild Flower,
> Hold Infinity in the palm of your hand,
>   And Eternity in an hour.

It is only in the last fifty years that he has been rehabilitated as a precursor of English romanticism.

William Blake (1757—1827), poet and painter, was born in London. He was an engraver by profession. From his earliest youth he was a seer of visions and a dreamer of dreams. But he was never detached from the revolutionary movements of the time: the American Declaration of Independence, the French Revolution and English radicalism. He was most creative during the French Revolution and he never lost his vitality during the Napoleonic Wars and the following years of reaction. He continued to write for nationalist independence and democratic revolution and dreamed of a better social order. Among his works are: *The Poetical Sketches*(1783), *Songs of Innocence*(1789), *Songs of Experience*(1794), *The Marriage of Heaven and Hell* (1793) and many other poems collectively known as *Prophetic Books*.

His early poems, fresh and direct, are easy to understand, whereas his later works are rather obscure. Blake was one of the most original poets — original in matter and form. He had his own myth, neither Hellenic nor Hebraic, and he wrote in his own way, sometimes in rhyme and metre, sometimes just the sort of prose much like Walt Whitman's.

In his *Prophetic Books* there are always visions of cosmic struggles between the Old and the New, between slavery and freedom, or (in his own language) between Urizen and Fuzon or Luvah. His *The Four Zoas* (1797—1802), for instance, contains nine visions about the liberation from all sorts of bondage. He wrote in the way in which Shelley was to write his *Prometheus Unbound* and Keats his *Hyperion*.

However, Romanticism was by no means a unified movement. Some eminent critics have proposed to speak not of Romanticism, but of

Romanticisms.

II Wordsworth and Coleridge

1. Wordsworth and His Early Poems William Wordsworth (1770—1850) was one of the poets that came under the influence of the French Revolution in their impressionable years. The son of an attorney, he was born in a small village in the Lake District. He was educated at Cambridge. In 1790 he took a walking tour on the Continent, when the French Revolution was in progress. France seemed to him to be "standing on the top of golden hours" and pointing the way to a new birth of human nature, as in *The Prelude*:

> Bliss was it in that dawn to be alive,
> But to be young was very heaven! — Oh, times,
> In which the meagre, stale, forbidding ways
> Of custom, law, and statute, took at once
> The attraction of a country in romance!
> ... The inert
> Were roused, and lively natures rapt away!
> They who had fed their childhood upon dreams,
> ...
> Were called upon to exercise their skill,
> Not in Utopia, subterraneous fields,
> Or some secreted island, Heaven knows where!

But in the very world, which is the world
Of all of us — the place where in the end
We find our happiness, or not at all!

Wordsworth was a follower of Godwin. “Throw aside your books of chemistry,” he said to a young student of the Temple, “and read Godwin upon Necessity.” For a time the French Revolution was his sole object, and the mighty happenings of the time his chief concern. His poem *Guilt and Sorrow* (1793—1794) was composed under the influence of *Caleb Williams*. It exposes the miseries of war, the injustice of the criminal law, and the wrongs inflicted by the privileged upon the defenceless poor.

2. Wordsworth as a Poet of Nature Wordsworth’s revolutionary fervour did not last long. By 1795 he had turned from the “world of man” to the “world of nature”. Gradually he took sides with English conservatism.

In 1798 Wordsworth and his friend Samuel Taylor Coleridge produced a little volume of poems entitled *Lyrical Ballads*. Most of the poems were written by Wordsworth, about simple life in simple diction — a little girl too young to understand death, an old huntsman with legs thin and dry, a worried mother who loves her idiot offspring, etc.

In 1799 Wordsworth retired to his native mountains in the Lake District, where he wrote poems and spent his long and uneventful life.

Wordsworth’s best poetry, mainly produced between 1797 and 1807, gives expression to objective truth about nature and about the ordinary men and women who lived in close touch with nature (e. g. the Lucy poems, *The Solitary Reaper*) or to his patriotic sentiment in his political sonnets. But in most of his poems he tends to mystify nature and to indulge himself in pantheistic revery. He ascribes to nature virtues that nature does not give. And he often sees the people of his chosen retreat through the Arcadian mist. The Lake District becomes for him an ivory tower.

Wordsworth wrote much about the traditional and stagnant features of the peasantry, eulogizing the non-resistance to evil, its poverty, ignorance and prejudice, and delighting in the intellectual backwardness of the people. During the last two decades of his life, he sought to preserve the past and outdated. He opposed parliamentary reform. He opposed the Catholic Emancipation. To the younger generation, he was a "lost leader".

3. Coleridge and Escapist Romanticism Like Wordsworth, Samuel Taylor Coleridge (1772—1834) had for a time high enthusiasm for the French Revolution. The son of a Devonshire clergyman, he was educated at Christ's Hospital and Cambridge. In 1789 he wrote *Destruction of the Bastille*, in which he exposed radical sentiment. Under the influence of Godwin's *Political Justice*, he and his friend Robert Southey planned to emigrate to America and to establish there a "pantisocratic" community free from prejudice and tradition and based upon "the generalization of individual property". They were, however, doubtful of the possibility of reforming their own minds, already warped by wrong education! They lectured at Bristol — Southey on history, Coleridge on politics and religion — as a means of raising money for their passage to America. Their utopian scheme was never realized, and soon both of them drifted away from the progressive movement.

Coleridge is a dreamer. He represents one trend of romanticism — the escapist trend. His representative poems — *The Ancient Mariner*, *Christabel*, and *Kubla Khan*—are poetic dreams, and the fragmentary *Kubla Khan* was actually composed in a dream, if we accept the author's statement. They are poems of escape — escape to the far-away and long-ago, escape to the realm of medieval romance. *Kubla Khan* presents an enchanting palace of the Oriental conqueror, *Christabel* describes a vampire-haunted castle, and *The Ancient Mariner* lures us to the demon-infested seas, nobody knows where they are.

In these poems, persons and characters are not real, but mystic and supernatural. They are not reflections of life, but shadows of imagination. They demand on the part of the reader a "willing suspension of disbelief".

III Sir Walter Scott

1. Literary Career of Walter Scott Walter Scott (1771—1832), son of a solicitor, was born in Edinburgh. He went through the "High School" in Edinburgh, but he got most of his education by himself. He read law and was admitted to the bar. He took various posts — as Sheriff of Selkirk at twenty-eight and as Clerk of Session in Edinburgh at thirty-five. He was a man of affairs as well as a poet and novelist.

As a poet, Scott matured late. He started as a collector and editor of ballads of the Scottish Border. In 1805 he leapt into sudden popularity as a modern imitator of medieval romance. His *Lay of the Last Minstrel* created a vogue. Other poems followed: *Marmion*, with its background laid in the time of Henry VIII; *The Lady of the Lake*, dealing with the clan warfare of the Highlands, etc. The picturesque, the supernatural, and the trappings of chivalry are presented in rapid and stirring verse.

Scott was beyond forty when he began his career as a novelist. He had public and domestic duties, and he was not healthy, yet he wrote a huge shelf full of novels at feverish speed. In seventeen years he produced twenty-six historical novels — sixteen of them pictures of various periods of Scottish history; six, of English; and four laid outside the British Isles. No man of letters, it would seem, ever lead a more crowded and prolific life.

Scott was not only interested in history, but gifted with a remarkable sense of history. His romance and fiction often contain an escapist element, especially in those dealing with the Middle Ages. But the best of his works (e. g. *The Heart of Midlothian*) gives pictures of the life of the real people, though often presented as romantic visions.

2. Romance, Ballad and Song Scott's romances are now seldom read except certain passages and many lyrics; e. g. *Lochinvar* (from *Marmion*); *Harp of the North*, *Soldiers, Rest, Thy Warfare O'er* (from *The Lady of the Lake*); *O Brignall Banks* (from *Rokeby*). Scott's patriotism is revealed in the short but characteristic specimen from *The Lay of the Last Minstrel*:

> Breathes there the man with soul so dead,
> Who never to himself hath said,
> "This is my own, my native land!"

Whose heart hath ne'er within him burned
As home his footsteps he hath turned
  From wandering on a foreign strand?
If such there breathe, go, mark him well;
  For him no minstrel raptures swells;
High though his titles, proud his name,
Boundless his wealth as wish can claim;
Despite those titles, power, and pelf,
The wretch, concentrated all in self,
Living, shall forfeit fair renown,
And, doubly dying, shall go down
To the vile dust from whence he sprung,
Unwept, unhonoured, and unsung.

Scott was a maker of tuneful songs strewn in his romances and in his novels. The song of Proud Maisie, the death-song of the unhappy, insane girl in *The Heart of Midlothian*, has much of the grim compactness of ancient popular ballads.

Proud Maisie is in the wood,
  Walking so early;
Sweet Robin sits on the bush,
  Singing so rarely.

"Tell me, thou bonny bird,
  When shall I marry me?"
"When six braw gentlemen
  Kirkward shall carry ye."

"Who makes the bridal bed,
  Birdie, say truly?"
"The gray-headed sexton,
  That delves the grave duly."

"The glow-worm o'er grave and stone
  Shall light thee steady;
The owl from the steeple sing,
  'Welcome, proud lady. '"

3. *The Heart of Midlothian* The novel opens with the story of the Porteous Riots of 1736. Sullen, determined and angry people broke into the Edinburgh prison Tolbooth (known as "The Heart of Midlothian"). They carried out Captain Porteous, who had fired on a crowd of people without sufficient justification, and hanged him. Against this background is presented the main story, that of Jennie Deans, a peasant girl. Jennie's half-sister Effie is imprisoned in the Tolbooth on a charge of child murder. Effie refuses to escape (Scott tells us why), and is put to trial. In a poignant scene, Jennie refuses to give the false witness which would secure her acquittal (again, Scott tells us why). But Jennie sets out on foot for London, makes a passionate appeal to Queen Caroline and obtains pardon for her sister. Scott not only presents a broad panorama of life, but also shows the social and historical forces that go to make the situation and lead the characters to act as they do in the novel.

The central part of the novel is the trial of Effie (Chapter 22), the causes which bring it about, and the consequences that follow from it.

Scott makes a serious attempt to capture realistically the strains and tensions of the experiences of the Scottish people. The trial is seen, not merely as a sensation, but as a significant event involving clashes of opposing cultures and differing values: humanity versus worldliness, peasantry versus town, Scotland versus England.

Scott was a man of the old order. He loved rank. He delighted in making himself a beneficent laird of his estate which he called Abbotsford. But with a sense of history he shows feeling for the plight of the Lowland peasantry and kinship with the people.

IV Jane Austen

1. Austen and Her World Jane Austen (1775—1817) was not a Romantic, though she lived and worked in what is known as the Romantic period. Her career was externally limited. She was one of a clergyman's large and lively family at Steventon not far from Winchester. At about twenty she started to write novels. Each of them underwent revision and none was published at once. Of her eight novels, only four appeared in her life-time, including *Pride and Prejudice* (1813) and *Emma* (1816—1816).

Jane Austen passed the greater part of her life in the country parishes at Steventon and at Kent. She had no experience with the great and the conspicuous. And she wisely confined her work to her own little world of country gentlemen and ladies together with snobs, bores and social "climbers". "Three or four families in a country village is," she said, "the very thing to work upon." With perfect modesty she called her work "small square two inches of ivory". She always wrote about what she knew and understood; that is, parish life with calls, walks, picnics, conversations, parties, balls, marriages. It has often been remarked that she never describes a scene in which no woman is present.

From Austen's little world the tremendous events of that times are excluded. Napoleonic wars swept past and left little trace upon her books, and the Industrial Revolution was not even mentioned. In her later life she received a message from royalty that she wrote about the House of Cobourg. But she was not enticed. Wisely she stayed "within the range of her imaginative inspiration".

2. *Pride and Prejudice* and *Emma* Of Austen's novels the most popular is *Pride and Prejudice*, and the most perfect in structure is *Emma*.

Pride and Prejudice begins with the well-known sentence of ironical amusement: "It is a truth universally acknowledged that a single man in possession of a good fortune must be in want of a wife." The Bennetts of Longbourn have five daughters to be married off, and single men in possession of good fortunes turn up at Longbourn or in its neighborhood. Bingley and Jane, the eldest Bennett girl, fall in love with each other. Darcy, Bingley's friend, is attracted to Jane's sister Elizabeth, but he offends her by his insolent behaviour at a ball. The repulsion is increased by the pride of the one and the prejudice of the other. But Darcy continues to be attracted to Elizabeth, in spite of himself. After some time, on a trip to the north of England, Elizabeth chances upon Darcy. Pride is checked and prejudice removed. The story ends with the marriage of Jane and Elizabeth.

Emma, too, is about marriage. Emma Woodhouse of Highbury, a clever and conceited girl, takes to match-making. She chooses for Elton, a local clergyman, not a girl like herself, but the amiable, soft but stupid Harriet of doubtful parentage. The bubble explodes when she realizes that her operations have encouraged Elton to aspire to herself. She next plans Frank Churchill for herself and Mr. Knightley for Harriet; while, in fact, Churchill is secretly engaged to Jane Fairfax, Emma's rival, and the elderly Knightley has been in love with herself ... Thus she makes one blunder after another. But she has one virtue: she is able to criticize herself and learn from experience. Illusion versus reality — this is the underlying idea of the novel.

In each novel there are eminent minor characters: the whimsical Mr. Bennett, his silly wife, the stupid Reverend Mr. Collins, the snobbish Lady Catherine in *Pride and Prejudice*; and the Quixotic Mr. Woodhouse, the loquacious Miss Bates, and the "climber" Mr. Elton in *Emma*.

3. Austen as a Novelist Austen's world, as has been pointed out, is a small world — world of Longbourn, or of Hartfield. She has been blamed for not having written about the battle of Waterloo, the French Revolution, or the Industrial Revolution. Such criticism is impertinent. Shc wrote about what she knew and understood, and no novelist can be expected to do more.

But Austen's world is not merely small but narrow. Her vision is limited by her unquestioning acceptance of class society — a society, in which a minority of the community lived at the expense of the majority.

Snobbery, smugness, condescension, lack of consideration, unkindness of any description — all these are indeed held to our scorn. But the fundamental basis of the class society is left unchallenged, and the value of Austen's fiction is seriously limited by the class basis of her standards.

Austen's strength lies in her realism, in her presentation of the actual problems of behaviour and sensibility in an actual, concrete society. Longbourn is offered as Longbourn, and Hartfield as Hartfield. She makes her readers acquainted intimately with the way men and women in a particular given situation work out their problems of living, particularly the problem of marriage. She has a genuine concern for human feelings, which she depicts with intensity and yet with detachment.

As an admirer of Jane Austen's art, Sir Walter Scott wrote in his Journal: "That young lady had a talent for describing the involvements, and feelings, and characters of ordinary life, which is to me the most wonderful I ever met with. The Big Bow-wow strain I can do myself like any now going; but the exquisite touch, which renders ordinary commonplace things and characters interesting ... is denied to me. What a pity such a gifted creature died so early." Austen was but forty-one at her death in 1817. Austen's range is not to be compared with that of Scott, which is vast, epic, and national. But she is one of the great masters of the craft of fiction.

CHAPTER IX

THE ROMANTIC PERIOD (II)

I George Gordon, Lord Byron

1. Early Career of Lord Byron George Gordon Byron (1788—1824), of an ancient aristocratic family, was born in London and brought up in Scotland. At the age of ten, upon the death of his great-uncle, he became Lord Byron of Newstead (Nottinghamshire). He was educated at Harrow and Cambridge. In 1807 he published *Hours of Idleness*, which was attacked by *The Edinburgh Review*. Byron replied with *English Bards and Scotch Reviewers* (1809), a vigorous satire on the romantics who had drifted away from the progressive movement of the time—Jeffrey, Southey, Wordsworth, Coleridge.

In 1809 he set out for the Mediterranean lands, about which he had read a great deal. He travelled by way of Portugal and Spain, sailed to Albania and at length to Athens. He came back in 1811, bringing with him the manuscripts of several poems. On 10 March 1812, when the first two cantos of *Childe Harold's Pilgrimage* was published, he (in his own words) "woke up and found himself famous".

Upon attaining his majority, Byron took his seat in the House of

Lords. In 1812 he spoke in the House in defence of the Nottingham frame-breakers and on behalf of the Irish Catholics. As an orator, he was noted for the sharpness of his tongue. The negroes, he pointed out, had been freed from oppression, but not the Irish. "I pity," he remarked, "the Catholic peasantry for not having had the good fortune to be born black."

For a few years Byron enjoyed an unusual popularity. In 1815 he married Anna Isabella Milbank. The marriage proved incompatible, and they separated the next year. Public sentiment was against him; and he, the proudest of the proud, experienced the fickleness of popularity. In 1816 he scornfully left England, never to return.

2. Lord Byron on the Continent Byron spent most of his remaining years in Switzerland and Italy. In Italy he composed the last two cantos of *Childe Harold* (1816), most of his poetic dramas, and his masterpiece *Don Juan*. He came in contact with the revolutionary organization called the Carbonari, which was working for the liberation of Italy. In 1821, war broke out in Greece against Turkish rule. Byron, who had been interested in the Greek cause, hired a company of soldiers, sailed in 1823 for the western coast of Greece. His prestige was high: he composed the differences between the revolutionary leaders. In 1824 he was struck down by a fever at Missolonghi.

Three months before his death, on the morning of his 36th birthday, he had written his last poem, which ends in the following stanzas:

If thou regret'st thy youth, why live?
  The land of honourable death
Is here: — up to the field, and give

Away thy breath!
Seek out — less often sought than found —
A soldier's grave, for thee the best;
Then look around, and choose thy ground,
And take thy rest.

Byron was one of the few modern English poets who enjoyed a high European reputation. Goethe, the great German poet, said that Byron "must unquestionably be regarded as the greatest talent of the century". He was impressed by the "daring, dash, and grandiosity" of Byron. "The English," he said, "may think of Byron what they please, but it is certain that they can point to no one poet who is his like. He is different from all the rest, and in the main greater."

3. *Childe Harold's Pilgrimage* *Childe Harold*, in four cantos, is a poem in the Spenserian stanza. The word "childe" is used in its medieval sense — i.e. a sort of knight. The poem starts as if going to be a story of Harold's adventures, but soon it resolves itself into a series of descriptions of spots of beauty and historic interest in southern Europe that Byron visited. In many places, description gives place to lyrical outburst concerning the great events and great men associated with them.

In the first two cantos, Byron deals with Portugal, Spain, Italy, Greece, and Albania during the Napoleonic wars. He condemns despotic rule and applauds the peoples struggling for freedom: Spanish guerillas, Albanian warriors and Greek patriots. In the third and fourth cantos, Byron sings of the greatness of nature — the Rhine, the Alps, the Mediterranean — of the great men in history like Rousseau and Voltaire, or architecture and sculpture, in Europe. Among the famous passages are: the thunder storm in the Alps, the descriptions of Waterloo, Lake Leman, Rome, Venice, and the apostrophe to the ocean.

From the long poem emerges the image of the Byronic hero Childe Harold — strong willed, friendless, always at war with the conventional world, always at one with the people's aspirations for freedom. Disgusted with the society as it was, he turns to nature in solitude.

> There is a pleasure in the pathless woods.
> There is a rapture on the lonely shore,
> There is society where none intrudes,
> By the deep Sea, and music in its roar:
> I love not Man the less, but Nature more.
>
> (Canto 4, Stanza 178)

4. *Don Juan*: an Epic of Satire *Don Juan*, Byron's masterpiece in 16 cantos, was composed between 1818 and 1823. The first five cantos were published between 1819 and 1821, the later cantos between 1823 and 1824. The name of the hero comes from a Spanish legend, but its character is Byron's own creation.

Don Juan is more of a story than *Childe Harold*. It tells of Juan's education, of his shipwreck and his idyllic love with Haidee (a pirate's daughter on a Greek island), of his stay with the Sultana at Constantinople, of his prowess in the Russian war, of his residence in Petersburg as the favourite of the Empress Catherine the Great, of his falling ill and being sent to England for a rest, of England as he found it.

"All things and a few others" — this was Byron's subject, a subject of epic grandeur.

The background of Juan's adventures is laid between 1780 and 1790 (Juan took part in the campaign of Ismail under Suvorov against the Turk in 1790), but the pictures of European society that the poem gives belong to the period of reaction and tyranny after the battle of Waterloo. Byron's attacks are directed against tyrants, war, reactionary politicians (e. g. Castlereigh and Wellington), non-revolutionary poets (e. g. Southey, Wordsworth, and Coleridge), and England in every aspect. Byron was the messenger of political freedom and national liberation of all the countries of Europe: "For I will teach, if possible, the stones to rise against the tyrants." (Canto 8, Stanza 135) Again:

> Raise but an arm! 't will brush their web away,
>   And without that, their poison and their claws
> Are useless. Mind, good people! What I say
>   (Or rather peoples) — go on without pause!
>
> (Canto 9, Stanza 28)

The poem is written in ottava rima — an Italian metre that Byron made his own. The style is conversational with the ease and naturalness of Byron's discourse. The poem flows like "a stream sometimes smooth, sometimes rapid, and sometimes rushing down in cataracts — a mixture of philosophy and slang — of everything".

5. Shorter Poems and Lyrics Aside from *Childe Harold*, *Don Juan*, and eight poetic dramas, Byron wrote a number of shorter poems, including *Prometheus* and *The Prisoner of Chillon*, both of them written in 1816. The image of Prometheus, the fire-giver in Greek myth, had always been in his mind, and he frequently alluded to him in his poems. To Byron, as to other revolutionary Romantics like Shelley, Prometheus is a rebel, who suffers for his service to mankind.

In the endurance, and repulse
  Of thine impenetrable Spirit,
Which Earth and Heaven could not convulse,
  A mighty lesson we inherit:
Thou art a symbol and a sign
  To Mortals of their fate and force;
Like thee, Man is in part divine,
  A troubled stream from a pure source ...

The image of a sufferer, at once beneficent and defiant, appealed to the passions and convictions of Byron and awoke his enthusiasm. Francois Bonivard (1493—1570) was such a sufferer. A prior of a small monastery in Switzerland, he joined the patriots who were trying to make Geneva a republic. He was imprisoned in the Castle of Chillon for six years. This is the subject of Byron's dramatic monologue *The Prisoner of Chillon* and his *Sonnet on Chillon*.

Chillon! Thy prison is a holy place,
  And thy sad floor an altar — for 'twas trod,
Until his very steps have left a trace
  Worn, as if thy cold pavement were a sod,

By Bonivard! May none those marks efface!
For they appeal from tyranny to God.

Among Byron's lyrics, *She Walks in Beauty*, *So, We'll Go No More A-Roving*, *Stanzas for Music*, *On This Day I Complete My 36th Year* are found in almost all anthologies of English verse.

II Percy Bysshe Shelley

1. Life of Shelley Percy Bysshe Shelley (1792—1822) was born in a family of propertied conservatism. At school from ten to eighteen, chiefly at Eton, he suffered much from tyranny. At Oxford, under the influence of Godwin's *Political Justice*, he published a leaflet entitled *The Necessity of Atheism*. Summoned before the authorities, he would not renounce his views and apologize to the University, and he was expelled.

Leaving Oxford, he drifted to London and wrote against tyranny and bigotry. At nineteen he married Harriet Westbrook, who shared his radical views. At twenty he was in Ireland, writing and working for Irish freedom. At twenty-two he gave up Harriet and eloped to Italy with Mary, gifted daughter of his master Godwin. Coming back to London, he endured most of the humiliation of poverty: his father had refused to provide him. He wrote against such institutions and usages as governments, laws, the use of force, private property, and matrimony. In 1818 he left England for Italy, never to return.

For a time Shelley saw a good deal of Byron. Like Byron, he was a rebellious soul. He was ever abreast with the progressive movements of the time: the Carbonari in Italy, the agitation for reform in England, and the struggle for independence in Greece. He wrote a good deal of poetry in Italy, including his masterpiece *Prometheus Unbound* (1820).

Shelley had always been fond of the recreation of boating. Early in July 1822 he sailed from Lerici to Leghorn to greet the arrival of his friend Leigh Hunt from England. On his return voyage he was caught in a squall and drowned. He was cremated and his ashes were buried in the Protestant Cemetery in Rome. Upon his gravestone were written the Shakespearian lines he loved:

> Nothing of him that doth fade,
> But doth suffer a sea — change
> Into something rich and strange.

2. *Queen Mab* and *Revolt of Islam* *Queen Mab* (1813) is the most important of Shelley's early works. It is a philosophical poem, in which he expresses his radical opinion about the society and orthodox Christianity of his day. Ianthe, the central figure, falls asleep and dreams that she is transported to the court of Queen Mab, where she is shown two visions — a vision of the human misery from war and superstition and trade, and a vision of man's recovery through reason, science, and purity of heart.

The poem shows the influence of Paine, Godwin, and the French Materialists. Shelley denies the existence of God and the deity of Christ.

He exposes the Christian Church as an ally of intolerance and oppression. He attacks the tyranny of kings and statesmen, the worse tyranny of priests, and the selfish greed of commerce. Let religion be abolished and reason reestablished, and mankind would speedily rid itself of such artificial institutions and customs as governments, laws, the use of force, private property, and matrimony, and enter into an era of freedom, love, and happiness.

Revolt of Islam (1818) was first entitled *Laon and Cythna*, the hero and heroine — brother and sister as well as lovers. This was too much for the publisher, and the relationship as well as the title of the poem was altered. The principal characters of the poem are: (1) a generous young man devoted to the cause of freedom and justice; (2) a generous and ardent woman his associate; and (3) a wise old man whose age and experience have freed him from all selfish motives. The poem sets forth in allegory the liberation of the world from tyranny through the love and martyrdom of the high-souled man and woman.

The poems were found objectionable, and *Queen Mab* was subjected to repeated persecutions. But they made their way in pirated editions and were widely read by the radicals of the day.

3. *Prometheus Unbound* *Prometheus Unbound*, Shelley's greatest work, is a lyrical drama. The story is based upon the Greek myth. Aeschylus, the Greek dramatist, had represented Prometheus as offending Jupiter (Zeus) by giving men the use of fire, and as chained to a rock in punishment; but ultimately Prometheus was to have been reconciled to Zeus by disclosing the secret of a danger to his empire. Shelley declared that he was "averse from a catastrophe as feeble as that of reconciling the

Champion with the Oppressor of mankind".

When Shelley's drama opens, Prometheus has suffered ages of pain and gained insight and wisdom. Jupiter demands that Prometheus disclose the secret, and when Prometheus refuses to bow to the unjust ruler, inflicts further tortures upon him. Far away, in an Indian vale, dwells Asia, the beloved of Prometheus, and the very spirit of love. She approaches Demogorgon, the Eternal Fate, to disclose the fate of Prometheus, and she is shown a vision of their future. Then follows the downfall of Jupiter, who has incurred the secret danger by marrying Thetis. Their child, Hercules, overthrows Jupiter and frees Prometheus, whereupon all the spirits of the universe chant a song of triumph over the downfall of tyranny and the victory of forgiveness, love, and unconquerable resistance to force.

Jupiter represents tyranny and autocracy and what has arisen under his sway—i.e. institutions and customs obnoxious to humanity.

> And those foul shapes, abhorred by God and man —
> Which, under many a name and many a form
> Strange, savage, ghastly, dark and execrable,
> Were Jupiter, the tyrant of the world;

Prometheus represents the liberator, the saviour of mankind.

> To suffer woes, which Hope thinks infinite;
> To forgive wrongs darker than death or night;
> To defy Power, which seems omnipotent;
> To love, and bear; to hope till Hope creates

From its own wreck the thing it contemplates;
  Neither to change, nor falter, nor repent;
This, like thy glory, Titan, is to be
Good, great and joyous, beautiful and free;
This is alone Life, Joy, Empire, and Victory.

As to Demogorgon, he is not merely the victor in a combat of gods. His victory suggests that while time may be on the side of man's oppressors, Eternity will bring triumph to his saviours.

Prometheus Unbound is, like *Revolt of Islam*, an appeal to the young and generous intellectuals not to yield to despair and cynicism in the age of reaction after Waterloo: a change is coming, thinks Shelley.

4. Shorter Poems and Lyrics The Manchester Massacre of 1819 aroused in Shelley "violent emotions of indignation and compassion". He wrote *The Mask of Anarchy*, in which he pictures the pageant and chariot of the skeleton Anarchy threatening to crush Hope, and exhorts the hosts of English labourers to resist such exploitation. In the same vein was written *Song to the Men of England*:

Men of England, wherefore plough
For the lords who lay ye low?

To these should be added *Ode... Before the Spaniards Had Recovered Their Liberty*, perhaps the finest of them all.

Shelley wrote exquisite lyrics of nature, which are never mere descriptions. In one way or another they are quickened by the sense of the contrast between the world of appearance and the world of reality, between the present and the future. The world of appearance weighs heavily upon his heart — the life of care which we have to endure, the misery and agony under tyranny. But the mood of melancholy is usually superseded by the recognition of the ideal realities and future promise that lie behind the veil. The West Wind, the harbinger of Winter and Death, will come; but just as certainly spring will not be far behind (*Ode to the West Wind*). We are earth-bound and our sweetest songs are sad; but the strains of the skylark suggest the reality of love and joy (*Ode to the Skylark*). If Shelley was at times gloomy about the present, he had never lost faith in the future. His poetry has for him this end: "to awaken public hope and to enlighten and improve mankind".

In his *Condition of the Working Class in England in 1844*, Engels wrote, Shelley, the genius, the prophet, Shelley and Byron, with his glowing sensuality and his bitter satire upon our existing society, find most of their readers in the proletariat; the bourgeoisie owns only castrated editions, cut down in accordance with the hypocritical morality of today."

III John Keats

1. Life and Character of Keats None of the great Romantics had so humble an origin as that of John Keats (1795—1821): his father was head-ostler in a livery-stable in London. He has only five years of formal education at school. At the age of sixteen, both of his parents being dead, he was apprenticed to an apothecary-surgeon. He took up medical studies in hospitals and was licensed in 1815 to practice surgery. But what really interested him was not surgery, but poetry.

In his last year at school and during his apprenticeship he read Spenser, Milton and other English poets, and he had glimpses of the art and literature of classical antiquity. He made the acquaintance of the progressive journalist Leigh Hunt and, through Hunt, of Shelley and Haydon the artist. In 1816 he wrote the famous sonnet *On First Looking into Chapman's Homer* — the first of his productions that received public notice.

Keats took up poetry as a profession. He read and re-read Shakespeare and gave much attention and thought to Milton. In 1818 he published *Endymion*, which was furiously attacked by reactionary critics. He was, however, not discouraged. "The road lies through application, study, and thought," he remarked.

It was in the last two and a half year of his life that nearly all of his best poetry was composed—e.g. *The Eve of St. Agnes*, the great odes and sonnets, and the two versions of *Hyperion*. But his health declined, and his financial difficulties increased. Under medical advice, he sailed to Italy in 1820 in the hope of restoring his health in a milder climate. In 1821 he died of tuberculosis, and his remains were buried in the Protestant Cemetery at Rome. Shelley, hearing of it at Pisa, composed his *Adonais*, a tribute of a genius to a genius.

Keats was an ardent liberal in polities. He was deeply interested in the social and political issues of the times. He was hostile to institutional Christianity, and he refused to accept its theology. His life was devoted to the search of beauty and love in life and art.

2. *Endymion* and *The Eve of St. Agnes* *Endymion* is a long narrative poem, the longest work of Keats. It tells the Greek myth of the shepherd Endymion's love for Cynthia the moon — a popular old legend of love between a mortal and an immortal. Its theme is the quest for the ideal of beauty and love. The opening lines of the poem express one of Keats's most profound convictions:

> A thing of beauty is a joy for ever:
> Its loveliness increases; it will never
> Pass into nothingness.

The glorification of love and passion in *Endymion*, as in Keats's early verse in general, was a lyrical protest against the puritanical bigotry and hypocrisy of the English bourgeoisie. Keats longs for a happiness, not for the fortunate few, but for all. The pleasure and enjoyment of beauty that he describes with sensuous details are available for all; the common folks share them with the gods and nymphs. This freethinking of the poet, no less than the hedonistic images of the poem, met with adverse criticism in the Tory journals, the *Blackwood's* and the *Quarterly* magazines.

The Eve of St. Agnes, a verse tale, is a glorification of beauty and love against a feudal background. According to Catholic tradition, if maids perform certain fond ceremonies on the eve of St. Agnes (21st January), they may in the night behold as in a vision their future husbands. On such a night in the time long ago — a bitter night in winter —

the maid Madeline does so dream and wakes to find her vision a reality. Above her bends her lover, Porphyro, with whose house hers is in deadly feud. And they elope:

> And they are gone: ay, ages long ago
> These lovers fled away into the storm.

The warmth of youthful love between Porphyro and Madeline is set against the cold of the night and the cold of feudal customs. The sensuous impression of the tale is unique in English poetry. One is reminded of Shakespeare's *Romeo and Juliet.*

3. The Two Versions of *Hyperion* Keats's most ambitious effort was to compose an epic: he felt that the greatest poetry was dramatic or epic. His *Hyperion* (1819) was originally planned to extend to about ten books, of which only two and a half were finished. The subject was the overthrow of the Titans by the true gods which he had read of in Chapman's "Homer" and in Greek poetry. He intended to interpret the downfall of the primordial rulers of the universe as a historical necessity. The Titans were fated to fall when there arose, in Apollo, a nobler type of power — a god whose strength lay in beauty, enlightenment, and poetry. In its cosmic span, in its philosophical implications, and in the Titanic images, *Hyperion* bears resemblance to the poems of Byron and Shelley (e. g. Shelley's *Prometheus Unbound*). To Keats, as to Shelley, the fall of gods means the inevitable change of all that exists: it signifies the development of life, a forward movement.

Hyperion exists in two versions. Artistically, the first version, entitled *Hyperion: a Fragment*, is more homogeneous and sustained. But the second version, entitled *The Fall of Hyperion: a Dream*, is more significant; for it includes Keats's maturest and fullest expression of his feelings concerning a problem which always seemed to him crucial —namely, what was the highest function of a poet, and what should be his attitude towards his fellowmen. The Introduction of *The Fall of Hyperion: a Dream* describes the stages in the development of a true Poet.

4. Sonnets and Odes In the sonnets and odes Keats found an outlet for his lyrical impulses. In the sonnet, Shakespeare was his chief inspiration and model; and a number of his sonnets are only next to those of his master. Critics have listed the following eight in order of merit as nearly flawless among the best in the English language.

Much Have I Travel'd in the Realms of Gold
When I Have Fears That I May Cease to Be
Come Hither All Sweet Maidens Soberly
Four Seasons Fill the Measure of the Year
Bright Star! Would I Were Steadfast as Thou Art
O Soft Embalmer of the Still Midnight
The Day Is Gone, and All Its Sweets Are Goner
As Hermes Once Took to His Feathers Light

The Lyric form, however, which was most congenial of all to Keats, was the ode. In his odes his strong personal feelings and preferences found direct, not allegorical utterance — his delight in the loveliness of autumn and the song of the nightingale, his melancholy over the evanescence of beautiful things, and his enthusiasm over their achieving a new and immortal life in art and literature (*Ode to the Autumn*, *Ode to the Nightingale*, *Ode to Melancholy*, *Ode to the Grecian Urn*). The informal ode, more spacious than the sonnet, dignified and exalted in tone, varied in metre and line — the ode was most suited to express the temper of Keats, his high seriousness, his meditativeness, his leisurely manner of approaching a thought, and his fondness for developing and enriching it with abundance of concrete imagery.

CHAPTER X

THE VICTORIAN PERIOD (I)

I "Cruel Thirties and Hungry Forties"

1. Popular Verse of Social Protest The three or four decades after the First Act of Reform (1832) were the age of industrial capitalism. The bourgeoisie grew and flourished by taking advantage of the new industrial and mercantile conditions, and emerged into wealth and importance. On the other hand, the labouring poor suffered from miserable exploitation by their employers, and the third and fourth decades of the century are known in history as "cruel thirties and hungry forties".

This "condition of England" gave rise to much poetry of social protest. In the thirties, Ebenezer Elliot, known as "Corn-Law Rhymer", wrote a couple of poems about unemployment (*Song*) and about the struggle between capital and labour (*Battle Song*). In the forties, Elizabeth Barrett's *Cry of Children* and Thomas Hood's *The Song of the Shirt*, *The Lay of the Labourer* and *The Bridge of Sighs*, all of them published in 1843, enjoyed wide circulation.

The Song of the Shirt was popular in France and Germany as well. It was printed on cotton handkerchiefs and sung about the streets:

With fingers weary and worn,
   With eyelids heavy and red,
A Woman sat, in unwomanly rags,
   Plying her needle and thread—
Stitch! Stitch! Stitch!
   In poverty, hunger, and dirt,
And still with a voice of dolorous pitch
   She sang "The Song of the Shirt!"

Engels remarked that the poem "drew sympathetic and unavailing tears from the eyes of the daughters of the bourgeoisie".

2. Chartist Songs and Poems The thirties and forties were the years of the Chartist movement, which has been defined by Lenin as the first extensive proletarian revolutionary movement, really mass in character and politically shaped. This movement gave rise to a lot of vigorous prose and some poetry. There were all kinds of popular songs, many of which have disappeared. A few can be found in Mrs. Gaskell's *Mary Barton*. One is preserved in the works of Engels:

Britannia's sons, though slaves you be,
God your creator made you free
To all he life and freedom gave
But never, never, made a slave.

Among the Chartist poets were Edward Mead, Ebenezer Jones, and Ernest Jones. Ernest Jones (1819—1869), the most remarkable of the group, suffered two years' imprisonment for his revolutionary speeches. For a time he was a follower of Marx and Engels. He was the author of *The Songs of Democracy*, of which *The Song of the Lower Classes* is the most vigorous and successful:

> We plough and sow — we're so very, very low
>   That we delve in the dirty clay,
> Till we bless the plain with golden grain,
>   And the vale with the fragrant hay.
> Our place we know — we're so very low,
>   'Tis down at the landlord's feet;
> We're not too low the bread to grow,
>   But too low the bread to eat.

In the same vein was written *The Song of the Wage-slave* with the following refrain, which is a call to action:

> The coming hope, the future day,
>   When wrong to right shall bow.
> And but a little courage, man,
>   To make that future now.

3. Rise of Critical Realism The "condition of England" found fuller expression in prose fiction, which was the most popular form of literature in the 19th century.

In England, as in other capitalist countries, there was the existence of two nations and two cultures; i.e. the backward and reactionary moneyed classes on the one hand and the progressive and revolutionary propertyless classes on the other. The best fiction of the age flourished not on the soil of the fashionable tastes of the bourgeoisie, but in protest against these tastes. It rendered a historic service by exposing to the whole civilized world the unsightly spiritual world of the bourgeoisie. Marx wrote in 1854:

> The present brilliant school of novelists in England, whose graphic and eloquent descriptions have revealed more political and social truths to the world than have all the politicians, publicists and moralists added together, has pictured all sections of the middle class, beginning with the "respectable" rentier and owner of government stocks, who looks down on all kinds of "business" as being vulgar, and finishing with the small shopkeeper and lawyer's clerk. How have they been described by Dickens, Thackeray, Charlotte Bronte and Mrs. Gaskell? As full of self-conceit, prudishness, petty tyranny and ignorance. And the civilized world has confirmed their verdict in a damning epigram which it has pinned on that class, that it is servile to its social superiors and despotic to its inferiors.

The following sections are concerned with the great realists of the period: Dickens, Thackeray, the Brontë sisters, and Mrs. Gaskell.

II Charles Dickens

1. Life and Works of Dickens Charles Dickens (1812—1870) had an unhappy childhood. His father, a navy clerk, amiable but not thrifty, was for years in a debtors' prison. At the age of eleven, young Dickens was subject to long and dreary labour in a blacking factory in London. Long afterwards, even when he was famous, Dickens never lost the memory of these horrible years.

Dickens had only two years of continuous schooling, though he made up most of his education by reading whatever he could find in his father's house. Leaving school at fifteen, he worked first as a lawyer's clerk, then as a newspaper reporter. From his early years he formed the habit of roaming London afoot, often a dozen or more miles a day, or preferably at night, observing the life of the poor and oppressed. He knew what suffering meant. All through his life he was to keep his sympathy for the poor.

At the age of twenty-four Dickens issued "in parts" *The Pickwick Papers* (1836—1837), a series of humorous and satirical sketches, which enjoyed a national success. It was followed by full-fledged novels: *Oliver Twist* (1837—1838), exposing the workhouse; *Nicholas Nickleby*(1838—1839), attacking the bullying schoolmaster, etc. At thirty Dickens had a five-month tour in the United States. His *American Notes* and *Martin Chuzzlewit* contain severe criticisms of the vulgarities and hypocrisy of the American bourgeoisie.

Everywhere Dickens witnessed the evils of bourgeois society, and he exposed and denounced them in a succession of novels: *Dombey and Son* (1846—1848), *David Copperfield* (1849—1850), *Bleak House* (1852—1853), *Hard Times* (1854), *Little Dorrit* (1855—1857), *A Tale of Two Cities* (1859) and *Great Expectations* (1860—1861). He published in all 22 novels in 29 years, of which 14 take ranks as major novels. Meanwhile, he edited periodicals, took an active part in philanthropies and amateurish theatricals, and undertook dramatic readings from his works. He died worn out at fifty-eight, with his last novel *The Mysteries of Edwin Drood* unfinished.

2. *Oliver Twist* In 1834 was passed the new Poor Law, in accordance with which was established the new poor-house, known as the workhouse. The indigent were no longer objects of charity, but were collected in the prison-like buildings, the Poor Law Bastilles, administered by officials who had no education and often no sympathy with the people under their care. *Oliver Twist* shows up the cruelty and meanness of such officials and authorities, high and low, who functioned under the Poor Law.

The novel opens with the birth of Oliver in a workhouse and the death of his mother who had been found on the road. He is brought up in a baby-farm, and at ten apprenticed to a workhouse undertaker. He runs away, drifts to London, and falls into the clutches of Old Fagin of a filthy den, where were gathered the homeless waifs and brutal thieves of London. Oliver is forced to help pick pockets by Fagin's crew or to creep into a window of a country house in order to admit the thieves. The sordid life of the underworld is vividly and truthfully pictured. Oliver is a figure of symbolic significance: he stands for all workhouse orphans, and his situation is pervaded with dramatic symbolic power.

Like many other Dickens's novels, *Oliver Twist* contains improbabilities. Oliver has the good fortune of being adopted by respectable people—first by the benevolent old gentleman who turns out to be the intimate friend of his father, and then by the benevolent lady who is discovered to be his aunt! These providential coincidences, together with false feelings and cheap sentimentality, constitute the weakest portions of the novel.

3. *David Copperfield* *David Copperfield* is Dickens's favourite novel. Under the image of one man's journey through life, it presents a many-faceted picture of real life of people in which Dickens wove a thread of autobiography.

David has an unhappy home life at the mercy of his step-father Mr. Murdstone and an equally unhappy school life under the heavy thumb of the brutal Creakle. Upon the death of his mother, David is set to work as a child labourer in a blacking factory. He makes the acquaintance of the inimitable Mr. Micawber, who reminds us of Dickens's own father. David makes his way to Dover, and appeals for help to his great-aunt, Betsy Trotwood, of whom he knows only by repute. His aunt decides to adopt him; and thereafter he begins a new life. From this point the main, autobiographical, thread ramifies into a succession of subplots. On the main line are David's adventures. He falls in love with Dora and marries her. After her death he marries the daughter of his aunt's lawyer-agent; and so he lives "happily ever after".

One of the sub-plots is that of little Emly, a charming orphan of a fisherman at Yarmouth. She is seduced and discarded by the handsome aristocrat Steerforth, David's quondam school-fellow. Another sub-plot is that of Uriah Heep, a lawyer's clerk — the humblest and the meanest creature on earth. Each of these sub-plots is, like the main plot, complicated further by subsidiary ramifications. Incidents and characters are multiplied and the novel becomes symbolical of the current of human life itself.

The class-orientation in *David Copperfield* is significant. The quasi-aristocratic characters—the Steerforths and a few others—fall definitely into the "bad" category. The well-to-do bourgeois characters are, with the exception of Betsy Trotwood and Mr. Dick, either scoundrels (e. g. Murdstone), liars (e. g. Mr. Spenlow), or moral weaklings (e.g. Mr. Wickfield). It is the lower middle-class characters (e. g. Micawber) and proletarian characters (e.g. the Peggotty family) who occupy the centre of the stage and enlist our sympathy. The juxtaposition of the Steerforth and Peggotty families' issues is something very near to natural class antagonism.

4. Dickens's Later Novels In his later novels Dickens tackles bigger and bigger problems arising from the fundamental composition of bourgeois society and shows himself more and more at odds with that society.

Bleak House is an attack on the law's delay. Dickens wrote, "The one great principle of the English law is to make business for itself. There is no other principle distinctly, certainly, and consistently maintained through its narrow turnings." There is an aggregate of the representatives of the law, including the Lord Chancellor, whose villainy conditions the whole action of the law.

Hard Times was based upon Dickens's own observations of industrial conditions in Manchester. The villain of the novel is the manufacturer-banker-employer Bounderby. The novel attacks the whole ethic of capitalism as represented by the Manchester school, laissez-faire, economics and ethics.

A Tale of Two Cities is the most successfully dramatized of all Dickens's novels. Its basic plot-theme is Dr. Manette's imprisonment and its consequences. The novel contains effective descriptions of the Faubourg Saint Antoine, of the preparations for the attack upon the Bastille, of its storming, of the September "Massacres", and of the revolutionary tribunal. The revolt of the masses is presented with historical truth, as a just and necessitated uprising of the people whose affliction and privation had grown to be such as could no longer possibly be endured. Tried by the standards of the then English contemporary opinion, Dickens went to extreme lengths in vindication of the French Revolution. But, following contemporary opinion, Dickens conceived the "victims" of the purge of the prisons to be mainly aristocrats guilty of nothing but aristocracy.

A Tale of Two Cities demonstrates unmistakably Dickens's sympathy with the people in revolt, with the revolt itself, and, within limits, even with their infuriated inflictions of vengeance upon their oppressors.

5. Dickens as a Novelist In *The Novel and the People*, Ralph Fox remarks, "In Dickens they [the Victorians] had a genius who restored to the novel its full epic character, whose teeming mind created stories, poems and people which have forever entered into the life of the English-speaking world. Some of his characters have assumed an almost proverbial existence, they have become part of our modern folklore, and that surely is the highest any author can achieve. He can only do it by genius, humanity and a feeling for the poetry of life."

Dickens enjoyed life, but he hated the social system into which he had been born. He exposed the workhouse, the debtors' prison, the private school, the factory system, the court of law. He attacked the hypocritical, the conventionally pious and their "philanthropy". He made most of his natural gift of observation — of seeing things in all their details and released his talent for satire and denunciation. Bumble, Murdstone, Uriah Heep, Pecksniff and other scoundrels are not only exposed but physically thrashed, so to speak, before the very eyes of the readers.

Dickens had his limitations. He had faith in the common people. In a speech given less than a year before he died, he affirmed that his faith in the people who governed the country was "infinitesimal", while his faith in the people who were governed was "illimitable". But somehow he felt that the only possible remedy for so vast an evil, the remedy of complete social revolution, was one that then seemed completely unattainable. He came under the influence of the Chartist movement, but he believed neither in its political programme nor in its methods of agitation.

As a writer of fiction, Dickens was hampered by his age which demanded sentiment and reticence and respectability. He had to accept the conventions of bourgeois society in morality and in language. Many an effective scene is damped by sentimentalism, many a bright page marred by melodrama.

III William Makepeace Thackeray

1. Life and Works of Thackeray W. M. Thackeray (1811—1863) and Charles Dickens were often compared. In some ways they were alike: each started as a journalist and each exposed the evils of the bourgeois order. But Thackeray was occupied with the manners of high life and pretensions of the middle class. He has always been less popular than Dickens, though he divided with Dickens the supremacy in fiction in the late forties and fifties.

Thackeray was born in Calcutta — the son of an East India Company official — and was educated at Charterhouse and Cambridge. After Cambridge he dawdled a while in Germany, where he met the aged Goethe, and turned to journalism. Under various pseudonyms he wrote sketches of high society — sketches of scoundrels, rogues, and thieves. In 1844 he gave up rascals and began to write about snobs. The age was a high season for snobs, and Thackeray studied them in all varieties and phases and exposed their pose and pretence.

In 1847, when Thackeray was thirty-six, appeared *Vanity Fair* which established his reputation as a novelist. It is a cynical satire on fashionable life. "I cannot help taking the truth as I view it," he said, "and describing what I see." In later years, as he passed the little house in Young Street, London, where he had once lived, he said to a friend, "Down on your knees, you rogue, for *Vanity Fair* was penned; and I will go down with you, for I have a high opinion of that little production myself."

Gorky named Thackeray among the most distinguished writers of Western Europe. "Swift, Rabelais, Voltaire, Le Sage, Byron, Thackeray, Heine, Verhaeren, Anatole France and many others," wrote Gorky, "were irreproachably truthful and rigorous exposers of the vices of the ruling class."

After 1848 Thackeray's realism declined. He was somewhat alarmed by the revolutionary movements of 1848: the Chartist petition in London and the July uprising of workers in Paris. He turned more and more from contemporary society to the historical past. His interest in the 18th century expressed itself in his lectures on *The English Humorists* and *The Four Georges* and also in his historical novels, *Henry Esmond* and *The Virginians*.

2. Story of *Vanity Fairy* Though *Vanity Fair* is "dated" by the battle of Waterloo; it is essentially a novel of contemporary life. The central character is Becky Sharp, a penniless orphan of not too respectable parentage. Only two courses are open to her: the passive one of submission to perpetual slavery, or the active one of independent rebellion. Becky takes the second course.

Leaving Pinkerton's school, Becky goes for a visit to the rich family of her fellow-pupil, the gentle Amelia Sedley. Here she meets Amelia's brother Jos — unmarried, fat, awkward and shy. She sets to work at once and just misses snaring him. She secures a position as governess in the household of Sir Pitt Crawley — a baronet, dirty, foul-mouthed, drunken, and without manner or decency. Here she captures Sir Pitt's son, Captain Rawdon Crawley, a gambler.

Then comes the calling of the troops for Waterloo. Captain Crawley, Amelia's newly-married husband Captain Osborne, together with England's thousands, are in the field. Becky goes to Brussels and becomes involved with the people she meets there. Thackeray's picture of Waterloo — not a description of the actual battle, but rather a vision of it through the eyes of the civilians awaiting the issue of the battle — is one of the supreme masterpieces of literature.

Captain Osborne is killed at Waterloo. The fortunes of the Sedley family decline, and Amelia is reduced to poverty. Her hand is finally won by the clumsy but kindly Captain Dobbin, a grocer's son, who had served and loved her for many years. Meanwhile, Becky continues her climbing. With Rawdon she sets up an establishment and lives precariously but fashionably. She accepts gifts and attentions from Lord Steyne, the top-most pinnacle of high society. This is discovered and Lord Steyne is knocked down and ejected by the disillusioned Rawdon. Becky disappears, taking with her all the money she can lay her hands on. Years later she gets into contact with Jos, who obliges her as best as he can, by insuring himself for her benefit and promptly dying. With the money Becky establishes herself in the respectable society of Bath, where she gathers about her a very strong party of excellent people who consider her to be a most injured woman.

3. *Vanity Fair* as a Social Satire *Vanity Fair* gives a vision of bourgeois society and of the personal relationships engendered by that society. Thackeray pierces the hypocrisies of Vanity Fair, reveals the disgusting, brutal, degrading sordidness behind and below its elegance and glitter.

In *Vanity Fair* Thackeray is chiefly concerned with people, who, as he says, have "no reverence except for prosperity, and no eye for anything beyond success". He is anti-aristocratic. When his "gentle" readers protested that Sir Pitt was "overdrawn", that it was impossible to find such coarseness in his rank of life, Thackeray replied, "That character is almost the only exact portrait in the whole book." Old Osborne reacting to George's death; Lady Bareacres sitting in her horseless carriage at Brussels; the description of Lord Steyne's house and family: such episodes are extremely successful.

As to Becky Sharp, she is one of the great characters in all fiction. She has vitality and fascination. One goes through Vanity Fair by following her progress. She is an unmistakable individual, and yet (like Oliver Twist) she has a typical symbolic quality: she is every woman of spirit rebelling against the humiliations forced on her by certain social conventions.

But Thackeray has his limitations. His satire on upper class society is constantly diluted by his comment of a loose and general cynicism. It seems that Thackeray has looked the world in the face and doesn't care to go on looking. The novel has the feeblest of endings: "Ah! *Vanitas Vanitatum*! Which of us is happy in this world? Which of us has his desire? Or, having it, is satisfied? — Come, children, let us shut up the box and the puppets, for our play is played out."

4. *Henry Esmond* When we turn from *Vanity Fair* to *Henry Esmond* (1852), we turn from the age of Waterloo to the age of Blenheim. The tale is told by Henry Esmond himself, in the form of memoirs of his boyhood and youth. As an illegitimate son of the old Lord Castlewood, Esmond grows up in the household of the new Lord. He is devoted to the young Lady Castlewood, befriends her boy Frank, and loves her brilliant daughter Beatrix. He goes to college, is mixed up with politics, takes part in the war with France, etc.

Part of the story concerns the career of Beatrix — the career of a "climber", as in the story of Becky Sharp in *Vanity Fair*. Like Becky,

Beatrix is calculating, selfish, bent only on making a great marriage. At length she captures the Duke of Hamilton. But on the very eve of marriage, Beatrix's dreams are shattered by the sudden death of the Duke in a duel at the hand of Lord Mohun.

The Castlewoods are Stuart sympathizers, and schemes are afoot to place James Stuart, son of James II, on the throne. Henry Esmond goes to France, and secretly brings back the Stuart prince. The reigning sovereign Queen Anne is on her death-bed. The prince is brought to her presence, and she seems to favour him. A day is set for the formal announcement of the prince as her successor. When the day comes, the Stuart sympathizers assemble — but the prince is missing. For Beatrix has lured him away to Castlewood. When he gets to London, it is too late, The Queen is dead and George I is king! The story ends with the marriage of Henry Esmond — not with Beatrix, but with her mother, for which many a reader has reproached the author.

The novel contains vivid descriptions of men and manners of English society under Queen Anne. Pictures are given of wars, duels, party politics, social evils and official corruption. Addison, Steele, Swift, the foolish and depraved Pretender, Mohun and Hamilton, and Duke Marlborough come to life under Thackeray's touch. The characterization of Beatrix as a "climber" is superb. Thackeray's weakness lies in his imperfect sense of history. While criticizing the corrupt aristocrats, the government system and the constitution based upon the Bill of Rights of 1689, Thackeray fails to present history as a process in which the people played a decisive role. With sympathy Thackeray speaks of the people, of their hard lot, but he does not find in the people a moving force that determines historical development.

IV The Brontës and Mrs. Gaskell

1. The Brontë Sisters The Brontë sisters — Charlotte (1816—1855), Emily (1818—1848), and Anne (1820—1849) — were brought up in a small parsonage named Haworth, close to a bleak, windswept village on the Yorkshire moors. The people thereabouts were farmers, hand-loom weavers, and wage-earning operatives of mechanized mills on the one hand and the new industrial bourgeoisie, the *nouveau riche*, on the other. The sisters had unhappy days at a Clergy Daughters' School in West Riding, Which had been the scene of Luddite riots.

For about ten years (1835—1845) the sisters made valiant efforts to gain their livelihood by teaching. Charlotte was twice, and Anne twice, governess in private families, and Emily taught in a girls' school for six agonizing months. In order to secure additional qualification for teaching, Charlotte and Emily went in 1842 to Brussels where they studied French and German under M. and Mme. Héger. They had intended to establish a school of their own, but the project was never carried out.

The Brontë sisters had "very early cherished the dream of one day becoming authors". In 1846 they published a volume of poems, under the pseudonyms of Currer, Ellis and Acton Bell. In their days a woman needed all the courage even to publish. A "female" writer could not expect a hearing, and must therefore win it before she was known to be woman. Of the poems, only two copies were sold. Meanwhile they had begun to write novels. In 1847 appeared Charlotte's *Jane Eyre*, Emily's *Wuthering Heights* and Anne's *Agnes Grey*. *Jane Eyre* was an instant and overwhelming success. In 1848 died Emily, in the next year Anne — victims of consumption. Charlotte, the most productive of the group, published *Shirley* in 1848 and *Villette* in 1853. She was married to Nicholls in 1854 and died a year afterwards.

2. Charlotte Brontë's *Jane Eyre* The novel opens with little Jane as a despised orphan in the house of her uncle's widow. Being rebellious, she is packed off to a "charity" boarding-school, which administers harsh discipline with especial vigour. Jane sets herself to learn, qualifies herself as teacher, advertises for a post, and is employed as governess of the illegitimate French daughter of Rochester in his country mansion, Thornfield. A love relationship develops between Jane and Rochester. Jane's resolute free spirit, her soul of fire, brings from the dominant Rochester a proposal of marriage. But at the very altar the wedding ceremony was interrupted, for Rochester is discovered to have a wife, now mad, at Thornfield.

Jane leaves Thornfield, wandering far away. She is rescued by the Rivers family and urged to marry the frigid St. John Rivers in order to undertake missionary work at his side. Almost she consents, but as she ponders, Rochester's voice crying her name resounds in her ears. She returns to Thornfield, but the mansion has been destroyed by a fire started by the mad wife. In a secluded country house nearby she finds Rochester, blind and alone; they marry and find happiness together.

The story is told with terrific intensity. The agonies of Jane are presented so powerfully and in such a simple but telling language that they cannot be read without emotion. It is not a romance. Like other novels of Charlotte Brontë, *Jane Eyre* is characterized by relentless truthfulness to ordinary reality. Even when the action is most exciting, its details are strictly true to real life.

Jane Eyre is unique in Victorian fiction; it is the first English novel, and perhaps even yet the most powerful and popular novel, which presents the free insurgent woman, free to feel and to speak as she feels. Jane is poor but independent. She can earn her own living and "need not sell her soul to buy bliss". She is not afraid to tell Rochester frankly that she loves him, but that she despises him for thinking of marrying a rich and beautiful but spiritually inferior girl. In *Jane Eyre* the woman becomes articulate, confronting man on equal terms.

3. Emily Brontë's *Wuthering Heights* The word "wuthering" is Yorkshire dialect for "weathering" — "a significant provincial adjective", as Emily says ironically, "descriptive of the atmospheric tumult to which its station is exposed in stormy weather".

The story is one of oppression and rebellion, of stormy weather and stormy passions. Mr. Earnshaw, a prosperous Yorkshireman of Wuthering Heights, brings home from the Liverpool slums a sallow ragged little boy, whom he calls Heathcliff. Heathcliff grows up with Earnshaw's son and daughter, Hindley and Catherine. Catherine loves Heathcliff, while Hindley hates him from jealousy of his father's affection. Upon the death of his parents, Hindley degrades Heathcliff to the status of a serf. Catherine stands for humanity and becomes Heathcliff's fellow-rebel under Hindley's tyranny. But Catherine is seduced by prospects of social comfort. She betrays Heathcliff and marries Edgar Linton of a rich landed family in a neighboring village at Thrushcross Grange. Upon which Heathcliff disappears.

Years pass. Heathcliff returns, rich, prosperous, and gentlemanlike. Between Heathcliff and Edgar Linton, Catherine becomes distracted. She gives birth to Edgar's daughter, Cathy, and dies. Heathcliff then sets himself to ruin both families in vengeance. He uses their own weapons against them — the weapons of money and arranged marriages. He buys out Hindley, turns him into a drunkard and gambler, so that Hindley's son Hareton becomes a pauper in Heathcliff's house. He marries Edgar Linton's sister Isabella, and after her death organizes the marriage of his ailing son to Cathy Linton. And he achieves the supreme ruling-class triumph of making Hareton, his old enemy's son, feel a passionate attachment towards himself. But all his revenge is foiled, because Cathy is devoted to Hareton, and the young lovers will struggle against their oppressors.

No question is solved, but much is revealed. A veil is drawn from the conventional face of bourgeois man. *Wuthering Heights* is an imaginative or symbolic expression of the stresses and tensions and conflicts, personal and spiritual, of 19th-century capitalist society. The men and women of *Wuthering Heights* are not of the imaginary world, but of the world that Emily Brontë knew, and their struggle against oppression is symbolic of the never-ending struggle in class society.

The novel is well constructed, and excitement is kept to the very end. Emily Brontë's manner of writing is austere and unadorned, but powerful. Her landscape painting is superb, unrivalled in English fiction.

4. Mrs. Gaskell's Novels Mrs. Gaskell, née Stevenson (1810—1865), was the daughter of a Unitarian minister and married a Unitarian minister. For the greater part of her life she lived in Manchester. In 1848, the Chartist year, she published her first novel, *Mary Barton*, which won the approval of Dickens and of the people at large.

Mary Barton is the first labour novel that presents the conflict between those who have and those who have not. It tells how a plain but honest man is falsely accused of murder and saved from the gallows by his daughter; and how this daughter, lured almost to her ruin by the dastardly guile of a rich manufacturer's son, struggles for independence and marries a stout, worthy labourer. Mrs. Gaskell handled with courage the crying industrial issues of the "hungry forties": low pay, squalor, strikes, and callousness of employers and government. The novel raised a double storm of praise and blame.

Mary Barton is followed by *Cranford* (1853), which is a series of sketches of simple, often humble, provincial people that Mrs. Gaskell knew in her early years at Knutsford. In 1855 Mrs. Gaskell turned again to the serious industrial condition of the age. *North and South* is a novel about the struggle between capital and labour. In this book is presented a contrast between the old agricultural gentry of the South of England and the new moneyed industrialists of the North. Among the typical characters are the clergyman who gives up his living because he cannot still his spiritual doubts and the trade-unionist official who combines social radicalism with atheism. This book has obvious connections with Dickens's *Hard Times* and Charlotte Brontë's *Shirley*.

Mary Barton and *North and South* are stimulating books, and they have not ceased to be stimulating. Mrs. Gaskell was the first to create the "operative" as a character in fiction. The remedy she suggested was the bringing about of a good understanding between masters and men — a bourgeois limitation which she shared with many critical realists of her time.

Mrs. Gaskell was also the author of *Life of Charlotte Brontë* (1857), a masterpiece of biography.

CHAPTER XI

THE VICTORIAN PERIOD (II)

I Tennyson, Browning and Poetic Retreat

1. Tennyson and His World of Romance Alfred, Lord Tennyson (1809—1892), son of a clergyman, was born and bred in a country rectory and educated at Cambridge. In the forties he established his reputation as a poet. Sensitive was his ear and fastidious his taste. But he turned from the ugly industrialism of his age to the world of romances: classical, medieval and English. What particularly fascinated him was the romance about King Arthur and the knights and ladies at his court. The background of Tennyson's *Idylls of the King* (1859, 1869, 1872) is neither that of ancient Britain, nor of medieval chivalry, but an imaginary world of romance in which the poet took refuge. In his hands poetry becomes a charmed and distant illusion.

In 1850 Tennyson was made Poet Laureate, in succession to William Wordsworth, and he became the "official" poet. He hated pacifism, and was always ready to sound the call to arms when the British Empire was threatened. He wrote for the Crimean War (*The Charge of the Light Brigade*, etc.) and he wrote against the Indian Mutiny (*The Defence of*

Lucknow). Tennyson always wrote with an eye on his bourgeois audience, and as Laureate he wrote with both eyes on Queen Victoria.

The Victorian world was a world of misery for the people at large. Tennyson was not undisturbed. In his early years he read about evolution and was personally acquainted with Darwin. But like Darwin and Darwin's followers of the time, he applied the theory of the individual struggle for existence to the interpretation of human society. He ascribed the ruthlessness of capitalism to the ruthlessness of Nature. In his later years he heard cries of anguish in individual lives, and the smooth harmonies, characteristic of his verse, began to be filled with a deeper and more turbulent music. But he clung to his faith and retreated all the more to his world of romance.

2. Browning and Italian Renaissance Robert Browning (1812—1889), son of an official in the Bank of England, was educated under private tutors and in the University of London. In his eager youth he wrote against the growing retreat of Wordsworth in a poem entitled *The Lost Leader*:

> Shakespeare was of us, Milton was for us,
> Burns, Shelley,
> Were with us — they watch
> from their graves!
> He alone breaks from the van and the freemen —
> He alone sinks to the rear and the slaves!

In 1846 Browning secretly married Elizabeth Barrett, author of the

Crying of Children, and took her to Florence. There, in 1848, they felt the revolutionary fervour which swept over Europe. Mrs. Browning was more interested in political liberty and in movements affecting social groups than her husband, who valued liberty chiefly as a means to the growth of the individual. Only individual freedom, he thought mistakenly, can bring social progress.

While Tennyson took refuge in his world of romance, Browning revolted from the drab present to Italian history and legends of the 16th century. He was interested in characters of the Italian Renaissance — aristocrats, ecclesiastics, alchemists, painters, musicians and charlatans. To recreate them imaginatively in the setting of their time; to recreate them, not by description, but dramatically — that is, to place them before us at some revealing moments of their life, to let them speak for themselves — that was Browning's way. Some of his "dramatic monologues", of which he wrote a number, are still worth reading; e.g. *My Last Duchess*, *The Bishop Orders His Tomb at Saint Praxed's Church*, etc.

Even more than Tennyson, Browning was detached from the Victorian world of misery. He knew little of evil and had a confident belief in progress as the solution for the ills which beset mankind, as in *Pippa Passe*:

> God's in his Heaven —
> All's right with the world.

3. Aestheticism and Decadence Aestheticism was a form of the

Victorian retreat. It found its apostle in Dante G. Rossetti (1828—1882), leader of a group of aesthetes known as the Pre-Raphaelites. Rossetti shut out from his work all the social and political interests with which much Victorian literature was concerned. For him life existed only to supply the images of art. He longed for a world of symbols, winds, dim moon-lit waters, strange, rich colours, seen in half-light, not the world of reality at all but the breath of spaces. Love and Beauty were the main themes which he pursued with the strange combination of the mystic and the sensual. In Rossetti and his followers (e. g. his sister Christina Rossetti, William Morris before he became a socialist, Walter Pater the critic, Oscar Wilde), the world of art is completely detached from the world of reality.

Aestheticism or "art for art's sake" is a form of what Marx called the "Commodity-fetishism" of capitalist society. Engels in *Anti-Dühring* very clearly explains the characteristic of that society:

> [It] has the peculiarity that in it the producers have lost control of their own social relationships. Each produces for himself, with the means of production which happens to be at his disposal and in order to satisfy his individual needs through the medium of exchange. No one knows how much of the article he produces is coming on the market, or how much demand there is for it; no one knows whether his individual product will meet a real need, whether he will cover his costs and even be able to sell at all. Anarchy reigns in social production. But commodity-production, like all other forms of production, has its own laws ... working blindly, the product dominates the producers.

"Man has lost control of his social relationships." And so has the bourgeois poet, who is separated from the world of reality, who is therefore separated from the source of art itself — who is anti-social. "The product dominates the producers." And so does a poem or a work of art. Technique and "tradition" are valued above everything else. Aestheticism, formalism, symbolism, etc. are but different types of poetic decadence.

II Carlyle, Ruskin and Huxley

1. Carlyle and His Hero-Worship Thomas Carlyle (1795—1882) was born of Scottish peasant parents and educated at the University of Edinburgh. One of the few students of German in the early 19th century, he rendered a great service to English literature by introducing Goethe and Schiller. In 1837 appeared *French Revolution*, which established his reputation as an author. Thackeray wrote an enthusiastic review for *Times*, and Dickens is said to have taken a copy of it everywhere he went.

Carlyle was not unaware of the "condition of England" — in fact, it was he who coined that phrase, which became the theme of many books. He opposed laissez-faire in economics, bourgeois democracy in politics, and mechanical materialism in philosophy. His heart ever went to the suffering and poor people, and in the Chartist years he wrote about them in books and tracts (*Chartism*, 1840; *Past and Present*, 1843). But he had no confidence in their power to manage their affairs. "The History of the World," he asserted mistakenly, "is but the Biography of great men." He evolved a mystical theory of the hero in his *Heroes and Hero-Worship*

(1840).

In a long article on the writings of Carlyle, Marx and Engels wrote:

> Thomas Carlyle has the merit of having opposed the bourgeoisie in literature at a time when official English literature was completely dominated by bourgeois attitudes, tastes, and ideas; and in a manner which at moments was even revolutionary. Thus, in his history of the French Revolution, in his apology for Cromwell, in his pamphlet on Chartism, in *Past and Present*. But in all these writings, criticism of the present is closely bound up with a curiously unhistorical glorification of the Middle Ages, something that frequently occurs with English revolutionaries, as, for example, Cobbett and some of the Chartists. While in the past he admires at least the classic epochs of a definite phase of social development, the present brings him to despair — and he is terrified of the future.

Carlyle exposed the evils of industrial capitalism and shabby commercialism, but he suggested no remedies except for a faith in what he considered the exceptional individual, the hero.

2. Ruskin and Medievalism John Ruskin (1819—1900), son of a rich wine merchant, was educated at London and Oxford, where he studied drawing and painting. He wrote voluminously on painting and architecture. His eye for colour and form was exact, and his vocabulary extraordinarily rich. He produced some of the most ornate passages on nature and art in English prose.

Ruskin attacked the industrialism and commercialism of his age in his *Unto the Last* (1862). He wrote a series of letters to the working men, entitled *Fors Clavigera* (1871—1887). All human work, he said, depended on the happy life of the workers. And the workers could be happy only if they lived as people had lived in the age of craftsmen, making everything that they needed with their own hands, taking pride in their work, and fulfilling the natural human instinct for beauty.

Ruskin made efforts to change the whole social and economic scheme of English life. He would abolish machines and machine-made goods. Life would become simple and natural once more, and every man, seeing clearly the purpose and end of all that he made and did, would be happy in the making and doing. Each man would be rewarded according to his labour, and the state would prevent any man from accumulating wealth at his neighbour's expense.

In an attempt to put his theories into practice, he spent a tenth of his fortune in the establishment of St. George's Guild, a co-operative agricultural and manufacturing organization. Essentially it was an attempt to revert to an irrevocable past, to establish a sort of neo-feudalism in industry. Profits were to be shared; but there were no profits to share. There were disagreements and disappointments. The whole scheme soon collapsed as it was bound to collapse.

3. Huxley and Popularization of Science One of the most remarkable essayists of the Victorian period was Thomas Henry Huxley (1825—1895), a scientist. Son of an unsuccessful assistant-schoolmaster, Huxley had a distinguished career as a student of science at the University of London. Upon graduation he entered the navy as assistant surgeon and joined a scientific expedition in New Guinea. The story of his struggle for recognition as a scientist is told with poignancy in his *Autobiography* (1889—1890).

When *Origin of Species* was published in 1859, Huxley became its effective defender and popularizer. A heated controversy followed. At the meeting of the British Association at Oxford in 1860, Bishop Samuel Wilberforce addressed a crowded lecture hall in ridicule of Darwin and in savage attack on Huxley. Towards the end of his speech he turned "with a smiling insolence" to Huxley and "begged to know, was it through his grandfather or his grandmother that he claimed his descent from a monkey". When Huxley was called on by the audience for discussion, he replied simply but dramatically that "he was not ashamed to have a monkey for his ancestor; but he would be ashamed to be connected with a man who used great gifts to obscure the truth". His first non-technical book, *Evidence as to Man's Place in Nature*, was very popular, selling like a novel and reaching both America and Germany.

Huxley wrote against religious dogmas and reactionary clerics. He also wrote against negro-slavery in America. Unlike Carlyle, he regarded hero-worship as a form of idolatry. He introduced the laboratory system into science instruction. He was a great apologist for science in the 19th century. "To learn what is true in order to do what is right," he said, "is the summing up of the whole duty of man for all who are not able to satisfy their mental hunger with the east wind of authority."

Like Darwin, and even more than some of Darwin's followers (e.g. Herbert Spencer), Huxley mistakenly applied the theory of evolution to the interpretation of human society (*The Struggle for Existence in Human Society*, 1888). He was not free from idealism; he called himself not a materialist, but an agnostic.

III George Eliot and Samuel Butler

1. George Eliot as a Realist George Eliot (Mary Ann Evans, 1819—1880) spent the early part of her life in a rural home on a great Warwickshire estate of which her father was agent. Under private tutors she stored up much knowledge of languages, literatures and music. At the age of twenty-two she left the farm and, as a result of contact with "advanced" circles, she broke with orthodox Christianity. At thirty-three she went to London as a journalist and made friends with "advanced" thinkers; e. g. Herbert Spencer, T.H. Huxley, and G. H. Lewes with whom she lived as his wife. She was the translator of Feuerbach's *Essence of Christianity* (1854).

When a middle-aged woman, George Eliot turned from the writing of philosophical essays to try her hand at fiction. Her early narratives bore the signature "George Eliot" — a name chosen almost at random. Dickens, Thackeray and Mrs. Gaskell were among her admirers. Her reputation was established by the publication of *Adam Bede* (1859), which was followed by *The Mill on the Floss* (1860), *Silas Marner* (1861), and *Middlemarch* (1871—1872).

As a novelist, George Eliot endeavoured to be true to life, Thus she says in *Adam Bede*:

> I aspire to give no more than a faithful account of men and things as they have mirrored themselves in my mind. The mirror is doubtless defective; and the outlines will be somewhat distorted; the reflection faint and confused; but I feel as much bound to tell you as precisely as I can what that reflection is as if I were

in the witness box narrating my experience on oath.

But George Eliot did more than that. She was a student of philosophy and psychology as well as a creative artist. She had trained her mind to analyze, to explain, to ask the why of things. While writing her novels, she was bent on explaining every step that her characters might take, all their feelings, all their inward struggles that led up to and bore fruit in a given act. She is a writer of what is called psychological fiction.

2. *Silas Marner* and *Middlemarch* Poor and misshapen Silas Marner, a linen weaver, is driven from his home somewhere in the industrial north by a false charge of theft. He takes refuge in the agricultural village of Revenoe, where he carries on his trade as weaver and keeps apart from his neighbours. He is left with no object in life but to save and hoard and count his money. One night his treasure disappears, and his happiness is gone. And then, on a New Year's Eve, a golden-haired foundling creeps into his cottage. Silas adopts her, calls her Eppie, and cherishes her as his own. And Eppie restores to Silas the happiness that he has lost with the gold.

Who has stolen Silas's gold? Where has Eppie come from? These remain mysteries until many years later. The draining of a pond near Silas's door reveals the body of the thief, still clutching the gold in his dead fingers. It was Squire Cass's reprobate son Dunstan. Moved by this revelation, Dunstan's elder brother Godfrey hastens to acknowledge himself the father of Eppie. For Godfrey had forsaken a woman, who died in snow in an attempt to force her way with her baby into Cass's house ... Much is revealed about the hidden motives and impulses of men under bourgeois order.

Middlemarch is a large novel, written on a scale unexampled in Victorian fiction. It contains a treatment of the problem of lost ideals. Dorothea Brooke, of the English landed class, aspires for something beyond the "genteel" selfishness of her class. She rejects a local aristocrat and accepts disastrously the hand of the impossible pedant Casaubon. Casaubon spends the honeymoon in research for his *Key to All Mythologies* and alienates Dorothea by his lack of sympathy. Meanwhile, Tertius Lydgate, an ambitious young doctor, animated by hopes of scientific discoveries and medical reform, makes the colossal mistake by marrying the pretty but commonplace Rosamond Vincy, whose mercenary motives bring about the failure of his hopes.

But these are not isolated episodes. The lives of Dorothea and Lydgate are inextricably bound up with many other lives of Middlemarch. "There is no private life which has not been determined by a wider public life," says George Eliot. One is impressed by the author's persistent idea; namely, the interrelatedness of social life, which she brings out through careful accumulation of detail and searching analysis of motives and actions.

The weakness of George Eliot lies in her idealistic philosophy. Under the influence of Comte and his positivism, of whom her husband G. H. Lewes was a representative in England, she believed in "the religion of humanity", which she thought erroneously could solve all the contradictions of social life. She shows the influence of the love of a child on the lonely and embittered nature of Silas. She expresses the opinion that the society of Middlemarch is to be rejuvenated by the principle of humanity. It is this idealism that diminishes the social significance of all the works of George Eliot.

3. Samuel Butler and His *Erewhon* Samuel Butler (1835—1902) was the son and grandson of clerics. In boyhood he suffered from the extremes of parental control and sanctimonious priggishness. He was destined for the church, but after graduation from Cambridge he refused to be ordained for conscientious reasons. In 1859 he emigrated to New Zealand, where he tried his hand at sheep-breeding, accumulated a small fortune and lost it through the indiscretion of a friend. Returning to England in 1864, he studied painting and wrote on diverse subjects: religion, evolution, painting and music, Homer and Shakespeare. Butler was one of the most versatile and original minds of his time. Of his literary works, the most remarkable are *Erewhon* and *The Way of All Flesh*.

Erewhon, or Over the Range, published in 1872, was the book that established Butler's reputation among his contemporaries. Mr. Higgs, the hero, traverses the mountains of New Zealand and finds himself in a hitherto undiscovered country among strange people — a country like and yet unlike England. One striking difference is the complete absence of machines.

Machines, it is argued, are a menace to man. Beginning in a humble way as his servants, they are rapidly becoming his masters and may in the end be able to dispense with him. Here Butler gives expression to the wide-spread horror of the Victorian intellectuals at the results of capitalist machine production. Butler does admit that machines, properly controlled, may enable man to increase his control over his environment, but he seems to have felt that the Erewhonians did better without machines.

Erewhon (Nowhere) is by no means an ideal state, though it has a number of good things — gracious usages and institutions. The Erewhonians regard ill health as a crime. They worship Ydgrun (Mrs. Grundy, i. e. respectability), whose religion consists in doing what the world does. They attend Colleges of Unreason, each containing a Chair of Worldly Wisdom.

Erewhon is a satire. It exposes the shallow inconsistencies and dubious values on which the confident action of Victorian society is based. Butler's fantasy resembles parts of *Gulliver's Travels* and is no less entertaining. It contains valuable criticism of the bourgeois order.

4. *The Way of All Flesh* Written between 1873 and 1885, *The Way of All Flesh* was not published until 1903. It is the most vigorous attack on Victorian conventions and respectability. Butler puts the following remarks in the mouth of his principal character in Chapter 84:

> There are a lot of things that want saying what no one dares to say, a lot of shames which want attacking, and yet no one attacks them. It seems to me that I can say things which not another man in England except myself will venture to say, and yet which are crying to be said.

The principal character of the novel is Ernest Pontifex, son of a pharisaical parson (Theobald Pontifex), grandson of a publisher of religious books (George Pontifex) and great grandson of a village carpenter (John Pontifex). In his childhood, Ernest suffers from the most unreasonable chastisements at the hands of his father. ("When a man is very fond of money, it is not easy for him at all times to be fond of his children also.") He is placed under a pompous master, who never understands his pupils, and then sent to Cambridge to be trained for the church. The reaction from suppression leads to sudden catastrophe. Upon leaving Cambridge, Ernest manages to insult a young woman whom he takes for a prostitute, and is sentenced to six months' imprisonment. Then he takes stock of his past and considers his future. He hates his father and mother and wants to have no more to do with them ... It is only by the unexpected bequest of his aunt that he is ransomed and given freedom and independence.

Much of the novel is autobiographical. Butler himself appears in two characters, the hero and the hero's counselor and friend. He puts into the book his parents and some other people that he knew. Some of the letters in the novel are letters actually written by his parents and himself! George Bernard Shaw described the novel as a "long drawn-out patricide and matricide". Nevertheless, the novel is not an autobiography: it is the way of all flesh. The realistic picture of family life in mid-Victorian England is a document as well as an indictment. Like *Wuthering Heights*, *The Way of All Flesh* shows that a full human life in a capitalist society was impossible of attainment.

Butler has a remarkable style. He wrote as he felt and had no patience for word-spinning. His patient sincerity, his downrightness, his wit, his grace, his hatred of cant: these qualities he shared with Dean Swift. In *Erewhon* and *The Way of All Flesh*, he revived something of the spirit of Swift.

IV Morris and Socialist Romance

1. The Progress of Morris William Morris (1834 —1896), son of a well-to-do London broker, was educated at Marlborough and Oxford. In his early teens he had developed a taste for the medieval and a love for the beauty fashioned by medieval hands. At twenty-four he published *The Defence of Guenevere and Other Poems* (1858), an Arthurian romance. Then he turned to decorative art. He built a workshop for the production of furniture, glassware, cotton goods, etc. with a new beauty in place of ugliness usual in such manufacture. He introduced a chair, designed to combine simplicity with comfort, which still bears his name.

Meanwhile, Morris produced more romances, Greek and medieval, in the Chaucerian manner. He was, as he confessed, a "poor idle singer of an empty day", singing only for the recreation of men "meshed within this smoky web of unrejoicing labour". But years of experience as a master-workman made him realize that true craftsmanship was impossible in the capitalist age which was sunk in greed and injustice and outward ugliness. He studied *Capital* and absorbed Marxist ideas. At forty-four he became a socialist.

In 1883 Morris joined the Social-Democratic Federation, the first English socialist party. He worked as an ardent leader, delivering addresses in halls and streets and writing poems and prose for *Justice*, the Federation periodical. In the next year, at the disruption of the Federation, he and his friends formed the Socialist League and wrote for *Commonweal*, the League periodical. When he died in 1896, Swinburne, his fellow-poet, sang his praises as the "warrior and dreamer" who strove to redeem the world "by sword and by song".

Among Morris's literary writings for the socialist cause are *A Dream of John Ball* (1886), *News from Nowhere* (1891), and *Poems by the Way* (1891), which contains *The Day Is Coming* and other poems he had published as *Chants for Socialists*.

2. *The Day Is Coming* and Other Poems *The Day Is Coming* (1884) was written in the trampling measure, a line of six beats in rising rhythm with frequent anapaests and extra mid-line syllables — a measure of Morris's own invention. It sings prophetically of classless society, when capitalism shall be abolished, and freedom and justice and happy fellowship return to the lives of the workers, who will inherit an earth beautified by Nature and Art:

> For all these shall be ours and all men's;
> Nor shall any lack a share
> Of the toil and the gain of living
> In the days when the world grows fair.

The poem ends up with a call for struggle, and so does *The Voice of Toil* (1884), written in octosyllabics, which gives a grim picture of the working men's life under the capitalist system:

> Where fast and faster our iron master,
> The thing we made, forever drives,
> Bids us grind treasure and fashion pleasure
> For other hopes and other lives.

Where home is a hovel and dull we grovel,
Forgetting that the world is fair;
Where no babe we cherish, lest its very soul perish;
Where mirth is crime, and love a snare.

On Sunday, 13 November 1887, which is known in history as the Bloody Sunday, took place in London a great parade of the unemployed in defence of the right of free speech. Morris marched in the parade, alongside G. B. Shaw, then little known. The marchers were attacked by the police, and Alfred Linnell, Morris's friend, was killed. This was the occasion of Morris's *A Death Song*, which was sold as a penny pamphlet to help the children of Linnell. The song contains the trumpet-like refrain:

Not one, not one, nor thousands must they slay,
But one and all if they would dusk the day.

3. Morris's Socialist Romances *A Dream of John Ball* is a reverie. The narrator returns in a dream to 14th-century England and finds himself in the midst of the Peasant Revolution. He hears a fiery speech by John Ball and afterwards talks long and earnestly with the peasant leader. He gives a vivid description of the battle at the township's end... Awaking, the narrator hears the factory whistles of modern industrialism calling people to work. There is thus a projection from the 14th century into the 19th. It is a work of lasting beauty and value.

But the best of Morris's works for the socialist cause is *News from Nowhere*, which appeared as a serial in *Commonweal* for 1890. Here we have again a dreamer, who this time finds himself in the classless future. Exploitation has vanished and men are happy in their work. The division between town and country is eliminated and the country of foul workshops surrounded by a poverty-stricken farm is converted into a garden:

> This is how we stand. England was once a country of clearings among the woods and wastes, with a few towns interspersed, which were fortresses for the feudal army, markets for the folk, gathering places for the craftsmen. It then became a country of huge and foul workshops and fouler gambling-dens, surrounded by an ill-kept, poverty-stricken farm, pillaged by the masters of the workshops. It is now a garden, where nothing is wasted and nothing is spoilt, with the necessary dwellings, sheds, and workshops scattered up and down the country, all trim and neat and pretty. For, indeed, we should be too much ashamed of ourselves if we allowed the making of goods, even on a large scale, to carry with it the appearance, even, of desolation and misery.

Gifted with an extraordinary visual imagination, Morris made the boundless possibilities of socialism pictorial and lifelike in *News from Nowhere*.

Morris's Utopia is not just another imaginary commonwealth detached from existing society. On the contrary, it grows out of existing society through struggle, bearing clear traces of that struggle and of its whole past. *News from Nowhere* contains a chapter called *How the Change Came*, which describes the revolution by which capitalism is overthrown and socialism established. Unlike the Fabians, Morris always held the Marxist view that socialism could only come by the seizure of power by the working class, which is what he always meant by revolution. Details of the revolution, which Morris put in the year 1952, are matters of imagination, obsolete and improbable, but the processes of the revolution that he outlines in *News from Nowhere* — the organization of the working class, the formation of a revolutionary party, and the overthrow of capitalism — show unusual discernment.

Though not free from utopian elements, *News from Nowhere* was the best of Morris's, which was given to the working class as ammunition for their daily battle. It is the embodiment of the deep, undying, hopes and desires not of an individual only but of a nation.

CHAPTER XII

SOME MODERN WRITERS

I Thomas Hardy

1. Hardy and the Hardy World Thomas Hardy (1840—1928), son of a small farm-holder and builder, was born near Dorchester and educated privately at local schools. He was intended to be an architect, but his natural bent was towards literature. In his early years he wrote a good deal of verse, but when he failed to find an audience for it, he turned to prose fiction. At thirty-one he published, anonymously, his first novel, *Desperate Remedies* (1871). For twenty-four years he wrote fourteen novels and four collections of short tales. The novels upon which his fame chiefly rests are: *The Return of the Native* (1878), *The Mayor of Casterbridge* (1886), *Tess of the D'Urbervilles* (1891), and *Jude the Obscure* (1895). Towards the end of the 19th century he returned to poetry, of which he published several volumes.

Hardy's novels and poems are intimately connected with the plain people of a single locality, that area of southwestern England, including the counties of Somerset, Dorset and Devon. At the time when Hardy was writing novels, this part of England, which he called Wessex, was rich in tradition and folklore and superstition. Hardy had a strong sense of the folkways: peasant songs and dances and old church music never failed to fascinate him. It was there, among his own people (peasants and lower gentry), that he passed the greater part of his life, and it was the plain lives of these people that furnished subject-matter for his novels and poems.

But the country was not an isolated "pocket" unaffected by the outside world. Even in Hardy's youth railways and the mechanized life of capitalism had begun to affect the country town of Dorchester and the peasantry had shown signs of decay. The whole social structure was full of tragic possibilities. Hardy had deep sympathy with the peasants, with their patriarchal order. But being unable to understand the nature and significance of the social changes of his age, he looked at man frequently as a determinist looks at him, the helpless plaything of forces outside himself. His novels of critical realism are marred by this "twilight view of life" or pessimism.

2. *Return of the Native* The novel opens with a masterly description of a desolate upland, Egdon Heath. There the heath-dwellers live out their simple lives, carrying on the tradition of an immemorial past (e.g. maypole dances, bonfires on 5th November, Christmas mummings). Hardy dramatizes his peasants and produces a remarkably complete picture of their lives.

Clym Yeobright has been away in Paris and has been back to his widowed mother and his cousin, the gentle Thomasin. He is attracted by the charm of Eustacia Vye, who has been brought there from a fashionable world and who hates the heath and rebels against its stern simplicity, its plainness. Disgusted with the vanity and uselessness of his occupation as a diamond merchant, Clym plans to start a school for the peasants and thinks that Eustacia would be a desirable assistant, while Eustacia yearns for "gay Paree" and thinks that Clym could be induced to go abroad with her. And they get married, to the great displeasure of Old Mrs. Yeobright.

Misfortunes come thick and fast. Clym's eyesight fails and becomes a furze-cutter, and Eustacia is depressed by languor. On a sultry day Mrs. Yeobright calls on a visit of reconciliation with her son, but by an unlucky combination of circumstances, Eustacia cannot admit her. In consequence, she goes away and dies on the road broken-hearted. Clym and Eustacia have a quarrel, followed by separation. Eustacia renews intrigues with her early lover Wildeve, a publican, who has married Clym's cousin Thomasin. On a stormy night Eustacia and Wildeve attempt flight, in the course of which both are drowned.

Here are the tragedies in the lives of the plain people of Hardy's rural Wessex in the period of its disintegration under capitalist conditions. The novel shows how, in a society based on egoism, enterprises of great pith and moment turn awry and hopes for happiness are frustrated.

Hardy, however, has his own interpretation. Clym, Mrs. Yeobright and Eustacia, in their struggle for happiness, are said to be alike up against untoward Fate, which from pure caprice makes a move and renders their efforts vain!

3. *Tess of the D'Urbervilles* The subject of *Tess of the D'Urbervilles*, according to Hardy, is the fate of a "pure woman". In fact, it is the disintegration of the English peasantry — a process which had reached its final and tragic stage in Hardy's time. *Tess* is the story and the symbol of the disintegration. More than any other Victorian novel, it has the value of a social document.

Tess Durbeyfield is a peasant girl, whose parents belong to a class ranking above the farm-labourers. By the opening of the novel the Durbeyfields have already fallen on hard times. In an attempt to solve the problems of domestic economy, Joan Durbeyfield persuades her daughter Tess to visit the Trantridge D'Urbervilles and to "claim kin" with that more prosperous branch of the family. This D'Urberville is, however, not a D'Urberville at all, but the son of the nouveau riche family, capitalists who have bought their way into the gentry. There, Tess becomes a worker, at the mercy of the ruling class. In spite of her effort to maintain her self-respect, she is seduced by Alec D'Urberville and gives birth to a child.

Upon the death of her child, Tess becomes a wage-labourer at the dairy-farm at Talbothays. There she meets and falls in love with the intellectual Angel Clare and thinks to escape her fate through marriage. But Clare turns out to be a prig, a hypocrite, a snob, even crueler than Alec D'Urberville. As soon as he is informed of Tess's past, he fulminates and leaves for Brazil. Tess is further degraded and becomes a wage-labourer under the hardest conditions. The threshing scene (Chapter 47) is a symbol of the dehumanized relationship at the new capitalist farm.

Misfortunes come in battalions. Tess's father dies and her family is expelled from their cottage. To support her folks, Tess is driven back to Alec D'Urberville. Then Angel Clare turns up, chastened and penitent. In her final attempt to maintain her self-respect, she kills Alec D'Urberville.

Law is against her. She is arrested, tried and hanged.

Much of what happens in the novel Hardy ascribed to Nature, to a cruel Fate. In his Preface to the novel he quotes Gloster's speech to King Lear:

> As flies to wanton boys are we to the gods;
> They kill us for their sport.

But the realistic picture of the destruction of peasantry under capitalist conditions survives the twists that Hardy gave to the interpretation of the story in accordance with his pessimistic and determinist view of the world.

In the subtitle of the novel — "A Pure Woman Faithfully Presented" — Hardy throws a challenge to the conventions of the Victorian age. While writing the story Hardy was approached by three publishers. Two of them rejected the completed manuscript on account of what they called propriety. For the sake of his livelihood, Hardy was forced to cut off the offending passages before it was published serially in *Graphic*. When the integrity of the novel was restored in book form, there was a storm of protest.

II John Galsworthy

1. Galsworthy's Literary Career John Galsworthy (1867—1933), of an old Devonshire family, was educated at Harrow and Oxford. After a trial of the law, with extensive travel for recreation, he settled down as a country gentleman to write books, which are eminently readable. In 1932 he was awarded the Nobel Prize in Literature.

In 1904 appeared the novel *The Island Pharisees*, which established Galsworthy as a critical realist. By "The Island Pharisees" Galsworthy meant the self-righteous and hypocritical bourgeoisie in England. The hero, Richard Shelton, starts as a conventional bourgeois, but after a course of disillusionment he becomes critical. He goes about England and feels disgusted with the cant, the narrow-mindedness, the conscious and unconscious hypocrisy and the stupidity of his own people. He embarks on a search for beauty, passion, justice and intelligence, and he finds none. A vain longing for good life in English society — this runs as an undercurrent in many of Galsworthy's novels.

In 1906 appeared *The Man of Property*, a treatment of the life of an upper middle class family, the Forsytes, in the late Victorian period. After a lapse of fourteen years, during which he wrote a number of other things, he took up the thread of the Forsytes and wrote two sequels. Together they formed the trilogy "The Forsyte Saga" (1922), upon which his fame chiefly rests. Two other trilogies followed: "A Modern Comedy" (1929) and "The End of the Chapter" (1934). But the first trilogy is his masterpiece, and of the first trilogy *The Man of Property* remains the highest point of Galsworthy's social criticism.

Galsworthy was also a prolific writer of plays, short stories and essays. His most important dramas are *The Silver Box* (1909), *Strife* (1909), *Justice* (1910) and *Loyalties* (1922). His short stories *Evolution*,

Conscience, *The Lost Dog* and *Quality* have found their way into anthologies.

2. "The Forsyte Saga" "The Forsyte Saga" is composed of three novels. *The Man of Property* (1906), *In Chancery* (1920), and *To Let* (1922). There are two interludes, or short stories, called *Indian Summer of a Forsyte* and *Awakening*. These narratives together make up a book of 900 pages — an epic of heroic proportions, an epic of the substantial bourgeois family in England.

The Forsyte family is bewilderingly large, and it has a sufficient variety. Three generations pass before the narrative is done. The first generation is represented by six brothers (Old Jolyon, James, Swithin, Nicholas, Roger and Timothy) and four sisters (Ann, Julia, Hester and Susan). When the narrative starts, most of the Forsyte brothers are married and have children, and some have grand-children aplenty. Different as they are from one another in many respects, all the Forsytes have a family likeness: they all exhibit the possessive instinct."A 'Forsyte' is a man who is decidedly more than a slave of property. He knows a good thing, he knows a safe thing, and his grip on property — it doesn't matter whether it be wives, houses, money, or reputation — is his hallmark."

Among the Forsytes there is a conflict of forces, which is a conflict between the sense of property on the one hand — British Philistinism or Mammonism — and the search for love and beauty on the other. The first force is represented by Soames Forsyte. He is rich and successful, but he never sheds the sense that he owns all that he owns. And his sense of property even extends to his wife Irene, who struggles to escape from his cold grasp. Irene is one of half-dozen women, charming and mysterious, in Galsworthy's fiction, who stands up against bourgeois "propriety" or "respectability".

Irene's first effort towards emancipation ends with the accidental death of the artist who loves her. Around the second part of the trilogy Irene and Soames are divorced and each marries again. The third part centres around the love that springs up between the children of these second marriages, Soames's daughter and Irene's son. Throughout, Irene stands outside the circle of the Forsytes and is seen only through the eyes of members of the family — a device of technique to which Galsworthy himself called attention.

Galsworthy's attitude towards Soames Forsyte is characteristic. He begins by detesting Soames Forsyte, the "man of property", but as he goes on, he somehow grows fond of Soames as he survives, almost the last vestige of Victorian stability, into the age of social disintegration after the First Imperialist World War. Realistic as he is in his treatment of the English family, pungent as he is in his satire upon the complacency and hypocrisy of the propertied class, Galsworthy is limited by his bourgeois outlook.

"The Forsyte Saga" covers the period from 1886 to the years immediately following the Armistice of 1918. The chronicle is carried into the age of the "bright young people" of the post-war world of which Galsworthy, a disapproving and bewildered spectator, knew little. The half-dozen later installments of this huge "novel in sequence" are on a much lower level than the original trilogy: they show the author's decline in realism.

3. *The Silver Box* and Other Plays As Galsworthy was educated to be a lawyer, there is always something legal about his plays. For in practically every play there is a case. *The Silver Box*, his first play, is concerned with the idea that the justice of the world exacts greater penalty from the poor than it does from the rich. A rich young gentleman has stolen a purse while drunk. A poor man steals it in turn while he is drunk. The poor man is sentenced to prison; the gentleman escapes with nothing worse than a scare. *Justice* is another case of law. William Falder, a lawyer's clerk is convicted of forgery, but he is punished out of all proportion to his crime, because his employer wishes to make an example of him. The drama is a poignant comment on the difference between rich and poor before the law, and its successful production led to some reform in prison-administration.

Strife, in three acts, is concerned with a great strike which has persisted in a northern factory town for months. It gives a realistic presentation of the class antagonism between capitalists and workers. The speeches of Roberts, the labour leader, contain an effective exposition of the case from the labourers' point of view, and the first two acts of the play are immensely successful. The ending, however, is artificial. The tale, full of sound and fury, ends in compromise!

Galsworthy's views were confined to the world of the well-bred and well-to-do upper middle class. His hope was in class conciliation, not revolution. But he was not unaware of absurd institutions and foul practice which he exposed and attacked in his dramas and stories. He had sympathy for the poor and downtrodden, and he had the desire to be just to the underdog. In spite of his limitations, he remains one of the last representatives of critical realism in English literature.

III H.G. Wells

1. Wells and Fabian Socialism Herbert George Wells (1866—1946), son of a small shopkeeper, was in his early years a draper's clerk and a school teacher. With the assistance of a scholarship he studied biology in the Royal College of Science, London, and graduated with honours at twenty-one. At twenty-seven he turned to literature and journalism and became a prolific writer. As novelist, biographer, essayist and pamphleteer, he enjoyed popularity in America and on the Continent as well as in England.

In 1903 Wells became a member of the Fabian Society, an organization of petty bourgeois intellectuals. He regarded himself, intermittently, as a socialist, but his socialism was derived from Saint-Simon and Comte rather than from Marx and Engels. To Wells, socialism was a principle not of revolution, but of love, and the duty of the socialists was merely "to talk, teach, explain, write, lecture, read, and listen". He had many dreams of an ideal state and wrote about many Utopias, for a large number of the hundred books of his are utopian or have a partly utopian character.

Friedrich Engels has given a classical treatment of the Fabians. He wrote in 1893:

> The Fabians are an ambitious group here in London who have understanding enough to realize the inevitability of the social revolution, but who could not possibly entrust this gigantic task to the rough proletariat alone and are therefore kind enough to set themselves at the head. Fear of the revolution is their fundamental principle. They are the "educated" *par excellence* ...
>
> With great industry they have produced amid all sorts of rubbish some good propagandist writings as well, in fact the best of the kind which the English have produced. But as soon as they get on to their specific tactics of hushing up the class struggle it all turns putrid. Hence too their fanatical hatred of Marx and all of us — because of the class struggle.

Wells was not unaware of the inevitable doom of capitalism, but he thought that salvation should be sought in technocracy, i.e. a state ruled by the specialists or the "enlightened" minority. In 1924 he visited the Soviet Union and had a long interview with Stalin. In that famous interview Stalin refuted Wells's utopian views of society and demonstrated the truth of the great principles of scientific socialism.

2. "Scientific" Fantasies and Bourgeois Realism With a lively imagination Wells loved to take trips to Mars and the moon just as Swift had travelled in Lilliput and Brobdingnag. He also loved to speculate on the shape of things to come. One of his better known fantasies is *The Time Machine* (1895), which tells of a marvellous contrivance able to carry its passengers not through space but through time. The narrator and the inventor decide to go forward rather than backward, and with very little delay they find themselves in the year 802, 701 A. D.. The only change they find on earth is about the class differentiation between the leisured few and the labouring many. One is said to be a race of delicate, mindless creatures inhabiting the face of the globe, and the other a race of bestial cannibals who come up when necessary from their homes underground and feed on their aristocratic victims!

The strength of Wells, however, lies not in his fantastic creations, but in his realistic presentation of bourgeois society. In a number of novels he made use of his own early experience, and the draper's clerk and the assistant schoolmaster and the student of science appear as principal characters. Perhaps the most remarkable, and the most popular novel of this category is *Tono-Bungay* (1909), which has for its theme the rise and fall of a business racketeer. George Ponderevo, the hero, tells how he and his uncle make a huge fortune out of a worthless patent medicine called Tono-Bungay, supposed to be of use as a tonic. They achieve their success by means of advertising and publicity. It is a picture of how science is prostituted in bourgeois society and how the people are swindled by capitalist methods of advertising. Summing up the whole humbug, George Ponderevo concludes: "Now it was open and manifest that I and my uncle were no more than specimens of a modern species of brigand, wasting the savings of the public out of sheer wantonness of enterprise."

Tono-Bungay is remarkable for its gusto and eloquence. But, like most of Wells's novels, it contains "all sorts of things" and lacks artistic unity. None of the characters of the novel, not even the hero, come to life.

IV George Bernard Shaw

1. Shaw, Dramatist and Publicist George Bernard Shaw (1856—1950) son of a civil servant, was Irish in birth but of Yorkshire blood. After his childhood in Dublin, his youth was a period of poverty and struggle in London as a journalist. In 1882 he proclaimed himself a socialist, and in 1884 became a member of the Fabian Society, for which he wrote *Manifesto*. Later he collaborated with Sidney and Beatrice Webb on *Fabian Essays* (1889). The Fabian ideology, of which Engels has given a critical treatment, furnished the guiding principles of all the works of Shaw.

After writing five unsuccessful novels, Shaw turned in 1892 to the drama. In half-a-century he produced more than thirty plays, some of which are still popular on the stage. With a brilliant wit he wrote against greed and hypocrisy and injustice of capitalist society. His satire ranged over the Church and State, the law, penology, medicine, pseudo-science and numberless other subjects. Among his important dramas are *Mrs. Warren's Profession* (1894), *Arms and the Man* (1894), *Candida* (1895), *Man and Superman* (1903), *Pygmalion* (1913), *Heart Break House* (1917), *The Apple Cart* (1930).

Shaw wrote a good deal on economics, politics, ethics and art. "For every play I have written," he said, "I have made hundreds of speeches and published big books on Fabian Socialism. There is behind my plays a thought-out sociology." He always had something to say on the problems of the day. In 1914 he made himself unpopular for a time by publishing *Common Sense about the War*, directed against the official justification of

England's entrance to the First World War. During the Second World War he held a unique position as a publicist who persistently wrote against Fascism and imperialism.

Though Fabian to the last, Shaw was a friend of the Soviet Union, when it was under the leadership of Lenin and Stalin. In the years following the great October Socialist Revolution, he fought against the anti-Soviet policy of the British government by advocating "Hands off Russia". In 1931 he visited Moscow where he celebrated his 75th birthday. Maxim Gorky, who was prevented by tonsillitis from attending the party, wrote him a letter of congratulations. During the Second World War Shaw sent greetings to the people of the Soviet Union. On 17th July 1941 he wrote to Fadeyev: "When Russia beats down Hitler, she will become the spiritual centre of the world."

2. *Mrs. Warren's Profession* *Mrs. Warren's Profession*, written in 1893 and 1894, deals with the problem of prostitution and the traffic of women in bourgeois society. With the rich Sir George Crofts as a partner, Mrs. Warren keeps brothels, of which she has two in Brussels, one in Ostend, one in Vienna and two in Budapest. Mrs. Warren's daughter Vivie, educated in a very moral atmosphere at a boarding college, is kept in ignorance. On graduating, she returns home and by accident discovers her mother's loathsome occupation. Vivie's conversation with Crofts reveals the cynicism of the propertied people:

> *Vivie.* My mother was a very poor woman who had no reasonable choice but to do as she did. You were a rich gentleman; and you did the same for the sake of 35 percent. You are a pretty common sort of scoundrel, I think. That is

my opinion of you.

Crofts. Ha! ha! Ha! ha! Go it, little missie, go it! It doesn't hurt me and it amuses you. Why the devil shouldn't I invest my money that way? I take the interest on my capital like other people: I hope you don't think I dirty my own hands with the work. Come! You wouldn't refuse the acquaintance of my mother's cousin the Duke of Belgravia because some of the rents he gets are earned in queer ways. You wouldn't cut the Archbishop of Canterbury, I suppose, because the Ecclesiastical Commissioners have a few publicans and sinners among their tenants ... And do you expect me to turn my back on 35 percent when all the rest are pocketing what they can, like sensible men? No such fool! If you're going to pick and choose your acquaintances on moral principles, you'd better clear out of this country, unless you want to cut yourself out of all decent society.

The play is a strong protest against bourgeois exploitation and the immorality of the ruling classes in England. A serious social problem is raised and discussed fully, but no solution is given. At the end of the play Vivie, Shaw's heroine, simply throws over her mother and goes to earn her bread by honest work. Mrs. Warren is left exclaiming, "Lord help the world if everybody took to doing the right thing!"

Mrs. Warren's Profession was published in Shaw's first collection of plays, *Plays Pleasant and Unpleasant* (1898). It was considered offensive and was banned by the British Censor from the public stage until 1926, though it was produced elsewhere in the early 20th century.

3. *Arms and the Man* While *Mrs. Warren's Profession* is an unpleasant play, which leaves a bad taste in the mouth, *Arms and the Man* is a pleasant play with a lot of fun and laughter.

Like Ibsen, Shaw was an iconoclast, an enemy of the false ideals and cheap sentiments of bourgeois society. *Arms and the Man* was meant to be a satire on the British army, of which the Duke of Cambridge was Commander-in-Chief. By the end of the 19th century British imperialism found its apostle in Rudyard Kipling, who in his poems and stories cast a new glamour round the national figure of "officer and gentleman". With keen humour Shaw demonstrated that the glamorous "officer and gentleman", the plumed and upholstered warrior from the best families, was dangerous to everyone but the enemy.

Two types of soldiers are presented in *Arms and the Man*. One (Sergius) is a pompous and pretentious man whom Shaw represents as an ornament of bourgeois society. The other soldier, Captain Bluntschli, is not a conventional figure on the stage.

> He suffers from want of food and sleep; his nerves go to pieces after three days under fire, ending in the horrors of a rout and pursuit; he has found by experience that it is more important to have a few bits of chocolate to eat in the field than cartridges for his revolver.

He says frankly, "What use are cartridges in battle? I always carry chocolate instead." And yet he gets the better of the pompous and pretentious officer.

In the play Shaw also satirized what he called the school girl's idea of love, romantic love — e. g. infatuation with "the noble attitude and the thrilling voice". The Chocolate Soldier wins the adoration of a young romantic lady through refusing to be impressed by her "noble attitude" and "thrilling voice".

Arms and the Man has its background laid in Bulgaria, and its characters are Bulgarian and Swiss. But people knew what the author meant. The play encountered a strong prejudice, not against its methods, but against its matter. It made fun of the British army and the long cherished ideals of romantic love.

4. *The Apple Cart* *The Apple Cart* has a subtitle: "A Political Extravaganza". It is an exposure of the crisis of bourgeois democracy. Prime Minister Proteus and his Cabinet attempt to force King Magnus to accept an ultimatum that would reduce the Crown to a cipher. The king's reply is that rather than be a cipher he would abandon his throne and go to the "democratic" poll and take up the premiership himself. And so the apple cart is upset and the ultimatum scrapped.

But, as Shaw points out in his Preface to the play, the conflict is not really between royalty and democracy, but between both and plutocracy, which has bought and swallowed democracy. "Money talks, money prints, money broadcasts, money reigns, and kings and labour leaders alike have to register its decrees, and even, by a staggering paradox, to finance its enterprises and guarantee its profits."

This play gives a vivid picture of the struggle of power among the bourgeois politicians. With an unusual insight he reveals that the Labourites, supposed to stand for the working class, are no more than adroit politicians who know how to keep snug jobs and take whatever portions they could of the state pie. This is what is said by the Labour member of the Cabinet:

> No King on earth is as safe in his job as a Trade Union official. There is only one thing that can get him sacked, and that is drink. Not even that, as long as he doesn't actually fall down. I talk democracy to these men and women. I tell them that they have the vote, and that theirs is the kingdom and the power and the glory. I say to them, "You are supreme, exercise your power." They say, "That's right, tell us what to do"; and I tell them. I say, "Exercise your vote intelligently by voting for me." And they do. That's democracy; and a splendid thing it is too for putting the right men in the right place.

In this play Shaw touches upon the sharp contradictions between England and the United States of America. The American ambassador Mr. Vanhatten approaches King Magnus for the formation of the Anglo-American political union in view of the fact that England has long been subject to the influence of the imperialist monopolies of America:

> Well, we find here everything we are accustomed to: our industrial products, our books, our plays, our sports, our Christian science churches, our osteopaths, our movies and talkies. Put it in a small parcel and say our goods and our ideas. A political union with us will be just the official recognition of an already accomplished fact. A union of hearts, you might call it.

5. Shaw as a Critical Realist Bernard Shaw was an enemy of the school of "art for art's sake". Unlike the aesthetes and decadents, who worked for an escape from the reality, he grappled with economic, social and political problems of his age. His dramas are problem plays, or "debated dramas" as he called them — i. e. discussions of economic, social and political problems. He had zeal for social reform. "Until Society is reformed," he said, "no man can reform himself except in the most insignificant small ways."

Being a Fabian and an idealist, however, Shaw had great limitations. He stood for piecemeal reform rather than for revolution, He disliked violence. He was under the delusion that the evils of capitalism could be removed through petty reforms, that public ownership and socialism would come gradually. A number of social diseases under capitalism are diagnosed in his dramas and essays, but few prescriptions are given and these few often misleading. Among his erroneous ideas is the idea of what he called the "Life-Force", which is supposed to direct woman more strongly than it does man towards procreation — the idea that marriage is "a man-trap baited with ... delusive idealizations". (*Man and Superman*, etc.)

Shaw's strength lies in his relentless exposure of English society. He revealed the evils and diseases of imperialistic England, fighting hard and generously against its gross injustices and its inhumanity. His best plays are plays of exposure, and even his lesser plays contain scenes of stark realism. "What is wrong with English society?" — This was his ever-recurring question which he discussed from many angles and with an intelligence unequalled in contemporary Britain. In a letter dated 28 July 1931, Maxim Gorky addressed Shaw as a "brave warrior and a gifted man". Gorky continued, "You have lived for three quarters of a century and your sharp intelligence has given numberless staggering blows to the conservatism and banality of men."

As a writer, Shaw has a manner of his own. His irony and contempt cut right and left. His style is sharp and final, with brilliant antitheses and with examples and illustrations drawn from many sources. In spirit Shaw is akin to Samuel Butler, author of *The Way of All Flesh*, and he is often compared with Jonathan Swift, the greatest satirist in English.

目录

第一章

乔叟以前的英国文学

一　古代英国诗——《贝尔武甫》

1. **口头文学与书面文学**　英国人民最初的文学与其他人民最初的文学一样，不是书面的，而是口头的。故事与传说先是口头流传，并在讲述中不断地扩大、改进。人民参与了这一类文学的创作。

自然，这类故事与传说都是由那些能说会道的人复述的，因此每个团体渐渐有了专门讲故事的人，称为“斯可卜”，意为歌曲的制作者。因为这些故事都是歌唱的，都是用一种吟诵体裁来讲述的。他们认为任何好故事，经过说唱或吟诵，就会更为动听。“斯可卜”（即诗人）以及“格利门”（即吟诵者）在氏族和封建社会里享有受人尊敬的地位。

在早期的撒克逊英国，“斯可卜”吟诵人民的英雄事迹的歌曲。他们对这些故事每唱一次就增饰一次，有时把几个不同的故事编成一个长篇纪事。这些故事在“斯可卜”之间通过口耳一代一代地传递下来，最后才有写本。但是写下来的只是其中的一小部分，而保存下来的又是写本中的一小部分。现存古代英国诗歌中最长最好的一篇就是《贝尔武甫》，它被称为英国人民的民族史诗。

2.《贝尔武甫》的情节 《贝尔武甫》讲的是一个冒险故事，一个传奇故事。英雄贝尔武甫是瑞典南部的高特族人，是斩杀妖魔的勇士。他听说有一个名叫格兰代尔的妖魔，一次又一次地夜袭丹麦国王的大厅，掳走在那里睡觉的武士，丹麦人民深受其害。于是，他就带领了十四名伙伴前往丹麦，去打格兰代尔。在一次可怕的短兵相接的夜战中，贝尔武甫扯下了妖魔的一只胳膊，妖魔身负重伤，逃回了他海底的窝窟。

格兰代尔的故事到此就结束了，可是格兰代尔的母亲却出来要为儿子报仇。她又来袭击大厅，贝尔武甫追赶她，一直追到一个荒湖激流下的洞穴里，和她搏斗。他用古时巨人留下来的魔剑砍下了这个妖魔的头。就在那里，他发现了格兰代尔的尸体，把他的头也割了下来。他带着这两个毛发毵毵的头，当作战利品，回到了丹麦大厅，在欢宴和歌声中庆祝胜利。

贝尔武甫回国后做了国王，治理人民五十年。后来竟发生了这样一件事：一条火龙在长眠中受到惊动，开始喷出火焰，焚毁它路过的一切东西。贝尔武甫虽已年迈，却只身和火龙搏斗。龙被斩了，贝尔武甫自己在战斗中也受了重伤。全诗以老英雄的葬礼和人民的哀悼结束：

他们，高特人，哀悼他们的亲人，

哀悼他们的王上；
宣称他是世上所有国王中
最善良的人，最温柔的人，
对人民慈爱，最渴望得到一个好的名声。

3.《贝尔武甫》所反映的生活习俗 《贝尔武甫》的题材是条顿族从他们欧洲大陆的故乡带到英国来的一种民间传说。现在我们所看到的诗是在8到9世纪期间，由一个英国诗人写定的。它反映了从氏族制到早期封建社会许多世纪中的生活习俗。

主要的故事，即贝尔武甫与格兰代尔、格兰代尔的母亲以及和火龙的搏斗的故事，显然是原始条顿族的民间传说。这些氏族，如我们所知，居住在欧洲大陆东北部沿海一带，从莱茵河口到日特兰半岛。他们居住在一些狭小的地方，后面是一片广阔无边的森林，前面是波涛汹涌的北海。他们必须与野兽搏斗，与神秘莫测的自然界的力量搏斗。当武士冒险远征或航海归来的时候，就会讲述那些住在海底下或大泽森林里的奇异妖魔的故事。他们很英武，但又心有余悸。这就是此类神奇故事的背景。

但是，《贝尔武甫》绝不是一首只反映原始时代的诗篇。它是在基督教已传入英国以后写定的，那时英国社会正在向封建主义过渡。因此，这首诗也反映出了7到8世纪英国的生活风貌，呈现出民间的一种新旧生活方式的混合，兼有氏族时期的英雄主义和封建时期的理想，即前一时期的刚毅和后一时期的柔和相结合，前一时期的勇敢带上后一时期的美德，显得更为高贵。《贝尔武甫》诗人喜爱的主题是采邑领主对国王的忠诚。领主和国王的关系极其密切。国王领导他们，在不友好的邻人中间保护他们，而他们也为国王而战斗，为国王而死。仇怨与阴谋，亲属谋杀与僭夺尊位是受到谴责的，因为这类行为在8世纪的撒克逊英国都要受到谴责。

《贝尔武甫》是封建主义黎明时期所复述的一个氏族社会的故事。贝尔武甫这位英雄不只是一个氏族的酋长，他体现了骑士的品德。

4. 语言与诗的形式 古英语在许多方面和近代英语不同。它是一种有强重音和很多辅音的语言，具有高度的屈折变化形式。像近代德语或俄语那样，它的意义不决定于词的位置而决定于词尾的变化。再者，古英语里有很多同义词，其中大多数很像近代德语中常见到的那一类复合词。例如海洋一语就有不少种说法："海豹浴场"、"鲸路"、"天鹅路"。

古代英诗的基本形式是头韵，即用来押韵的单词都以同一辅音开始。每一行通常有四个重读音节，在第二与第三重读音节之间有一个停顿，这样就把一行分为两个部分。通常头三个重读音节，更多的是头两个重读音节(其中一个照例就是第三个重读音节)，都用头韵，如：

Steap stanlitho — stige nearwe.
(陡峭的石级——狭窄的小路。)

Tha com of more under mist — hleothum
Grendel gongan; godes yrre bar.
(从云雾迷茫的荒野
格兰代尔走了出来，他忍受着上帝的愤怒。)

在我们看来，这些诗似乎生硬单调，但是在当时也许未必如此。我们无法想象早年的歌手（斯可卜或格利门）吟诵时，那些年轻武士在他们主人宴会大厅里倾耳聆听的情景与感觉。

二　古英语的散文：比德和阿尔弗雷德

1. 比德和他的《教会史》　比德（673—735）是在耶罗修道院里教养起来的，是一位博览群书的学者，相传著书四十部，都是用拉丁文写的。其中最有名的是《英国人民教会史》，原用拉丁文写成，后来译为英文。

《教会史》所讲述的早期英国历史比其他任何著作更为详细。它叙述了最初的征服与定居，异教与基督教诸小王国之间的斗争，罗马教团的来临，修道院与新文化的建立。书中记述了很多不可思议的神迹和令人难以置信的奇闻，但也包含了描绘当时生活风情习俗的美妙图画。关于诗人开德蒙的记载是常被引用的。

开德蒙是一个牧童，没有受过什么教育，生活贫苦，在欢乐集会里他不像别人那样能歌善舞，常常在羞愧中溜回家。一天夜里，他躲在熟悉的牛棚里睡着了，这时有个生人出现在他面前，说：

“开德蒙，给我唱点什么。”

“我不会唱呀！”开德蒙回答说，“这就是我为什么要离开桌子，走到这里来的原因——因为我不会唱歌。”

那人又马上回答说：“不，你总要为我唱支歌儿。”

“唱什么呢？”

“唱众生的起源。”

开德蒙就遵照这话，开始唱起赞美造物主上帝的诗歌，这些诗是他以前从来没听过的。就这样，开德蒙成了诗人。人们说：“上帝赐给他天恩。”

这种牧童的幻想是古代人试图解释诗歌灵感的来源所常用的一种方法，在许多国家和许多文学中，都有类似的传说。

2. 国王阿尔弗雷德与《古代英国编年史》 阿尔弗雷德（849—899）是一位优秀的军人和杰出的学者。他与丹麦人抗战七年，巩固了西塞克斯王国。为了教育人民，他将许多拉丁文著作译成英文。为了使他的臣民知道他们自己的过去，他为比德的《教会史》提供了英译本。出于同样的目的，他修订并续编了《古代英国编年史》——这部书逐年记录英国史实，由后人续编直到1154年。

《编年史》早期部分没有正确的历史观点，将日蚀、月蚀、彗星出现、地震、年岁歉收与社会和政治事件等量齐观。但755年以后，《编年史》开始表现出较多的真实感。有关阿尔弗雷德抵御丹麦人的记录尤为突出，现略举几段简短的范例如下：

公元875年　是年夏，国王阿尔弗雷德率领一支舰队出海，与七艘兵船交战，俘获其中一艘，并把其余船只赶走。

公元897年　国王阿尔弗雷德下令建造长船以抵御丹麦船。船身较其他船只长一倍；有些船有六十支桨，有的更多，较其他船只快速平稳,而且也较高,其外形不像弗里斯兰的和丹麦的船,他要建造在他看来效率最大的船。

公元901年　阿尔弗雷德逝世。……除去丹麦人统治的那部分以外,他统治了全英国,在位二十八年半,后由其子爱德华继位。

《古代英国编年史》的风格是简朴的、原始的,往往重复笨拙,但有时显得质朴有力。在阿尔弗雷德的作品中,可以看出英国散文文学的开端。

三　骑士制度与传奇

1. 封建主义、骑士制度与传奇　封建制度开始于撒克逊英国的后期,在诺曼征服以后加强了,并且完善了。一种新的社会等级制度产生了:顶层是以国王为首的封建主,其次是骑士,又其次是封臣,底层是奴隶或农奴。

骑士是那个社会的中心人物。他们承诺为他们的封建主服兵役。在战争时期,他们穿上盔甲,带着刀剑和长矛奔赴沙场,封臣和弓箭手跟随其后。在和平时期,他们比武竞赛。这就是所谓骑士精神。

但是,骑士不仅要效忠于封建主,勇敢善战,而且要风流倜傥,对妇女多情。这种爱情崇拜的风气起源于意大利和法国,是对修道院禁欲主义的一种反抗。北方的骑士精神和南方的爱情崇拜两者相结合,从而产生了骑士制度。

骑士制度产生了大量的诗体传奇，这种传奇起源于12世纪的法国。法国的传奇有两个主题——英勇的作战和想入非非的爱情。它们多数是在诺曼女王和盎格鲁—诺曼贵族的赞助下在英国创作的。后来，才逐渐出现了英文写的传奇，但几乎所有英文传奇都来源于法国。

传奇故事中，有些是关于希腊和罗马武士的（如亚历山大），有些是关于法国国王查理曼和他的追随者的，有些是关于古代不列颠的。所有传奇中最杰出的是那些与名叫亚瑟的一位传说中的古代英国国王有关的故事，即所谓亚瑟传奇。

2. **语言与诗歌形式** 在诺曼征服之后的两百年，英国语言发生了巨大的变化。古老的屈折变化——为了表示一个词与句子中其他部分的关系而引起的词形变化——开始消失。英语原是一种综合性语言，逐渐变为分析性语言。在词汇方面，它吸收了成千上万色彩显著、音调铿锵的法语单词；语言的骨干、框架与结构，仍然是英国的；但那些外来词却使它更加充实，具有多样性和法国诗歌优雅的风格。

在法语的影响之下，一种新的诗体流行起来。盎格鲁—撒克逊诗歌的头韵体逐渐让位于复杂的韵律模式。通行的诗体，特别是在传奇中，为每行八个音节或四个重读音节的两行联韵体，这是法国古诗体的常见形式。至于头韵，已不多见，虽然有些传奇还是继续运用这种韵律，但也不同于古代的音步，因为语言已经变了。

总的来说，13和14世纪的文学手段几乎是一种具有新的音调的新语言。

《高文爵士和绿衣骑士》是英国传奇中最精美的作品，大约写定于1370年，产生于英国西北部——柴郡或兰开夏郡。

3.**《高文爵士和绿衣骑士》** 当亚瑟王和他的骑士以及夫人们在新年欢宴的时候，有一个彪形绿衣骑士穿着一身华丽的衣服，拿着一把绿斧头，骑着一匹绿马走进了大厅。"谁要用这把绿斧头砍下我的头，而让我一年后在绿色教堂里砍下他的头？"年青的高文接受了这个挑战，他用力一挥，脑袋从地板上滚了过去。绿衣骑士拾起了他的头颅，跨上马鞍，驰骋而去。

在11月里，高文在北威尔士荒山中开始了他的漫长、荒凉、寂寞的旅程。圣诞前夕，他来到一座美丽的城堡，受到了热烈的欢迎与豪华舒适的款待。城堡的主人愿意引他到绿衣骑士那里去，但劝他留在城堡里，等到新年再走。主客两方开了个玩笑，约定在随后几天中，每个人无论得到什么东西都要交给对方。

城堡的主人每天出去打猎，高文就待在房里。城堡女主人每天都来看高文，向他卖弄风情，和他接吻。每天夜里高文热烈地吻他的主人，以报答主人带回来的麋鹿、熊和狐狸。但是第三天他经不起诱惑，接受了女主人的丝腰带，据说这条腰带有种力量，可以使人刀剑不伤。

元旦那天，高文被带到悬崖峭壁间一个堆满积雪的荒谷里。绿衣骑士手里拿着斧头，冲了出来。一斧下来高文受了轻伤。高文跳起来自卫，但绿衣骑士不慌不忙地说明他不是别人，正是城堡的主人，是他叫他的妻子勾引高文的，又说，高文的错误在于接受了女主人的腰带，以致受了轻伤。高文带着羞愧与宽慰交集的心情，经过长途跋涉，又回到了亚瑟的朝廷。

这个故事写得有条不紊，是亚瑟传奇中不可多得的。它具备诗体传奇的各种传统元素——惊奇的冒险、宫廷生活和风流韵事。它描绘骑士社会，不是照它本来的样子，而是照它可能的样子来写的。像其他传奇一样，这个故事几乎完全脱离了现实生活。

但是，对于高文爵士漫游途中的景色，诗中都有出色的描写——不是想象中的景色，而是具有亚瑟时代的不列颠的特征。猎捕麋鹿、熊、狐狸的情景，也写得很真实。

四 民间故事与民间歌谣

1. 民间故事 诗体传奇原本是为宫廷和城堡里的骑士和贵妇人写的，而以民间传说为基础的民间故事，则是为一般人民创作的，篇幅较传奇短得多，其内容自动物寓言以至平民生活琐事——例如傻丈夫被聪明的妻子愚弄，或者贪财的人被戏谑的流氓欺骗。

关于动物寓言，《猫头鹰与夜莺》可以作为一个典型的例子。它的写作时期在1200年前后，写的是这两只鸟之间的一场长期争辩。夜莺说，猫头鹰是一种黑暗之鸟，瞎眼睛，叫声粗哑，好像一只迷失在雪里的母鸡；但是她，夜莺，歌声悦耳，有用，为人们所喜爱。猫头鹰反驳说，夜莺生性贪玩，没有用，像教士一样唠叨，乡土气很重；而她，猫头鹰，愉快地唱歌，能够未卜先知，劝世教人，甚至死后还有用处，可以当作稻草人！它们辩论了一整夜。刚刚破晓的时候，夜莺自称胜利了，周围所有会唱的小鸟都齐声歌唱，支持夜莺。但聪明的鹪鹩要求判决，于是它们都飞去找一个好法官。

但是它们怎样飞走了，

来到鲍狄桑那里，有何裁决，
我不知道，所以就不能讲了，
故事就到此结束。好吧，再会。

这里反映了一个普遍的问题，也是一个常见的问题——青春对老年，欢乐对节制，尘世对修道院。幽默之中掺杂着讽刺。这首诗是早期中世纪文学中许多主题的一个集中体现。

2. **民间歌谣**　英国民歌早在诺曼征服以前就有了，但是记录下来的为数很少。这是因为民歌不见于笔录，而是口耳相传的，作者逸名，因为好歌谣不是属于个别作者，而是属于人民。

民歌传统在诺曼征服以后继续下去。据说，12 世纪有一个教士，当村民在教堂院子里通宵歌舞的时候，他没有合过眼。第二天早晨做礼拜时，他应该像通常一样这样开始："愿主和你们同在。"可是他却复述了夜里所听到的话："亲爱的心上人儿，发发慈悲吧！"全教区传为丑闻。

13 世纪留传下来的少数民歌中有一首《布谷鸟歌》。这首歌在它铿锵的音调中保存着一种简朴有力的节奏：

夏天啊，夏天已经来到！
　布谷鸟儿高声歌唱！
草地花开，种子茁壮，
　树木也长得莽莽苍苍，
　布谷鸟儿歌唱！

这里有来源于民间舞蹈的赞歌和舞曲；有劳动歌，特别是妇女纺织和缝衣歌；有情人在黎明听到巡逻人的叫喊而分手时对唱的歌曲；有女子遇人不淑，而想另结新欢之歌；有青春之歌；还有如下格调的奇逢巧遇之歌：

几天前我出去游荡，
碰巧看见一位漂亮的姑娘……

这里应当提一提法国普罗旺斯诗歌的影响，因为这些抒情诗都是起源于普罗旺斯，而又是从普罗旺斯传到法国北部和诺曼英国的。关于普罗旺斯民族，恩格斯说："它在近代的一切民族中第一个创造了标准语言。它的诗当时对拉丁语系各民族甚至对德国人和英国人都是望尘莫及的范例。"[①]

① 《马克思恩格斯论艺术》卷2，人民文学出版社，1963年，第100页。

第二章

乔叟与15世纪

一　朗格兰、威克利夫与罗拉德派

1. 朗格兰与《农夫彼尔斯之梦》 14世纪是黑死病与农民起义的时代，它在文学里有很好的反映。《农夫彼尔斯之梦》是这个时代杰出的诗篇，共有三个稿本流传下来，大约写于1363年、1377年和1393年。作者不明，一般认为是一个名为威廉·朗格兰的人。诗篇用头韵体，其语言来自英国西部。

这篇诗写的是一系列的梦境——写梦境是中世纪文学通用的一种手法。梦中出现的人物主要是一些抽象概念的人格化，例如真理、贪婪、虚伪、理性与贪吃。但是这些抽象人物却写得栩栩如生，而这些人物活动的场面也生动难忘。

这首诗是对当时社会的邪恶，如贵族的懒惰、有钱僧侣教士的穷奢极侈的生活、商人的寄生恶习的深刻尖锐的讽刺。它描绘贫苦农民为着苟延残喘而斗争的生活：

……茅屋里的穷人
负担着一大堆孩子，和地主的租税。
他们纺织挣来的钱，原想做些乳糊
去喂那些嗷嗷待哺的婴儿，
可是这些钱他们只能用来支付房租。
唉，他们自己忍着饥饿，
冬天苦苦地半夜起身
在狭小的屋子里摇着摇篮，
理呀，梳呀，补呀，洗呀，擦呀，卷呀，剥蒲草呀。
农妇的悲苦看了叫人伤心，
唉，还有许多别的人，强作笑脸，
耻于乞讨，不好意思让邻居知道
他们早晚缺少的东西。
那么多孩子，只靠一个人的手
为他们忙穿忙吃；挣来几个钱，
一下子就被许多张嘴吃得光光。

作者并没有推翻社会秩序的意图，但他赞扬穷人和被压迫者，并认为劳苦农民最接近神圣的真理和拯救。这首诗在“下层”阶级极为流行；农民彼尔斯的名字变成了1381年农民起义的口号。

2. 约翰·威克利夫与反教权主义 约翰·威克利夫（约1320—1384）出身于刚毅的约克家族，在牛津大学受教育，后任该校院长和教授。他对于普通人民具有信心，撰文反对普通人民的压迫者，并付诸行动。他到处看见教会的腐败现象——教皇、主教、僧侣、修道士，由于富有、安逸而堕落无行。他攻击修道院占有土地，认为土地原本是应该用来维持广大人民生活的。他对教会的古老教义进行诘难，而将圣经译为英文，以便一般人都能阅读、解释，并自行思考。

于是，反对“异端”的呼声甚嚣尘上，威克利夫和他的追随者只好逃离牛津大学。但是，他继续传道、写作，启发了许许多多的追随者，即所谓“罗拉德派”。他们衣履不周，赤足走遍全国各地，传布教义，为老百姓做好事。他的教义就是宗教改革前的新教。

威克利夫对文学有很大贡献。除了学术著作以外，他还写了两卷布道词——“为人民而作的简朴的布道词”。他的散文正如其人——朴实无华、文理清晰、论证扎实，而且极其有力。略举简短的两则范例如下：

主啊，人们都在这样的奴役中，哪里有基督的自由？

所以要摆脱虚伪，勉力学习真理；要么就伪装，要么就表里如一。

3. 约翰·保尔与1381年的起义 约翰·保尔是威克利夫派的“穷教士”之一。他宣传反对权贵和富人的腐败，唤起农民去结束这种腐败现象。他所传布的精义保存在弗鲁依萨尔特[①]的《史纪》中：

---

① 又译傅华萨。——编注

我的好朋友，英国的情况不会好的，除非一切财物都归公有，那时没有奴仆，也没有老爷；那时老爷们不能够再做主人，驾凌我们之上。他们对待我们多么凶恶！他们为了什么理由这样奴役我们？我们不都是同样的祖先亚当和夏娃的子孙吗？他们为什么应该做我们的主人，他们凭的什么，或者能够举出什么理由？他们一身锦绣，饰以貂皮或别的毛皮，而我们都褴褛不堪。他们有美酒佳肴，而我们只能用糟糠果腹，只有清水可喝。他们住高楼大厦，而我们在田野里胼手胝足，栉风沐雨。他们是靠我们的劳动来维持豪华生活的。我们被称为奴隶，假如我们不做工作，就要挨打，我们没有君主可以向他诉苦或者愿意倾听我们申诉。让我们到国王那里去向他申辩吧；他年轻，我们可能从他那里得到一个有利的回答，假如不能的话，我们自己必须设法改善我们的境遇。

这不是一个向压迫者要求改革的呼吁，而是一个向被压迫者要求采取行动的号召。

保尔被投进麦司顿监狱，他常常用双句联韵的诗体发出秘密信号，号召人民武装起义。在1381年，他“被两万人民”释放出狱，与瓦特·泰勒和杰克·斯特劳在一起，领导农民，向伦敦进发。在布莱克希斯那个地方他发表一篇布道词，以古老的诗句作为标题：

当初亚当挖地，夏娃编织，
那时谁又是什么老爷绅士？

这篇布道词的要义就是，在上帝面前人人平等和部分的财产均等的思想。起义被镇压后，保尔被捕，并被处以绞刑。

二 乔叟和他的《坎特伯雷故事集》

1. **乔叟生平及其早年作品** 乔叟（约1340—1400）是一个酒商的儿子，与宫廷有联系。青年时期曾当过王妃的侍从。英法百年战争中，曾在法国服兵役，并曾被俘一年。他在1366年以前结婚，他的妻子和宫廷也有来往。在14世纪70年代，他几度参加驻外使馆工作，曾两次驻意大利。后来，又历任各种官职，当过议会议员，又任皇家工程总管，但也受过几年贫困。他于1400年逝世，安葬在威斯敏斯特教堂，在现在所谓的"诗人角"。

乔叟有好几幅画像留传下来。他身材比较矮小，有一副沉思的面容，目光向下，是一个羞怯沉默的人，但又精明敏锐。他是一个书生又是一个通达世务的人。工作之余，他就到他藏有六十卷书的书房里——这在当时就算是一个相当大的图书馆了——去读书和写作，直到深夜。他通晓拉丁文、法文和意大利文，熟悉法国和意大利的大作家，包括佩脱拉克[①]、薄伽丘和但丁。他曾翻译并改写过他们的一些作品，其中有骑士传奇、爱情幻梦和民间故事。在这些作品中最出色的是《特洛伊罗斯与克丽西达》，那是根据薄伽丘的《爱的摧残》改写的。但是，他最著名的作品是《坎特伯雷故事集》，这是他一生中最后十二年费尽心力而完成的。

2. **《坎特伯雷故事集》的计划** 春天的时候，人们开始出游。一天晚上，三十个香客停留在伦敦南岸萨得克的泰巴客店，准备骑马去朝拜六十英里外坎特伯雷的殉道者圣托马斯的圣祠。这群人光怪陆离，各式各样——贵贱不一，良莠不齐，有活泼伶俐的，也有呆头呆脑

① 又译彼特拉克。——编注

的——除去皇族和最贫苦的农民以外，其他各个阶层都有代表人物。同时，这又是一群丰富多彩的人物。有的穿着长袍，戴着平常的兜帽；有的穿着短外套、紧身长筒花袜；有些人“把自己的产业都穿在背上”。年轻人都是新奇的打扮。时髦男女都戴着奇形怪状的大头饰，像牛角，或者像头巾，或者像宝塔。

晚饭过后，客店主人提议，每个香客在去的路上讲两个故事，回来时再讲两个，作为旅途中的消遣。主人自愿作调度人，由他逐一指派，谁的故事讲得最好，就由大家合伙请他吃一顿盛餐。这个倡议被接受了，次日就开始讲故事。

这就是总引中所规定的《坎特伯雷故事集》的计划——一个庞大的计划。但是后来乔叟只完成了计划的四分之一，以及一个总引和十个左右的断片。但是这些故事已经足以勾勒出一幅 14 世纪英国社会的图画。

3. **坎特伯雷香客**　香客可分四类，列示如下：

(1) 上层人士

① 骑士。一位伟大的战士，一个富有骑士风度的人物。（“他举止温柔，像一位姑娘。”）

② 骑士的侍从。容貌漂亮，衣冠楚楚，娴于武艺、诗歌、绘画，通晓礼仪。

③ 小地主。一位头面地主，胡子泛白，讲究吃喝。（“他常常就是代表自己郡里的议员。”）

④ 女修道院院长。年轻，出于名门，喜爱漂亮的衣服和狗。（她也可以列入教士一类。）

(2) 教士

① 修道士。酷嗜打猎，讲究生活。（“烤菜中他最爱吃肥天鹅。”）

② 游乞教士。一个寻欢作乐的流氓，女人和酒店老板都是他的熟人。

③ 教会法庭的差役。一个酒鬼，教会法庭里的恶棍官吏，他把一些犯了清规戒律的人叫到法庭上来，但又可以接受贿赂把他们放走。

④ 牧师。虽然贫穷，但对穷人很慷慨。（“他是一个牧师而不是唯利是图的商人。”）

⑤ 修道院中⑤的修女和三个教士。

⑥ 赦罪教士。一个骗子，满头黄发，说起话来是一副假嗓子。

（3）自由职业者

① 医生。一个骗子，精通星相学，靠瘟疫赚钱。

② 律师。所有法律条文都熟记在心。

③ 牛津学者。贫穷，瘦弱，但很有学问，喜爱书籍。（“他喜欢学习，又乐于教人。”）

④ 乔叟本人。总引里没有提及。

（4）商人和手工艺者

① 商人。富有的样子，留着叉形的长胡须。

② 巴斯妇人。一位织布能手，戴着沉重的阔边大帽，穿着红色长袜，嫁过五个丈夫，把他们都送终埋葬了。

③ 针织用品商、木匠、织工、染工和家具商。富有的市民。（“他们每一个人看起来都配做一个好市民。”）

④ 厨司。品酒的好手。（“他会烤、炖、焙和煎炒。”）

⑤ 船夫。一个被太阳晒黑的水手，一个走私犯。（“他顾不上讲什么良心。”）

⑥ 磨坊主。结实，粗壮，硬脑壳，红胡子，鼻子上有一个瘤。（“他懂得怎样偷谷子，并从中搜刮三倍于他所应得的数量。”）

⑦ 庄稼汉。工作勤苦，自己虽不富裕，但对穷人很慷慨。

⑧ 管家。一个庄园的管理人。

⑨ 自耕农。棕色皮肤，圆脑袋，一个很巧的射手。

⑩ 哈利·贝雷。旅店老板，身材魁梧，快活有趣，自任旅途中的向导和指挥。（“谈吐豪爽，聪明温雅。”）

⑪ 伙食经理。法学院里的一个管事人，精明干练，能够哄骗他们所有的人。

4.《坎特伯雷故事集》中故事的类型与形式 《坎特伯雷故事集》实际上包括了中世纪文学的所有主要类型——骑士与贵妇人的传奇、含有道德寓意的以及有趣的民间故事、寓言，等等。有些是高雅的，或者极为有趣，也有些是平淡无味的，还有些甚至是粗陋俚俗的。这些故事都是古老的——也就是说，以前都有人讲过。然而乔叟喜欢古老的东西：

> 常言道，从古老的田地里
> 一年又一年长出新的谷粒，
> 说句真话，人们学习的一切新科学
> 都是来自古老的卷帙。

有时，香客们讲故事互相取笑，例如磨坊主和庄园管理人、游乞教士和教会法庭的差役。有时，若干故事形成一个系列。其中最引人注目的是那个所谓的“婚姻问题组”。起初，巴斯妇人描述她自己的婚姻经历，并认为幸福的婚姻取决于丈夫顺从妻子。然后那个学者告诉大家，妻子怎样顺从她的丈夫才能得到幸福。最后，那个地主现身说法，表明家庭生活应该以相忍相让、互信互爱为准则。

乔叟的语言是近代英语——然而还不是很近代的。近代英语是从他用的语言演变出来的。乔叟的文笔精练优美，流畅自然，他把语言提升到一个较高的文学水平上。

乔叟对英诗韵律作出了很大的贡献。他创立了英雄诗行，即五步重音节抑扬体，这已成为英诗中最常用的体裁。他就是这种英雄偶句体的一位宗师。

5. 乔叟是一位现实主义大师 《坎特伯雷故事集》不仅是一个故事集，也是14世纪英国生活绚烂壮丽的展览，是一部人间喜剧。其中来自不同阶层的三十个人扮演着不同的角色，而把他们自己显示出来——他们的私人生活和习惯，他们的好的和坏的品质。这种生活很多不是通过他们讲的故事，而是通过他们沿途的行为展现出来的。

乔叟描绘的人物栩栩如生。他可能是从他广阔的世界中，挑选出某些具有特色的原型作为起点的。在伦敦南岸萨得克确有一个泰巴客店，也的确有一个名叫哈利·贝雷的有名的旅店老板，也有一个流氓似的采邑管理人和一个海盗似的船夫，这些人是乔叟所认识的……但乔叟笔下这些画像不仅是具有鲜明特征的个人，而且是“典型环境中的典型性格”—— 一个典型的旅店老板，一个典型的船夫等等。如高尔基指出的，乔叟是英国现实主义的奠基人。

在世界观方面，乔叟代表贵族、富商和发迹的“公务人员”，他不是罗拉德派。然而没有人像他在《坎特伯雷故事集》里那样把神职人员，特别是教会法庭差役和赦罪教士的贪污腐化和各式各样无法无天的行为，更赤裸裸地揭露出来；也没有人把新兴资产阶级，如商人、手工艺者以及自由职业者的贪婪、自私和不讲信义，更加巧妙地暴露出来。在坎特伯雷这群人里，在总引中没有受到鞭挞的只有那个骑士、那个牛津大学穷学者、那个牧师和那个庄稼汉。值得注意的是，乔叟对最后两个角色特表同情。

三 民谣

1. **民谣：主题与形式** 民谣的起源一直是一个有争论的问题。有些人认为民谣是在跳舞和其他民间集会中创作出来的，并非出自哪一个作者之手，而是集体创作，每人贡献几行。另有些人认为民谣像所有其他的诗歌一样，是作家的个人作品。但是无论我们采取集体或个人创作说，民谣总是一种民间文学，因为个人不过是多数人的代言人，而且大多数民谣是经过若干世代在民间口传以后才写定的。

英国民谣盛行于 12 世纪至 15 世纪。在这时期，贵族以谈骑士传奇为消遣，而一般人民则用一种形式简单得多而感情比较真挚的诗歌来表达他们的爱好和理想。民谣反映人们所看到的那个时代的生活。

所有民谣的主题都是一般人民喜闻乐见的：(1) 英雄业绩，例如《帕特里克 · 斯彭斯爵士》；(2) 上流社会的爱情悲剧，例如《快活的巴巴拉 · 阿伦》、《朗代尔勋爵》；(3) 家庭悲剧，例如《爱德华》中的杀父，《两姊妹》中的杀姊；(4) 民间传说，里面的角色是神仙、鬼魂或妖怪；(5) 滑稽歌谣，在这里面怕老婆的丈夫成了讽刺家特别取笑的对象。

民谣是戏剧性的。动作从一个生动的或震撼人心的事件向另一个事件迅速有力地移动。民谣里对话用得很多,许多民谣通篇都是对话。同时也常常运用悬而未决和达到高潮的手法来取得感情上的效果。

民谣差不多常用简单的四重音诗节(即四行诗节),这种诗节常称为“民谣体”:

各位自由的勇士,来听我讲,
　你们爱寻欢乐的都来呀,
我给你们讲一个好汉的故事,
　他住在诺丁汉郡。

2. **罗宾汉歌谣**　最杰出的是罗宾汉歌谣,形成于1400年前,普遍流传于15世纪。罗宾汉是个人民英雄,在他周围聚集着一帮逍遥法外的自耕农,也就是生而自由的农民。他们劫富济贫,并以此为生。他们特别仇恨上层贵族——伯爵、男爵、大主教、主教和修道院院长,以及皇室官宦。另一方面,这些法外之徒对于农民,即他们自己的人,表现出特别的关爱。罗宾汉对小约翰这样说道:

但是对犁田的庄稼汉
　当心不要触动,
也不要伤害绿林丛中
　行走的自耕农。

如果要知道产生罗宾汉和他党徒的历史根源，那应当在受压迫者永远反抗压迫者的情况中去寻找——农民反抗他们的庄园地主，反抗宫廷指派的地方官吏，反抗皇家的法官，因为在皇家法庭里农民竟是不受法律保护的。

在罗宾汉的思想方式中有些特别之处。一是罗宾汉对待宗教的态度。他似乎是虔诚的，正统派的。他对圣母马利亚极为虔诚，而且为了她的缘故，不准他的党徒在路上劫掠妇女。但同时并不禁止他们抢劫教徒，特别是修道院院长。

另外，罗宾汉对国王的态度也很特别。《罗宾汉的事迹》是有关罗宾汉歌谣中最好的作品，其中国王好像是法外歹徒和官府之间的调解人——好像他竟然是这些法外歹徒的实际的恩人。国王被看作凌驾于社会上所有敌对阶级之上。这是当时农民中普遍的幻想。

四　早期戏剧的形式

1. **奇迹剧（或神秘剧）**　从13至15世纪，奇迹剧大约在一百二十五个村镇里演出。它们取材于圣经故事，如世界的创造、诺亚与洪水、基督诞生，通常在节日，如圣诞节、复活节、基督圣体节上演。演出是由当地市镇政府负责的，市政当局在市镇各行各业公会内分配剧目。到了节日，装有车轮的戏台就在市内驶往指定各站表演；这样，人们就可以从这一站到另一站，想要看多少就看多少。这种演出常常连续三天。舞台设计是简陋的，重要的是服饰和化装。

奇迹剧并不都是以宗教为内容的。圣经里的故事通常都经过改编，由普通人表演，也是给普通人观看的。超自然的部分常常巧妙地和最平凡的现实主义结合在一起。

在那出名为《牧人》，原由威克菲尔德行会演出的戏里，就饶有真实生活的风味。时间是夜晚，在一个荒山坡上，牧羊人躺在地上。其中一个人说："主呵，天多么冷啊！我快要冻僵了，直挺挺的，我已睡得太久了。这场雨，就下个不停吗？这个日子难过呀，要完税呀，而地主老爷又那样对待我们。前几天，有一位老爷来向我借车和犁。我怎么办呢？我要对他说个不字，倒不如被绞死算了！"另外一个牧人接着讲下去，说天气坏透了，生活又很艰难。他说："在这天气里我们在外面，饿得要命，而有钱人吃好东西，还睡舒服的床。"

这个剧本写于14世纪后期，反映了当时的情况，那时农民被苛捐杂税和豪绅的压迫压垮了。

2. **道德剧** 道德剧出现于1400年左右，是奇迹剧的一个分支。道德剧的作者不再沿用圣经里的人物，如亚当、夏娃、诺亚、亚伯拉罕、犹大，而给他们的人物以这类名字，如仁慈、恶行、良心、愚蠢、力量、知识、善行。仁慈自然总是说好话、做好事；愚蠢总是说蠢话、做蠢事；他们争夺人的灵魂。《每个人》是道德剧中最杰出的。在这个剧本里，死亡把"每个人"叫来，要他到坟墓里去。他求助于他在世上的朋友——戚谊、美丽、五觉、力量、知识，但都属徒然。他最后才发现只有"善行"愿意陪他前往。

在戏剧的发展中，道德剧好像是倒退了一步。因为奇迹剧试图通过对话和动作（这是戏剧的要素）来展示性格，而道德剧里面却没有多少实际的故事情节，只有每一个人物的滔滔不绝的演说和没完没了的说教。然而，道德剧有其重要性。道德剧的主题是文学中一个古老的主题，即所谓“灵魂的斗争”。既然是一种斗争，它就包含着高度的戏剧发展的前景。莎士比亚的悲剧和一些近代戏剧在本质上都属于这一类。

此外，在道德剧中圣经的材料被抛弃了，戏剧作家将找到他的自由创作的道路。

第三章

文艺复兴

一　英国的人文主义

1. **恩格斯论文艺复兴**　文艺复兴开始于13到14世纪，是欧洲的一场伟大的文化运动。这场运动是由于在封建社会里孕育的生产力的成长以及新型社会关系的发展而产生的。它标志着封建制度开始瓦解。

恩格斯在《自然辩证法》的导言中对文艺复兴时期作了经典性的论述：

> 这是一次人类从来没有经历过的最伟大的、进步的变革，是一个需要巨人而且产生了巨人——在思维能力、热情和性格方面，在多才多艺和学识广博方面的巨人的时代。给现代资产阶级统治打

下基础的人物，决不受资产阶级的局限。相反地，成为时代特征的冒险精神，或多或少地推动了这些人物。那时差不多没有一个著名人物不曾作过长途的旅行，不会说四五种语言，不在几个专业上放射出光芒。……那时的英雄们还没有成为分工的奴隶，分工所具有的限制人的、使人片面化的影响，在他们的后继者那里我们是常常看到的。但他们的特征是他们几乎全都处在时代运动中，在实际斗争中生活着和活动着，站在这一方面或那一方面进行斗争，一些人用舌和笔，一些人用剑，一些人则两者并用。因此有了使他们成为完人的那种性格上的完整和坚强。[①]

2. **英国的人文主义者** 文艺复兴运动始于意大利。在13和14世纪，意大利出现了一批进步思想家——但丁、佩脱拉克、薄伽丘等人，他们译述了荷马、苏格拉底、柏拉图、西塞罗等古代希腊、罗马思想大师的著作，使他们获得了新生。他们运用关于这些经典著作的知识来和当时的因循守旧、愚昧无知以及阻碍人的自由发展的宗教狂热作斗争。他们为了自由和启蒙而努力。他们被称为“人文主义者”。

在15世纪，一些英国人到了意大利，他们尽其所能汲取了当时的“新学问”，行囊满载书籍而归。在16世纪初期，英国出现了一批叫作“牛津改革派”的人文主义者——如研究希腊的学者威廉·格罗辛、医生托马斯·林纳克尔、圣保罗大教堂的教长约翰·科列特。他们全都通晓希腊文。通过他们，来自古代世界和来自意大利和法国的新知识、新思想在都铎王朝时代的英国传播开来。荷兰的人文主义者伊拉斯默斯来来往往，在剑桥大学教授希腊文。他是那个时代最杰出的学

① 恩格斯：《自然辩证法》导言，见《马克思恩格斯选集》，中共中央马恩列斯著作编译局，人民出版社，1972年，第444—445页。

者。他所著的《愚人颂》是一部针对教士们的腐败堕落和愚昧无知进行讽刺的作品。

在英国人文主义者中，最优秀的是托马斯·莫尔爵士（1478—1535），他是伊拉斯默斯的亲密朋友。他是学者、律师，又是下院议员和杰出的政治家。在牛津学者之中，他是唯一具有创作天赋的人。他所著的《乌托邦》已成为一本世界名著，这本书可以视为英国文艺复兴运动的真正开端。

3. **托马斯·莫尔的《乌托邦》** 《乌托邦》（1515—1516）用拉丁文写成，并在整个欧洲流传。它的第一个英文译本于1551年由拉尔夫·罗宾逊完成。全书分为两卷，这两卷有意地、巧妙地使新旧两个世界形成对照。

在上卷里，人文主义者和航海家希斯洛德向我们讲述了当时英国的状况。在各种社会罪恶中，他提到残酷的法律（例如绞死窃贼）、无止境的贪婪（例如圈地和赶走农民）、民族主义的野心、自私自利的战争、苛捐杂税和财富分配的不平均。书中没有提出特殊的解决办法，而是指出了造成这些罪恶的根本原因。这就是私有财产的支配和商品的私有制。“只要私有财产依然存在，人类大多数和最优秀的部分就会在不可避免的忧虑烦恼的重压之下受到压迫。”上卷结尾的这些话是全书的中心思想。

下卷是关于“乌托邦”的描述。它是新世界里某个无人知晓的海洋中的一个理想国度。在“乌托邦”里，一切土地属于公有。这里没有私有财产，也没有随之而来的种种罪恶。劳动是由国家组织进行的，而生产、消费、贸易和商业也是如此。人人都工作，但一天只工作六小时，而且“许许多多各行各业的人，不分男女，都去听讲”。在这里宗教信仰完全是自由的。莫尔的结论是具有讽刺意味的:他不能同意希斯洛德所说的全部事情,又不得不承认,“乌托邦”里的许多事情对英国来说是可望而不可即的。

4. 莫尔与空想社会主义 《乌托邦》是资本原始积累时期的一部伟大的社会文献。作者对都铎王朝时代的社会进行了分析,把它称为“富人反对穷人的一个阴谋”。这个论断是根据他对周围世界的社会发展所亲眼观察到的事实——圈地运动、小佃农被人驱逐、土地上农业工人的需求的减少、人民群众的贫苦和悲惨的境遇。他指出,与劳动人民相比,“连牲畜的生活,似乎也是令人羡慕的”。

莫尔是一个极其博学而有见识的人。他熟知柏拉图的《理想国》,熟知那个想象中的国度。他也读过当时那些描述美洲和西印度群岛土著民族的著作,这些土著民族的土地房屋都是公共所有,并且不分“你的”和“我的”。与此同时,他看到周围人民群众的苦难生活,深有感触。他对于他所看到并谴责的那些社会矛盾,找不到一种力量来加以解决——资产阶级制度还尚在形成之中。他只能在头脑中设想出一个社会平等和人与人之间和谐一致的想象中的国度。他的《乌托邦》是一部深邃透辟而令人惊叹的著作。

莫尔已被公认为空想社会主义鼻祖,并且也是空想社会主义最伟大的代表之一。“乌托邦”(Utopia)和“乌托邦的”(Utopian)这两个词就来自他那本小小的经典著作。

然而,决不可以认为莫尔的思想完全是现代的,在许多方面他的思想是中世纪的。他在《乌托邦》一书中赞成宗教宽容,反对禁欲主义,但是他本人却是一个顺服的天主教徒,身穿粗毛衣,并且作为亨利八世的大法官迫害了英国最初的新教教徒。当英国国教与罗马教庭分离时，他拒绝服从，并为自己的信仰而殉难。

二　诗剧以外的诗歌

1. 歌曲与十四行诗　英国早期的歌曲传统在文艺复兴时期得到了发扬。中世纪的禁欲主义过时了，人间世俗之美和感性的培育和享受在音乐和诗歌中得到了更充分的表现。16 世纪下半叶，通常叫作伊丽莎白时代，那是一个歌曲盛行的时代——一个产生了著名音乐家和作曲家的时代，例如威廉·伯尔德、约翰·道兰德、托马斯·坎平等。在这个时代，人们对音乐和歌唱的爱好之普遍，超过了之前英国历史上的任何时期。

伊丽莎白时代的戏剧里穿插着不少歌曲，其中有许多至今仍为人们所歌唱，有的是按照当时谱写的古老的曲调，有的是按照现代作曲家谱写的曲调，例如《谁是西尔维亚》(见《维洛那二绅士》)、《在那蜜蜂采蜜的地方》(见《暴风雨》)、《听吧，听那云雀》(见《辛白林》)。

十四行诗是一种形式谨严、抑扬格五音步、押韵格式复杂的十四行的诗体。它在意大利诗人佩脱拉克的手里达到了完善的程度，并在 1557 年之前就已经传入英语诗歌之中。在随后的半个多世纪中，十四行诗是最流行的诗体之一。当时诗人中有一股写十四行诗“组诗”的风气——每首诗自成一体，但“组诗”之内各首的主题多少有些关联——献给某一位令人心醉而又负心或冷漠无情的美丽女子。

伊丽莎白时代的抒情诗歌的基调是多种多样的，但有两种基调是特别代表这一时代的：一是慨叹人生的短暂，渴望抓住转瞬即逝的片刻欢娱——比如说，今朝尽情作乐吧，因为明天我们都将死去！二是逃避现实，梦想一种纯朴的乡村生活（例如马洛的《牧羊人恋歌》）。这两种情调都是从希腊和拉丁诗人那里继承过来的，但同时也反映了时代的精神——标志着创业者和冒险家时代的激情和冒险精神，以及试图逃避当代各种各样动乱的遁世思想。

2．斯宾塞的《仙后》 在诗剧以外，伊丽莎白时代最长的诗歌是埃德蒙·斯宾塞的长达六卷的《仙后》（1590—1596）。这首长诗谁都知道一些，但是很少有人通篇读完。如斯宾塞自己所说的那样，这首长诗的主旨是"塑造一位道德高尚、秉性温和的绅士或贵人"。这首诗是奉献给"世上最杰出、最光辉的人"，即伊丽莎白女王的。

全诗的主题是以一种奇特的方式展开的。斯宾塞没有定下什么条条框框。他没有说这位绅士或那位贵人应该这样做或不该那样做；相反，他把读者带进一个梦境，在那里什么事都会发生，而事实上确也发生了许多极不寻常的事。诗中有一连串骑士，其中每一个骑士在他的冒险中体现了一种美德，一种正当生活的原则。例如，一个骑士象征神圣，另一个象征节制，再一个象征贞洁，等等。这些骑士身穿闪闪发光的铠甲跟浑身长鳞的妖怪和巫师对抗，这同中世纪诗体传奇中描写的差不多。

但是《仙后》的思想与其说是封建的，还不如说是资产阶级的。骑士们作为一个整体代表英国或英国国教，而他们所遇到的种种邪恶人物、困难和危险则代表西班牙国王菲利普、苏格兰女王玛丽，或者罗马教会。而且这些骑士本身并不怎么像诗体传奇中的冒险者，而是更像伊丽莎白的朝臣。

值得注意的是，这篇诗作具有一种可以配合仙境生活的、柔和动听萦绕耳际的音乐性。每节诗有九行，韵律复杂（ababbcbcc），最后一行较长，从此称为“斯宾塞诗节”。拜伦的《查尔德·哈洛德游记》里用的就是这种诗歌格律形式。

三　都铎王朝时代的散文

1．伊丽莎白时代的翻译　伊丽莎白时代是一个翻译蓬勃发展的时代。通过翻译作品，古代的、意大利的和法国的文化渗入了英国文学的发展。在为数众多的翻译作品中，必须提一下廷德尔和科弗代尔翻译的圣经以及托马斯·诺斯爵士翻译的普鲁塔克的《希腊罗马名人传》。

英文版的圣经是新教改革的重要思想武器。同威克利夫和他的信徒们罗拉德派人一样，宗教改革者们坚信圣经不应该沿用中世纪的拉丁文，也不应由教皇和高级教士们所垄断，而是必须使用人民都能通晓的语言。

1525年，威廉·廷德尔（卒于1536年）在科隆出版了他翻译的《新约》。他说：“如果上帝让我活下去，无须多年我就会使耕田的孩子比神学家更懂圣经。”他的工作后来由迈尔斯·科弗代尔完成。1537年科弗代尔出版了他翻译的《旧约》。在随后半个世纪里，出版了不少其他译本。但是他们两人的译本则成为直至今日英文译本所遵循的基础。由于它的语言雅俗共赏，它深入了英文散文和诗歌的骨髓。

普鲁塔克是公元1世纪的希腊作家。他的《希腊罗马名人传》是希腊、罗马时代的壮丽画廊。古代的伟大人物（例如恺撒、克利奥佩特拉、安东尼）在他笔下的大量轶事中都显得栩栩如生。托马斯·诺斯爵士翻译的此书于1579年出版。他不仅仅是翻译，他还以生动有力的、口语化的语言进行了再创造。这本书读起来令人兴趣盎然——毫无疑问，伊丽莎白时代的人们是这样想的。莎士比亚罗马剧中的许多情节、人物和用语都可以追溯到诺斯所译的普鲁塔克的《希腊罗马名人传》。

2. 伊丽莎白时代的航海发现　伊丽莎白时代是一个地理大发现的时代。佛罗比歇、霍金斯、吉尔伯特、德雷克，以及华尔特·雷利爵士等英国航海家带回了有关遥远国度的神奇传说。这些传说变成了酒店旅馆、街头巷尾、礼堂民宅或剧院中人们热议谈论的话题。

1589年，理查·哈克路特出版了卷帙浩繁的集子《主要的航行、航海与大发现》，虽然他本人从未出海航行过。这个集子后来又再版并增订。它包括了一百多个英国和外国的航海发现的故事。这本集子中的故事质量参差不齐：有些表现出极为卓越的技巧，有些则是粗制滥造和未完成的。但是，即使在写冒险和发财的最平淡无奇的叙述中，也不乏浪漫的情节穿插其中。哈克路特的本意并非仅仅记录这些业绩，而是旨在鼓励他的同胞们去创造业绩，去发现未知的国度和进行殖民，并鼓励与地球上遥远的地方进行贸易。这些航海家的记叙曾唤起诗人迈克尔·德雷顿的激情，他写道：

勤劳的哈克路特，
　致力于航海的故事！
　人们听了你的话语，
将去追求荣誉；

还将称颂你的才德

作为师表于万世。

3. 伊丽莎白时代的散文小说 伊丽莎白时代的小说可分为两类：(1)为“文雅读者”写的小说；(2)关于市民生活的平易故事。约翰·李利的《尤菲绮斯》(1579—1580)属于第一类。尤菲绮斯是一个雅典青年，他去了那不勒斯，坠入情网，被情人抛弃，后来到了英国。书中情节并不多，但关于爱情和习俗的谈论却滔滔不绝。《尤菲绮斯》是以一种独特的文体写成的，被称为“尤菲绮斯体”，它的特点在于运用对仗、头韵和比喻。以下是两个例子：

> Let my rude birth excuse my bold request.
>
> （请为我鄙陋的出身而原谅我冒昧的请求。）

> Although I have shrined thee in my heart for a trusty friend, I will shun thee hereafter as atrothless foe.
>
> （尽管我在心中一向把你当作我可信的朋友，可是从今以后我将把你当作无信的敌人而避开你。）

与《尤菲绮斯》相类似的还有菲利普·锡德尼爵士的《阿卡狄亚》(1580)。两位王子到了阿卡狄亚，在森林里碰见了两位公主。他们坠入了情网——当然最后是缔结良缘。但是其中充满了乔装打扮、张冠李戴、侠义打斗，构成了一部长篇大著。其文笔有些尤菲绮斯色彩。一位少女绯红的面庞被描绘为就像“微风轻拂叶儿时玫瑰花儿在微笑”。同《尤菲绮斯》一样，《阿卡狄亚》也似乎是形式重于故事。

更值得注意的是第二类小说——即关于现实生活的不加粉饰的故事。托马斯·纳希的《杰克·威尔顿》(1594)就是这样一本小说。书中讲叙的是一个书童的故事,他随主人历游欧洲各个城市,“见识见识生活”。这部中篇小说开创了一种做法,即将一位冒险的主人公置于一连串的经历之中,而所有这些经历都是真实的。主人公处于形形色色的人们之中,这些人又都非常逼真,因而就勾画出了一幅广阔真实的当代生活的画卷。后来的小说家如笛福、菲尔丁、萨克雷都继承了这一传统。

同样有趣的是一本名叫《体面的手艺》(1597)的小书,作者是诺里奇的一位纺织工人托马斯·德洛尼。书中有三个故事,其中一个讲的是“西蒙·埃尔是怎样从一个鞋匠起家,后来当上了伦敦市长”。这个简单质朴的故事成了后来一长串小说的先驱,这些小说都以真实描写普通百姓及其日常生活而引起读者的兴趣。

四　莎士比亚的先驱

1. 多种多样的戏剧形式　都铎王朝时代的戏剧采取了多种多样的形式。奇迹剧在宗教改革之前一直流行,而道德剧则一直流行到16世纪中叶。与晚期的道德剧同时,兴起了另一种形式的戏剧,叫作“幕间剧”。这种剧中的人物是社会生活中的典型,而不再是善行和邪恶的化身。

“幕间剧”的一个典型是约翰·海伍德的名叫《四个P》的一出小戏(大约1530年)。剧中的朝圣者(Palmer)、赦罪教士(Pardoner)、小贩（Pedlar）和药剂师（'Potecary = Apothecary）展开了一场争辩，看谁撒的谎最大。小贩充当裁判，取胜的是朝圣者——他庄严地声称在他交往过的各种各样的女性中，他从来没有见过一个女人会失去耐心！

同时，通过古典文学的复兴，剧作家们接触到了希腊和拉丁的戏剧。他们从这里学到了关于结构和风格的所有重要知识，关于悲剧和喜剧的更确切的概念，并且也找到了用之不竭的题材。他们学会了一出戏要有条有理地分成五幕。他们也学会了运用一些惯用的角色，如狡诈的恶仆、漂亮的情人、暴躁的父亲、趾高气扬的军人等。他们还看到了怎样有效地运用鬼魂、"合唱"，以及喧闹的台词。在16世纪中叶，充斥了模仿拉丁戏剧的悲剧和喜剧。

奇迹剧、道德剧、幕间剧、古典剧以及当时流行的各种戏剧的混合物——这些便是伊丽莎白时代早期的戏剧形式。马洛和莎士比亚的戏剧就是从这些形形色色的戏剧之中产生的。

2. 剧院、演员和观众 在早期，戏剧是在旅馆的庭院里演出的，表演时搭起临时舞台。伦敦有些老的旅馆，由于经常演戏，基本上成了剧院。

约在1576年出现了正规的剧院。它们分成两类：私人剧院和公共剧院。私人剧院，其中"黑衣修士"剧院是第一家，有房顶，收费高昂，拥有由男孩扮为演员的剧团。公共剧院，如"大剧院"、"帷幕剧院"等，被看作是不体面的场所。它们被拒于城外，先是在泰晤士河北岸，后来又在南岸。但它们的发展却是迅速的，到了16世纪末就已有八座。这对一个人口不到二十万的城市是个惊人的数字，证明戏剧演出已博得人们的喜爱。著名的"环球"剧院——莎士比亚的剧院——是在 1599 年建立的。

舞台几乎是空荡荡的，帷幕是挂在靠舞台后面的地方，而不是像现代舞台那样挂在前面。舞台两边的门用作通道，而在王政复辟时期之前，几乎不使用活动的布景。

在几乎光秃秃的舞台上，演员的表现显得格外重要。他们的艺术因而就达到了很高的水平。当时没有女演员，女角色是由男孩扮演的。尽管演员是些社会上的流浪者，但他们不仅受到人民大众的欢迎，而且也受到贵族们的庇护。其中有些人名噪一时，如伯贝奇父子以及在马洛的戏剧中担任主角的爱德华 · 艾伦。

拥进伊丽莎白时代剧院的观众来自各个阶层、各行各业。“一般人”通常是在戏池里站着看，富人贵族坐在楼座上观看，而放荡无礼的纨绔子弟就在舞台上带着皮壳的食物边嗑边看。然而，大部分观众是简单朴实的老百姓，他们富于好奇心和想象力，也很容易为剧情所感动。

3. **马洛和文艺复兴** 在莎士比亚之前的许多剧作家之中，最有才华的是克里斯托弗 · 马洛（1564—1593）。他是坎特伯雷一个鞋匠的儿子，就学于剑桥大学并得到硕士学位。1587 年他到了伦敦，在随后的七年里写了七个剧本和许多诗。1593 年 5 月的一天，他卷入一场酒馆里的殴斗，被刺身亡。他的一生虽然短暂，但是非凡。

马洛是一位学者，是他那个时代最正直的学者之一。他通晓古典著作，并在他的剧作中充分利用了这种知识。他具有文艺复兴时期的学者对真理的热爱，并认为在学术争论中必须持公正态度。他挺身而出为异族和异教辩护。他说，一个诚实的土耳其人，或一个守信的犹太人，也要比一个不讲信用的基督徒为好。正是由于这样的观点，顽固派污蔑他为“宗教自由论者”和“无神论者”。

马洛是文艺复兴的化身，在他的身上体现了这样一种认识，即人类具有无穷无尽的潜力。他通过帖木儿大帝的口说道：

构成我们的自然四要素，
渴望统治而在胸中斗争，
教导我们都须有凌云壮志：
我们的心灵能充分领悟
这个世界上奇妙的结构，
测量运行着的行星的轨迹，
永远攀登无穷无尽的知识的高峰，
随着永不静止的宇宙而运动。
我们的灵魂叫我们
自强不息，永不休止，
直到摘到那最成熟的果实……

除了其他优点之外，马洛最为人称道的是他的“雄伟的诗行”。他能以最少的语言表达最广博的思想，这种本领其他诗人中没有几个能和他相比。虽然在他之前就已经有人写过素体诗——不用韵的抑扬格五音步诗行，但是只是到了他的笔下素体诗才成为英诗中最富有表现力和最雄伟的格律形式。

4. 马洛的代表作 他的七个剧本中，三个最为突出：《帖木儿大帝》(1587)、《浮士德博士》(1588)和《马耳他岛的犹太人》(1589)。它们都反映了文艺复兴时期那种永无止境的探索精神和极端的个人主义精神。《帖木儿大帝》分为两部，共十幕。它是一部展示这位鞑鞑征服者战胜欧亚弱小国家的极为壮观之作。它的主题是追求无限权力的欲望——征服世界：

我们要一直进军到南极，
征服一切人，把他们踩在脚下，
我们将威名远扬，使一切帝王黯然失色！

《马耳他岛的犹太人》刻画了一个贪婪、阴险、奸诈的有钱人巴拉巴斯。剧本的主题是资本主义萌芽时期那种对财富的贪求。马洛最著名的著作是《浮士德博士》，其主题是追求无限的知识以及这种知识和魔法给予人类的巨大能力。

浮士德年轻、聪明、富于求知欲，他发现自己对轻易取得成就感到厌烦。他梦想得到超人的能力，他想要去知道，去理解，并在这个意义上去占有地球上所有的王国：

在寂静的南北两极之间的万物，
都将听命于我。皇帝和国王
只能在他们各自的领土上发号施令，
他们不能唤来大风，也不能撕裂云层；
但是具有叱咤风云本领的人，
他的统治将远及人类思维所至之处。

浮士德为了取得他所渴求的一切，宁可把灵魂出卖给魔鬼以换取二十四年的魔力。他一取得这种魔力，就立刻蔑视一切传统，一心一意为了知识而追求知识，或是为了财富而追求知识。他追求政治和军事力量，追求人生的欢乐。但他的内心是矛盾的，他感到烦恼、厌倦，幻想破灭，并不时陷入焦虑之中。可是他仍然无止境地追求他尚未得到的东西——直到魔鬼把他带走。

浮士德的故事是以一个德国民间传说《浮士德故事》为素材的。但这一传说到了马洛的笔下就反映出时代的渴求和向往——一种强烈的个人主义、怀疑主义，一种对人类具有无穷无尽的潜力的认识。

第四章

威廉·莎士比亚

一　莎士比亚与文艺复兴

1. **莎士比亚生平事迹**　莎士比亚于1564年4月（历来以4月23日作为他的诞辰）生于艾冯河畔斯特拉福德——那是一个大约有两千人口的繁荣小市镇。他的父亲约翰·莎士比亚是一个富裕的商人，经营羊毛和皮革生意，一度任首席市参政员之职。莎士比亚年轻时上过斯特拉福德镇的文法学校，受过良好的拉丁文训练。他十八岁时娶了安·哈撒薇为妻，她是农家出身，比他大八岁。

大概在1585年，莎士比亚到伦敦，开始剧院生涯。在1592年之前，他在伦敦的所作所为很少为人所知。据说，他一度在剧院管过马，当过听差。到了1592年，他作为剧作家和演员已经声名大噪，引起老戏剧家罗伯特·格林的嘲讽，被叫作“一只暴发户似的、用我们的羽毛装饰起来的乌鸦”。

其后二十年，他当演员，改编和写作剧本。他演戏好像不很成功，但他写戏的天才却很快得到了公认。他的事业得到了成功，成了著名的“环球剧院”的股东。他不时回到斯特拉福德镇探望，并在那里买了一所宽敞的住宅。大约在1613年他不再在伦敦工作，回到故乡以度余年。他死于1616年4月23日（照我们现在的历法应为5月4日），葬于斯特拉福德教堂。这个地方已经成了文学朝拜的圣地。

莎士比亚是一个“漂亮的、体格匀称的人，很好相处，才智敏捷，性情愉快、平易”。本·琼生对他在艺术上虽有所批评，但是，尽管他有失误，对琼生来说，他是戏剧作家中最伟大的人。

1623年，莎士比亚著作的第一部合集出版了，叫作“第一对折本”。莎士比亚的全部著作包括两篇诗作、一百五十四首十四行诗和三十七部剧本。

2. 莎士比亚与文艺复兴时期的文化 看来莎士比亚在伦敦的头几年就和当时大学生的圈子有所接触。他的早期戏剧《错误的喜剧》（1592）就是属于传统的“学院戏剧”，亦即在中学和大学里创作和演出的戏剧。直到今天还保存着一份布告，证明该剧曾在伦敦四个法学院里业余上演。而且，他跟学生界的这种接触继续着。大学生们给他提供的环境对他汲取当时的进步文化是有帮助的，否则他的创作是难以想象的。

此外，在1592年之前，莎士比亚就已是戏剧界的一位赞助人南安普敦伯爵家的座上客了。莎士比亚的诗篇《维纳斯与阿多尼斯》（1593）和《鲁克丽丝受辱记》（1594）就是题献给这位爵爷的。在宫廷生活的圈子中，他一定接触过文艺复兴时期的艺术：意大利绘画和意大利音乐。他的作品中的许多段落都证明了他爱好绘画,尤其爱好音乐。他不仅熟悉意大利文化,并且熟悉法国作家和古典作家。他一再从意大利、法国和古典作家的故事中汲取自己创作的素材。第三章中提到的诺斯译的普鲁塔克的《希腊罗马名人传》就是他编写剧本时汲取题材的主要来源之一。

但是这位诗人兼戏剧家,对本民族的文化也具有深厚的修养。他的青少年时代是在乡下度过的,他从乡间带来了一份丰富的宝藏:这就是,民谣、民歌,以及和他一起生活过的人们的风俗习惯。在他的剧本中可以看到他早年生活的经历和他所熟悉的人们:市镇的警察、教师、教区牧师、工匠、村民、乡绅等。

3. **莎士比亚"打开了自己的心扉"** 很遗憾,莎士比亚从来没有写过他自己的生活。关于他的生平,后世所知极少。也许我们可以从他的十四行诗中了解一些情况。在这些诗中,正如华滋华斯所说,他"打开了自己的心扉"。

莎士比亚写十四行诗是按照当时的风尚。文艺复兴时期绝大多数诗人都写过十四行诗,这些诗的内容是向自己的心上人倾诉衷肠,抱怨她冷漠无情,变幻无常。但是莎士比亚在许多十四行诗中,却抒发了自己真实的感情。他觉得自己智力高超,然而又深感自己社会地位低微,这种矛盾的心情反映在某些十四行诗中(例如第二十九首十四行诗),另外一些十四行诗则述说了当时社会的不公平。下面的几行诗(第一百一十首十四行诗)倾诉了他作为演员和剧作家的生涯的苦恼:

唉,我的确曾经常东奔西跑,

扮作斑衣的小丑供众人赏玩，
违背我的意志，把至宝贱卖掉，
为了新交不惜把旧知冒犯。[①]

下面是著名的第六十六首十四行诗，反映了社会的不公平：

厌了这一切，我向安息的死疾呼，
比方，眼见天才注定做叫化子，
无聊的草包打扮得衣冠楚楚，
纯洁的信义不幸被人背弃，
金冠可耻地戴在行尸的头上，
处女的贞操遭受暴徒的玷辱，
严肃的正义被人非法的诟污，
壮士被当权的跛子弄成残缺，
愚蠢摆起博士架子驾驭才能，
艺术被官府统治得结舌钳口，
淳朴的真诚被人瞎称为愚笨，
囚徒“善”不得不把统帅“恶”伺候：
　厌了这一切，我要离开人寰，
　但，我一死，我的爱人便孤单。[②]

莎士比亚写这些十四行诗时还是一位青年，诗中涉及了他个人的私生活。但是这些诗是他去世前七年才发表的，这时，他已经是一个成功而杰出的公民了。

---

① 见梁宗岱译本。

② 见梁宗岱译本。

二　早期的悲剧和喜剧

1.**《罗密欧与朱丽叶》** 作为戏剧家，莎士比亚是从习作开始的。他的早期剧本不少是旧剧新编，而且绝非本本都是杰作。他是在写了一些失败的和不太成功的剧本之后，才学会了写戏的艺术。

《罗密欧与朱丽叶》(1595—1596)是他最早获得成功的一部悲剧。故事取自意大利，发生在维洛那。这部悲剧揭露了古老的封建社会里无穷无尽的内部斗争以及人与人之间的不近情理的关系。

罗密欧与朱丽叶是一对情人，他们的家族蒙太古族和凯普莱特族是世仇。他们互相爱慕，但不可能结合。罗密欧因杀死了凯普莱特族的一个成员而被放逐；朱丽叶则被许配给一个她所不爱的人。朱丽叶问计于劳伦斯神父。为了帮她摆脱包办婚姻并使罗密欧有机会把她带走，劳伦斯神父想出了一个大胆的计策。她吃了一种药，假死四十二小时。她被送往殡宫。这时罗密欧知道了她的葬礼，赶回来，到了墓地，并在朱丽叶快要苏醒过来之前殉情自杀了。后来朱丽叶醒来，看到罗密欧已死，于是也自杀了。

罗密欧与朱丽叶是坚贞不渝的爱情的化身和象征——这是莎士比亚的诗歌和戏剧中喜用的一个主题。罗密欧与朱丽叶是文艺复兴时期的产儿，悲剧的背景是阴暗的封建家庭，父母偏狭固执，对爱情和婚姻采取封建的态度。

《罗密欧与朱丽叶》这出富有诗意和浪漫色彩的悲剧是当时英国青年所喜爱的一出戏，在英国革命爆发之前一直如此。17 世纪牛津大学好学的学子几乎把印有该剧的“第一对折本”翻烂了。

2.**《威尼斯商人》** 《威尼斯商人》(1596—1597) 是莎士比亚一

出深受欢迎的喜剧。故事也取自意大利,发生于威尼斯。一位名叫巴萨尼奥的富于冒险精神的威尼斯青年准备向鲍西娅求爱。鲍西娅是一个出名的美人,住在一个叫作贝尔蒙特的地方(该地究竟在哪里,暂且不管)。他需要钱,因而求助于他的朋友,商人安东尼奥。但是安东尼奥的钱都已投资在商船上,而那些商船还在海上。为了使巴萨尼奥有钱去求婚,他便向放高利贷的犹太人夏洛克借债。夏洛克曾经在基督徒的手上吃过苦头,这时他同意借给所需要的款项,但有条件,即如若到期不还,他便从安东尼奥身上割取一磅肉。巴萨尼奥到了贝尔蒙特,跟鲍西娅结了婚。但是安东尼奥却处于危险之中:犹太人要割取他的一磅肉。

在这千钧一发之际,一位法学博士来到威尼斯。他审理了这件案子,判定犹太人有权履行原约。但是这位才学出众的博士也警告犹太人,必须完全按照契约的文字执行,所要割的肉不能多也不能少,并且不许流一滴血,否则他必须偿命。这些不可能做到的条件挫败了犹太人,他恼怒之余撕毁了契约,离开了法庭。原来这位才学出众的博士不是别人,正是女扮男装的鲍西娅!全剧在谈情说爱和喜悦的歌声中结束。

这出喜剧描绘了封建—资产阶级社会中及其典型人物的特点:富商大贾(安东尼奥)、放高利贷者(夏洛克)、希望得到嫁妆致富的求婚者(巴萨尼奥)等。这出戏揭露了这个社会的罪恶:贪婪、恶毒、种族偏见、拜金主义、不讲道义和残暴。然而,这种阴霾的气氛却被一位妇女的光辉形象所驱散,她就是鲍西娅,一位文艺复兴时期的女性——美丽、端庄、有教养、彬彬有礼,并且具有临危不惧、应付裕如的才干。她是莎士比亚笔下理想女性之一。

3. **犹太人夏洛克** 《威尼斯商人》一剧中最值得注意的人物是犹太人夏洛克。莎士比亚淋漓尽致地刻画了夏洛克的卑鄙、奸诈和残忍，然而他所描绘的这个犹太人却又引起我们的同情。这个犹太人并非一个大恶棍。

《威尼斯商人》上演之前几年，有一位名叫洛佩斯的医生以图谋毒死伊丽莎白女王的罪名受审，他是御医，是葡萄牙籍犹太人。罪证不足，女王似乎相信他无罪。但是当时反犹太人的情绪很高，结果他被处以绞刑，并被开膛和肢解。

莎士比亚的《威尼斯商人》不是反犹宣传。相反，他为受到迫害的犹太族说了许多话。夏洛克犯有高利贷者的一切罪过，但是，“别人对他犯的罪过比他犯的罪过更多”。他怨恨基督教徒商人是有道理的：

> 难道犹太人没有眼睛吗？难道犹太人没有五官四肢、没有知觉、没有感情、没有血气吗？他不是吃着同样的食物，同样的武器可以伤害他，同样的医药可以治疗他，冬天同样会冷，夏天同样会热，就像一个基督徒一样吗？你们要是用刀剑刺我们，我们不是也会出血的吗？你们要是搔我们的痒，我们不是也会笑起来的吗？你们要是用毒药谋害我们，我们不是也会死的吗？那么要是你们欺侮了我们，我们难道不会复仇吗？要是在别的地方我们都跟你们一样，那么在这一点上也是彼此相同的。要是一个犹太人欺侮了一个基督徒，那基督徒怎样表现他的谦逊？报仇。要是一个基督徒欺侮了一个犹太人，那么照着基督徒的榜样，那犹太人应该怎样表现他的宽容？报仇。①

① 《威尼斯商人》，第三幕，第一场。见朱生豪译本。

这就是夏洛克所说的话——或者毋宁说是莎士比亚借那个受到迫害的夏洛克之口所说的话。是莎士比亚使我们在这个犹太人退场时不禁喊了出来："天啊，这个人受到了冤枉！"

三　历史剧

1. **莎士比亚和历史剧**　莎士比亚开始学习写戏时，英国人民还在为击败西班牙无敌舰队而欢欣鼓舞。历史题材适合他们的自豪感，因而这类题材常常被编成戏剧，搬上舞台。这类戏剧称为"纪事剧"，无非是把这位或那位国王统治下的事迹串编起来，只是一些杂乱无章的盛装演出，编得很粗糙。

莎士比亚在1590年至1599年之间，写过若干出这样的戏：《约翰王》以及一系列从理查二世到理查三世之间的戏[—即《理查二世》、《亨利四世》（上、下部）、《亨利五世》、《亨利六世》（上、中、下部），以及《理查三世》]——这一系列的戏写的都是约克家族和兰开斯特家族之间的斗争。

莎士比亚早期的历史剧比起老的纪事剧并不高明多少。但是他后来写的历史剧却大有改进。他删去了编年史中不必要的场面，变动或甚至更改了某些历史情节，因而使故事的发展具有了真正的戏剧性。此外，他在剧中写进了各式各样的普通人物，描绘了他们的风俗习惯，甚至于他们的荒诞可笑之处，他把他们的所作所为跟重大的宫廷事件和战争编织成为一体。因此，在莎士比亚笔下，老的纪事剧变成了历史剧，揭示了真实人物的内心世界。

2.《亨利四世》上部　莎士比亚最值得注意的历史剧之一是《亨利四世》(1597—1598)。这出戏写的是一个纷扰不安的朝代。亨利四世继理查二世之后成为英王，但他在王位上一刻也不觉得安稳。他的臣民起来造反，使他不得安宁。不仅强大的贵族在北方造反，而且像珀西家族这样的贵族也跟威尔士人联合起来反对国王。叛乱最后被国王的小儿子哈尔亲王，即未来的亨利五世领导的军队所平息。莎士比亚是根据霍林谢德的编年史和一出老戏写成的，但是他却使老的纪事剧具有了新的生命。国王的形象疲惫、怯懦、多疑；亨利·珀西是一个“非常勇敢的叛逆者”；哈尔亲王是一个粗野鲁莽的青年，但能改正自己的缺点。

莎士比亚在这出戏中，描述了封建制度下封臣割据与君主集权两个对立的原则之间的斗争。跟伊丽莎白女王时代的资产阶级一样，他拥护王权与秩序。在很出名的第三幕第一场中，他以机智和幽默的笔调揭露了叛逆者瓜分英国的阴谋：这一部分归我，那一部分给你，留一小部分给英格兰名义上的国王。在这里，他好像是在说，这就是封臣一旦得势以后要干的事情。这在莎士比亚的时代是不会不受到观众的欢迎的。

3. 约翰·福斯塔夫爵士　剧中最令人难忘的人物是一位又老又胖的骑士，即约翰·福斯塔夫爵士。他是哈尔亲王寻欢作乐时的朋友。他肥胖臃肿、又老又丑、品行不端、自私狡黠、懒惰畏缩；但有时候他也能表现得机警、灵巧、欢快。他是一个十分矛盾的人物，历来关于他的论述可以说是不可胜数。

战争爆发以后，哈尔亲王统率全军，福斯塔夫也带领一队乌合之众前往参战，但他的那一队人只有“一件半衬衣”。当叛军的一位首领攻击他时，他就躺下“装死”。当哈尔亲王杀死了亨利·珀西时，他就一跃而起，大言不惭地说珀西是他杀死的。他总是要无赖而又使人觉得他和蔼可亲、无忧无虑、机智诙谐。他确实具有一种独特的魅力。

约翰·福斯塔夫爵士是莎士比亚的一个伟大创造。他不仅出现在《亨利四世》下部中，而且还出现在一出十分逗笑的喜剧——《温莎的风流娘儿们》之中，在这出戏中他常常使人捧腹不止。

恩格斯在给拉萨尔的一封信中写道：“我们可以看到，在封建主义关系解体的这个时期，关于身无一文的国王、穷困潦倒的雇佣骑士，以及形形色色的冒险家，关于这些奇特有趣的典型人物，有着多么丰富有趣的描写啊。”福斯塔夫就是这样一个典型人物。他是封建主义关系解体时的一个封建骑士。他看上去也像一个资本家。他大腹便便、游手好闲、吃喝玩乐、无所事事。他是社会上的一个寄生虫。马克思认为他是资本原始积累时期的一个资本家，即资本主义萌芽时期资本的化身。

四 伟大的悲剧

1. **悲剧的阴暗气氛** 迄今为止，我们讨论了约1600年以前的莎士比亚代表作。这个时期的作品充满了青春的气息，明媚而又欢畅。甚至悲剧《罗密欧与朱丽叶》也闪烁着南方的春天与和煦的阳光。然而，到了1600年，莎士比亚的创作活动似乎蒙上了一层风暴的阴云。他开始深入透彻地观察生活，无情地揭露伊丽莎白时代的社会矛盾。

这就是伟大悲剧的时期:《哈姆雷特》(1601)、《奥赛罗》(1604)、《李尔王》(1605),以及《麦克白》(1605)。

莎士比亚的阴暗悲剧气氛也见于17世纪初与他同时期的剧作家的作品中。舞台上出现了这样一些男女主角:他们是社会不公平的牺牲者,他们满怀怨愤地谴责当时的社会秩序,并要求报复。甚至喜剧也蒙上了一层阴暗的色彩。

这种阴暗的悲剧气氛反映了伊丽莎白统治末期开始的经济和社会危机,这个危机一直持续到英国革命的开始。王权与资产阶级的联合是伊丽莎白统治的基础,到了1600年,这种联合已成过去。皇室要专制,资产阶级则力求自由发展。议会里发出了反对政府经济政策的抗议。同时还出现了反对伊丽莎白女王的阴谋。1601年2月,伊丽莎白女王失势的宠臣艾萨克斯伯爵发动叛乱,结果被判斩首。伦敦的小业主日益沦为资本主义剥削下的雇佣工人,他们也举行了起义。莎士比亚就是在这种社会的普遍动荡不安中创作了他的伟大的悲剧。

2. **《哈姆雷特》** 《哈姆雷特》一剧的情节——儿子向谋杀自己父亲的凶手复仇——取自13世纪古老的丹麦传奇故事。1599年之前已经有人(大概是托马斯·基德)用这个题材写了一出戏,莎士比亚必定是看到过的。这是一出充满了“雷暴与血腥”的悲剧。莎士比亚在1601年到1602年间所写的《哈姆雷特》一剧虽然保留了老戏的某些痕迹,但已不再仅仅是一出复仇剧了。

戏剧开始时笼罩着一片骚扰不安与阴暗沉闷的气氛。年轻的哈姆雷特王子为了父王暴殁与母后匆匆再醮叔父而郁闷沉思。父王的鬼魂告诉他,自己是死于伤天害理的谋杀。于是王子装疯卖傻,想方设法证明父王是被谋杀的。他的叔父起了疑心,多次派朝臣找出他发疯的原因。有一阵哈姆雷特和他叔父的斗争似乎势均力敌。哈姆雷特思索得很多,想象得很多,准备采取行动,但似乎又犹豫不决。最后,哈姆雷特在由他叔父安排的一次击剑比赛中被毒剑刺中而死,但他在临死前终于复了仇。

这就是全剧的故事梗概。哈姆雷特企图解决内心世界和外部世界的矛盾,然而却悲壮地失败了。剧本以极大的洞察力揭示了人的动机与激情,揭示了使无辜与有罪同遭无情毁灭的可怕的力量。所有这一切使《哈姆雷特》成为世界上最伟大的悲剧之一。

3. **哈姆雷特的问题** 关于哈姆雷特的性格,论述极多,都是为了“解开他内心的秘密”。为什么哈姆雷特不能当机立断?是否因为他想得太多?他是否是一个秉性懦弱的人?……

哈姆雷特可以看作是莎士比亚时代的一位人文主义者。像其他的人文主义者一样,他看到了丑恶的现实,梦想人与人之间能有健康的关系,但是不能实现他的梦想。梦想愈美丽,他就愈感到周围的现实黑暗,他的内心冲突就愈尖锐。

> 活下去还是不活:这是问题。
> 要做到高贵,究竟该忍气吞声
> 来容受狂暴的命运矢石交攻呢,
> 还是该挺身反抗无边的苦恼,
> 扫它个干净? ①

这出悲剧反映了莎士比亚所生活和进行创作的那个时代的矛盾。

---

① 《哈姆雷特》,第三幕,第一场。见卞之琳译本。

《哈姆雷特》里一段很有意义的文字重复了托马斯·莫尔在《乌托邦》中所说的话。莫尔写道："全世界是一座监狱。"莎士比亚的哈姆雷特完全重复了同样的话："丹麦是一座监狱。"又说："全世界是一座了不起的大监狱，里面有许多禁闭室、监房、暗牢，丹麦是其中最坏的一间。"

哈姆雷特能杀死篡夺王位的叔父，从而实现了个人的复仇。但是，他还只是朦胧地意识到那个伟大的任务——重建世界——却是他力不能及的。他看不到重建世界的道路，莎士比亚也看不到，他同时代的人也看不到。这不是因为他们主观方面的无能，而是由于那个时代的人们思想形态上所存在的历史局限性。他们只能在梦想中追求人与人之间的健康关系。

4. 《李尔王》 李尔王及其女儿的传说起源于古代不列颠，很可能是在罗马人入侵之前。在莎士比亚大约于1605年以它为题材写戏之前，它就已经不止一次出现在诗歌和散文中了。

古代不列颠的李尔王是一位老耄、执拗的专制君主，他有三个女儿。他把他的王国平分给长女高纳里尔和次女里根，并打算轮流和她们居住。他跟最小的女儿断绝了关系，因为她的直言不阿触怒了他。不久，脾气暴戾的李尔王跟专横成性的高纳里尔和里根发生了冲突。他被她们从她们家里赶了出去，在一场雷电交加的暴风雨中发了疯。他最小的女儿考狄利娅已经嫁给了法兰西国王，这时率领军队回国，却被打败，死于狱中。

剧中还有一个平行发展的次要情节。李尔的朝臣葛罗斯特听信私生子的谗言，使嫡出的长子不得不出走并乔装疯丐。葛罗斯特因为好心照料李尔，被李尔的女婿残暴地挖去双眼。

这出戏的主题不仅仅是悖逆不孝，它更描绘了巨大的社会动荡。李尔和葛罗斯特的悲惨遭遇揭示了一个腐败社会的本质，在这个社会中，人人都随时准备消灭对方。剧本中最经常出现的形象是一些动物，如狗、马、牛、羊、猪、狮子、熊、狼、狐狸、猴子、老鼠、青蛙、蛆虫。《李尔王》是莎士比亚最悲惨的悲剧之一。

5. **李尔与“贫无栖身之地”** 莎士比亚的时代是原始积累的时代，其标志是人民群众的赤贫。这在暴风雨一场中描述得最为尖锐有力。

剧本开始，李尔王被描绘成一个完全无视旁人的专横暴君。他脱离现实，每一个行动都激起我们的愤慨。但是当他从女儿家里被赶出之后，当他踯躅在凄凉的荒野上，亲眼看到他最贫困的臣民的生活之后，他开始对他所说的“贫无栖身之地”有了同情：

> 衣不蔽体的不幸的人们，无论你们在什么地方，都得忍受着这样无情的暴风雨的袭击，你们的头上没有片瓦遮身，你们的腹中饥肠雷动，你们的衣服千疮百孔，怎么抵挡得了这样的气候呢？啊！我一向太没有想到这种事情了。安享荣华的人们啊，睁开你们的眼睛来，到外面来体味一下穷人所忍受的苦，分一些你们享用不了的福泽给他们，让上天知道你们不是全无心肝的人吧！[①]

在这里李尔有了转变，因此我们对他的感情也有了转变。杜勃罗留波夫这样说：

① 《李尔王》，第三幕，第四场。见朱生豪译本。

我们初看他[李尔]时，痛恨这个乖戾的暴君。但是，随着剧情的发展，我们愈来愈同情他作为一个人的遭遇。最后，我们充满愤慨，满腔怒火，但**不是痛恨他，而是为了他**，为了全世界而感到愤怒；我们对于能够把甚至像李尔这样的人变成乖戾暴君的那种野蛮的非人境况感到愤慨。

“衣不蔽体的不幸的人们”不是针对古代不列颠而发出的，而是指伊丽莎白统治后期的英格兰。

五　莎士比亚的艺术

1. 莎士比亚作为现实主义作家　在《哈姆雷特》一剧（第三幕第二场，第二十四至二十八行）中，莎士比亚谈到他对戏剧演出的看法。他说，演戏的目的是，“仿佛要给自然照一面镜子；给德行看一看自己的面貌，给荒唐看一看自己的姿态，给时代和社会看一看自己的形象和印记”[①]。这个演戏的原则也就是他进行戏剧创作的原则。这实质上也就是现实主义的原则。

莎士比亚了解他的时代及其矛盾。他戏剧中的许多段落都反映了托马斯·莫尔所说的“富人反对穷人而进行的阴谋”。在《配力克里斯》(1607年底或1608年初)一剧中，一个渔人问另外一个渔人，“鱼在海里是怎样活的？”那个渔人是这样回答的：

① 《哈姆雷特》，第三幕，第二场。见卞之琳译本。

嘿,它们也正像人们在陆地上一样,大的拣着小的吃。我们那些有钱的吝啬鬼活像一条鲸鱼,游来游去,翻几个跟斗,把那些可怜的小鱼赶得走投无路,到后来就把它们一口吞下。在陆地上我也听到过这一类的鲸鱼,他们不把整个的教区、礼拜堂、尖塔、钟楼和一切全都吞下,是决不肯闭上嘴的。[①]

莎士比亚也淋漓尽致地反映了在资本主义发展时期金钱能够改变一切的力量。在《雅典的泰门》(1606)一剧中,关于金钱的腐蚀力就有以下一段著名的文字:

金子!黄黄的、发光的、宝贵的金子!……这东西,只这一点点儿,就可以使黑的变成白的,丑的变成美的,错的变成对的,卑贱变成尊贵,老人变成少年,懦夫变成勇士。……这黄色的奴隶可以使异教联盟,同宗分裂;它可以使受咒诅的人得福;使害着灰白色的癞病的人为众人所敬爱;……来……,该死的土块,你这人尽可夫的娼妇,你惯会在乱七八糟的列国之间挑起纷争。[②]

马克思在引述泰门的这一段独白时写道:“莎士比亚多么精辟地描述了金钱的本质啊!”

2. 莎士比亚作为人物性格的塑造者 莎士比亚的戏剧并不总是取材于英国,他的人物常常穿着外国的服装——意大利的、法国的、丹麦的、凯尔特的、罗马的,等等,但是人物的思想感情,他们对生活的态度和对彼此的态度,却属于莎士比亚的时代。莎士比亚写的是自

① 《配力克里斯》,第二幕,第一场。见朱生豪译本。

② 《雅典的泰门》,第四幕,第三场。见朱生豪译本。

己的人民，并且是为自己的人民而写。

莎士比亚的主要人物塑造于**典型的**真实环境之中：封建的城堡、中世纪的城市、富丽堂皇的宫廷，等等。他们的基本性格是在他们跟环境的冲突中，在他们跟其他人的关系中揭示出来的（例如，李尔王性格的发展、哈姆雷特的悲剧，等等）。他们每一个人都是某一社会—历史倾向的维护者，都是某一类型的人的代表，而这些人的所作所为在很大程度上表现出了他们的**典型**性格（例如，人文主义者哈姆雷特、放高利贷者夏洛克、末代封建骑士福斯塔夫，等等）。然而他们又并不仅仅是“时代精神的代言者”（恩格斯语）。他们每人都具有个人特质，这就使他们有血有肉，栩栩如生。例如，夏洛克是一个放高利贷者，但又不是一个一般的放高利贷者；福斯塔夫可以说是一位堂吉诃德式的人物，但又不完全像堂吉诃德，等等。莎士比亚从来没有因为人物的精神因素，而忽视社会现实因素。这就是马克思所说的“莎士比亚化”。

莎士比亚是马克思和恩格斯所喜爱的作家，他们的著作中许多地方都提到莎士比亚戏剧中的情节和人物。下面这段保尔·拉法格的话可以说明马克思是多么喜爱莎士比亚：“他详尽地研究过莎士比亚，无限爱慕莎士比亚，熟悉莎士比亚戏剧中即使是最微不足道的人物。马克思一家是真正的莎士比亚崇拜者，马克思的三个女儿都很熟悉莎士比亚的戏剧。”

在过去三个世纪中，有许多男女演员，由于扮演莎士比亚戏剧中的角色，而誉满剧坛。例如，18 世纪的加里克，19 世纪的基思和欧文。而且莎士比亚不止在英国深受欢迎，他是一个世界著名的伟大作家。

3. **戏剧形式和语言** 莎士比亚戏剧的形式完全适合表达其内

容。剧情自由发展,不受古典“三一律”(地点、时间与情节一致)的限制。剧情的发展可以从一个城市换到另一个城市,从一个国家换到另一个国家,或者从皇家宫室换到战场;可以经历几天、几个星期,甚至许多年。一切取决于剧情的特点、主题的性质。有时一出简单的戏包含不止一个主题;主要情节与次要情节并行发展。戏剧的形式与结构服从于主题与内容的需要。

莎士比亚力求再现生活的多方面的形象,生活中的差异和矛盾。这就使他的戏剧具有一种特有的复杂性——既辉煌壮丽又诙谐可笑,既有帝王将相又有市井小民,既富有诗意又平易近人。他的戏剧是人文主义的宝库,为马克思、恩格斯、普希金和其他许多评论家所赞赏。

莎士比亚是运用雅俗共赏的英语的大师。他剧中人物的语言适合各自的社会地位,并能表现出各自性格的特点。例如,从哈姆雷特的语言可以看出这位人文主义者的高度文化教养、他的多方面的兴趣、他的天赋、他的才智的深度。

莎士比亚所掌握的词汇量大于任何其他英国作家。他使用过一万六千个词语(当然他知道的就更多了)。他喜欢做文字游戏,玩弄声韵和双关语。这些技巧他常常用得过分,显得晦涩或过于微妙,难以理解。但是他用的新词语和新表达法丰富了英语。以下是《哈姆雷特》中的几个例子:“简洁是智慧的灵魂”;“多一点实质内容,少一点技巧形式”;“一般人不赏识的鱼子酱”;“绞尽脑汁”;“活下去还是不活”;“蒙上了一副惨白的思虑的病容”;“要讲得一丝不苟”。

莎士比亚是多种诗歌形式的大师——歌曲、十四行诗、双行联韵体、四行诗、素体诗。他特别擅长素体诗。在他的戏剧中,素体诗的运用总是适应于剧中人物情绪的变化。“从单纯的口语对话到充满激情的独白,从妙趣横生的应对到慷慨悲壮的雄辩,从短小精悍的警句到详尽细致的描绘。”

这里还必须说一下散文。莎士比亚也是一位散文大师。他的散文富于变化,有时平易质朴(例如,“谁在那儿?”),有时则慷慨华丽(例如,“人是多么了不起的一件作品!”,见《哈姆雷特》第二幕第二场。)

莎士比亚时代最卓越的散文家就是莎士比亚。

第五章

17 世纪早期

一　弗兰西斯·培根

1. **培根与近代唯物主义**　弗兰西斯·培根（1561—1626）与莎士比亚完全是同一个时代的人。培根出身在一个与宫廷有关的家庭。他十二岁至十四岁就读于剑桥大学，十五岁专攻法律，二十三岁进入议会，是当时最有学问的政治家和法学家，享有该盛名达三十年。他五十七岁出任大法官，三年后因受贿被捕入狱，褫夺一切公职。老年受尽屈辱，去世时六十五岁。

培根是近代科学的奠基人，毕生致力在各个知识领域中进行改革，并制定比较完善的调查研究方法。他说，无论在哪一门学问中，人们都喜欢把事情看成是想当然的；他们接受古人留传下来的学说或原理，并力图使事实适应这些学说或原理。培根却反其道而行之。他坚持要擦亮眼睛，决不接受任何未经证实的观点，并逐步建立理论，使之符合事实——他认为，这才是寻求真理的唯一方法。1605年他发表了《学术的进展》，以清算传统学者的种种谬论。1620年，他发表了拉丁文著作《新工具》，在其中阐述了归纳法。

马克思和恩格斯写道：

> 英国唯物主义的真正祖先是培根。在他看来，自然哲学是唯一真正的哲学，而基于感觉经验之上的物理学，则是自然哲学的最重要的部门。……照他看来，感觉是正确无误的，是一切知识的源泉。所有科学都是以经验为基础的，是在于以理性的研究方法去整理感觉所提供的材料。归纳、分析、比较、观察、实验，就是这种理性方法的主要形式。

2. 培根和英国散文　培根是个天才的演说家。本·琼生说："他的演说富有吸引力。他说话干净、利落、紧凑、庄重，并不落空泛，无人可以企及。他说的每一句话无不表现他个人的特有魅力。"

培根写文章跟说话一样，干净、利落（即紧凑、简练），庄重、严肃也是他的文章的重要特点。大多数跟他同时代的人所写的散文多半冗杂、雕琢、声调铿锵。培根却喜欢写得明白晓畅，直截了当，然而并不缺乏魅力。这在他的《论说文集》中特别明显。《论说文集》是培根写的随笔，于1625年汇集出版。《论说文集》题材广泛，内容包括婚姻、爱情、高官显爵、友谊、园艺、读书、荣誉以及"事物的变迁"。

培根的许多精辟文句已经成为格言。比如关于读书，他曾在《论读书》中写道：

有些书可以浅尝；有些可以囫囵吞枣；少数则须咀嚼消化。换言之，有的书只须读一部分，有的只须大体涉猎；少数则须通读，而读时须全神贯注，孜孜不倦。……读书使人饱学，讨论使人敏捷，写作使人准确。

培根有一部未完成的乌托邦著作，叫作《新大西岛》，大概是在英国人开始向新英格兰移民时写的。关于他的乌托邦，最值得注意的是：他的理想国是在太平洋中，上面有一所学院或学会，叫作“所罗门之家”，是一所科学研究学会。众所周知，《新大西岛》对 17 世纪英国和欧洲大陆上各种科学团体的产生起了激励和推动的作用。

二　本·琼生和约翰·邓恩

1. 琼生和讽刺喜剧　本·琼生（1572—1637）是与莎士比亚同时代的人或晚辈中最有名的作家之一。他早年做过泥瓦工，三十多岁一跃成为当时最重要的戏剧作家。据说，他和莎士比亚曾多次在美人鱼酒店“斗智”，“就像一艘西班牙大帆船和一艘英国战舰一样”互相攻击。琼生精通古典文艺，而莎士比亚更是位伟大的天才。

跟莎士比亚一样，琼生也是一位现实主义作家，但有所不同。莎士比亚剧作的场景遍及全球——威尼斯、维罗纳、亚登森林、波希米亚海岸，或者是一座孤岛。而琼生所描绘的主要是他周围的世界，也就是 17 世纪初的伦敦——沿街叫卖的小贩、栉比鳞次的店铺、趁火打劫的流氓、吵吵闹闹的交易所、上层人士之家和殷实的商人富户、博览会、美人和丑八怪，以及卖弄才学的书呆子——五光十色的人物交织成琼生喜剧中一幅纷纷攘攘的伦敦风俗画。他最杰出的喜剧有《人人高兴》（1598）和《炼金术士》（1610）。

琼生在喜剧中所抨击的人物主要是贵族和资产阶级；装腔作势的宫廷大臣，他们“衣冠楚楚，照着镜子练习礼仪，说一口人们用惯的好听话”。宫廷贵妇，她们“在日常谈话中特别留意遣词造句，话要说得纯正，词要选得精致，不亚于阿卡狄亚的任何人”。还有穷奢极欲、贪得无厌的艾壁鸠尔·买蒙爵士。

我的肉食端进来时，要用印度的甲壳，
还有那镶金的玛瑙盘子，就是那
装饰着红的、绿的、蓝的各色宝石的盘子。

琼生的作品，还有几出供宫廷演出的假面剧和以古希腊罗马戏剧为模式的悲剧。

2. **诗人和批评家琼生** 琼生是一位大学者，具有超人的智力和记忆力，也是一位多产的天才诗人，写下了不少抒情诗（例如，《致西莉亚》）。但是跟伊丽莎白时代的多数作家不同，他不能忍受多愁善感和浪漫的狂放激情。他力求艺术上的完美，他认为一首诗要有周密的计划，一环紧扣一环，做到意尽即止。他努力创造突出而鲜明的形象，虽不那么洋洋洒洒，却十分谨严。下面几行诗句可以用来说明他的简练和纯朴：

让我看一张脸、一副神色，

纯朴率直构成它的魅力。
长袍飘飘,发也不结,
吸引我的正在它不加修饰,
形形色色的矫揉造作
使我注目,却没有乱我心曲。

琼生在诗歌创作上始终是一位刻意求工的艺术家。

当琼生在艺术上臻于成熟的时候,在他的周围聚集了一批诗人。他们在伦敦的酒店里喜欢坐在他的脚下,自命为“本·琼生的孩子们”。诗人罗伯特·赫瑞克就是其中之一。他写过《玫瑰堪折君可折》和《柯瑞娜欢庆五月节》等抒情诗。

琼生还是一位优秀的批评家。他的《发现集》(1641)中有许多令人难忘的文段。关于莎士比亚,他是这样说的:“我记得演员们在恭维莎士比亚时,说他写东西(不管写什么)从来没有抹掉一行。我曾经回答说‘但愿他抹掉过一千行’……”他的散文风格清晰简练,很像弗兰西斯·培根。

3. 邓恩和“玄学派”诗歌 约翰·邓恩(1573—1631),伦敦富商的儿子,是一个神童。他十一岁进牛津,十五岁入剑桥,学过法律,当过军人,还写过讽刺诗。经历了一段冒险生涯或者说是不幸的遭遇以后,邓恩被授职为牧师,后来任圣保罗大教堂的教长,一直到逝世。

邓恩的诗是所谓学人之诗。他的愿望似乎是言前人之所未言,他的语言里充满了别具匠心的暗喻和幻想,有时鲜明新颖,有时牵强难解,有时甚至卷入荒诞不经的隐喻。譬如,他想象一对情人在相对凝视:

对着一望，我们的眼睛
就穿在一根双股的线上。

然而，只要他愿意，他也能写出可爱的诗句，譬如《黎明》：

且慢，亲爱的，不要起床，
发亮的不是晨光而是你的眼光。
夜幕未破，我的心却破碎难受，
因为你和我啊，必须分手。
　且住，否则欢乐就会消亡，
　就在襁褓之中消亡。

邓恩的追随者如理查德·克瑞肖、乔治·赫伯特和亚伯拉罕·考利，他们写诗也采用同样的方法。他们都是所谓“玄学派”诗人，而邓恩则是它的创始人。

玄学派诗歌是书斋里的诗，是为少数人写作的。在斯图亚特王朝统治下，诗人似乎离开了宫廷和大众生活而转向了书斋。因为他们的诗篇是在书斋里写的，所以从中可以闻到书斋的气味。

三　弥尔顿和英国革命

1. 弥尔顿的家世、教育和早期诗歌　约翰·弥尔顿（1608—1674）在伦敦市中心出生并长大成人。他父亲是新教徒，是伦敦一个小银行的公证人，颇有成就，业余爱好音乐并善作小曲。老弥尔顿鼓励儿子学习语言，如拉丁语、希腊语、法语、意大利语、希伯来语，还教导儿子热爱美好的事物。

弥尔顿先在家里跟随家庭教师读书，接着进圣保罗学校，然后进入剑桥大学攻读七年。对于学校指定的功课他并不十分感兴趣，然而在那里他接触到培根的哲学著作。1631 年，他在学完剑桥大学的课程以后，退居距伦敦二十英里他父亲在霍顿的乡间住宅，继续学习。在那里，他写下了早期的重要作品：《快乐的人》、《幽思的人》和《利西达斯》。

《快乐的人》和《幽思的人》是姊妹篇，文笔优美，分别描述快乐的心情和幽思的乐趣。《利西达斯》(1637) 是弥尔顿哀悼他的剑桥同学爱德华·金的挽诗。但它不同于传统的挽诗，而是反映了弥尔顿对英国国教教会所犯的错误的看法。他预见到议会和国王之间要发生战争，他写道：

> 但是那有着两只手的兵器正在门侧，
> 准备一击，一击足矣，无需再击。

正如评论家指出的，“有着两只手的兵器”指的是英国议会的上下两院。

2. 为言论自由声辩：《论言论自由》 英国革命是从 1640 年召开长期议会时开始的。1642 年发生内战，战争的结果是国王的军队败绩，查理一世被处斩首 (1649)，护国公奥利弗·克伦威尔执掌了政权。

在这场斗争中，弥尔顿是用笔而不是用剑来参与战斗的。他发表了大量小册子，其中最有名的是《论言论自由》(1644)——它要求思想自由和出版自由。

先是保皇党人使用星法院压制思想自由。1640 年，长期议会召开时，星法院被撤销了，人人都可以有思想自由和出版自由。但在 1643 年，议会里的长老派通过了一项法案，规定未经过官方检查官审阅和发放许可，不得印刷任何书籍和小册子。弥尔顿的小册子是写给英国的最高权力机关"上、下两院"的。英国的上、下两院相当于古代雅典的最高权力机关战神山议事会，因此这本小册子就叫作《战神山议事会录》(即《论出版自由》)。

弥尔顿的主要论点是这样的：任何检查都不能决定什么是真理，什么是谬误，因为真理只能通过自由讨论达到。他说：

> 一个人能够理解并考虑到罪恶的一切诱惑和虚假的欢乐，却能洁身自好，分辨是非，并一心向善，那他就是一个真正斗志昂扬的基督教徒了。我不能推崇一个躲躲闪闪的、与世隔绝的有德之士，既没有活动，也不敢喘息，从来不敢冲出去面对敌人，而是偷偷地逃避战斗。世上不朽的荣誉，本来需要争夺，其中也不无尘土飞扬、汗水淋漓的场面……尽管世上各派学说风靡一时，只要真理仍在战斗，那么我们不论是许可或者禁止，都是怀疑真理的力量，因而造成很大的危害。让真理与谬误搏斗吧。在自由而公开的斗争中，有谁知道真理曾经败过呢？

3. **弥尔顿与共和国**　1649 年查理一世被处死刑，这使反动的欧洲感到震惊。查理死后不到两星期，弥尔顿就发表了《论国王与官吏的职权》。他的主要论点是：(1) 政府的成立须经被统治者同意；

(2)臣民没有忍受不公正统治的义务。这就是约翰·洛克在《论政府》一文中所阐述的资产阶级革命的理论。

弥尔顿的《论国王与官吏的职权》很快就受到共和国政府的赞赏。弥尔顿即被任命为国务委员会的外文秘书。其职责为：(1) 翻译外国官方信函；(2) 将国务委员会致外国官方的信函译成拉丁文；(3) 回应国外敌人对共和国所进行的攻击。最后一项职责使弥尔顿在政治和宗教问题上参与了许多次激烈持久的论战。

弥尔顿在任拉丁文秘书期间写了许多论文，其中最杰出的是《为英国人民辩护》(1651) 和《再为英国人民辩护》(1654)，作为对国外敌人攻击共和国的回应。后者中有一段著名的文字，这一段文字是弥尔顿作为一个革命者向他的对象——力量无比的群众讲的：

> 我仿佛站在高处俯瞰着幅员广阔的海洋和陆地，还看到数不清的人群，面带喜色，他们的兴趣，他们的激情都跟我的非常一致。我在这里看到孔武有力的日耳曼人蔑视奴役；也看到慷慨大度的法兰西人的激烈感情的表现。这边有镇定而庄严的西班牙勇士；那边有泰然自若、谨慎宽宏的意大利人。热爱自由和善行的人，慷慨而明智的人，不管他们在什么地方，都是有的暗地里赞成，有的则是长时期不信奉上帝，最后还是屈服于真理的力量。我的周围结集着大队群众，我在想象，从赫克里斯之柱到印度洋，我看到世界各国都在恢复他们久已失去的自由……

4. **弥尔顿与十四行诗**　在英国革命时期，弥尔顿除了写过几首十四行诗以外，没有写过任何诗歌。弥尔顿的十四行诗不是爱情诗，也不自成一组，而是一些即兴诗，精雕细琢，达到完美的地步。其中最优秀的是关于政治题材的以及关于争取自由的。他写诗反对议会里的长老派，管他们叫作“把良心强加于别人的人们”。他在有名的诗句中总结了他的抨击：“新长老不过是旧日僧侣一词夸大的别名。”

他写了反对在皮埃蒙特迫害新教徒的诗歌（《哀最近的皮埃蒙特大屠杀》）。他还作诗献给克伦威尔并对当时主要的将领进行规劝。在这些诗中，他唱出了庄严肃穆的新曲调。华滋华斯说：

> 在他手里
> 这东西［指十四行诗］变成了号角；他吹奏出
> 激动人心的调子——可惜为数太少了。

此外，他还写了一些抒发个人情感的十四行诗，《咏失明》是其中最杰出的诗篇。他在担任拉丁文秘书长期间，力疾从公，眼力消耗过度。1654 年，他不顾医生劝阻，奋力撰写《再为英国人民辩护》一文。文章写完了，眼睛也瞎了，那时他才四十五岁。他写了十四行诗《咏失明》诉说失明后的心情。

弥尔顿的十四行诗为数不多，但在英国诗歌史上占有重要地位。它们被后来的浪漫派诗人华滋华斯、拜伦和雪莱奉为楷模。

四　《失乐园》和《力士参孙》

1. **《失乐园》：主题与风格**　1655 年，弥尔顿担任的拉丁文秘书一职责任有所减轻。他有较多的空闲，同时由于失明，思想更为集中，于是开始就名为《失乐园》的一首诗进行构思。1658年他开始写作，或者说由他口述，请秘书笔录。王政复辟后，他失去了拉丁文秘书的职务，也失去了财产，仅仅免于一死，获准回家赋闲。五年中这首长诗逐渐扩写。1663年全诗十二卷完成，1667年出版。

这首诗的故事取自圣经和人们根据圣经精心加工过的许多故事。其中包括：上帝创造世界；撒旦和他那一伙天使在天上造反；他们失败后被逐出天国；大地和亚当、夏娃的创造；撒旦引诱夏娃；人类离开伊甸园。在我们听来，所有这一切很像是一种寓言，然而弥尔顿却非常认真。正像他在诗开始时说的那样，他写诗的目的是"为了证明上帝对待人的行为是正确的"，这就是说，要顺从全能的上帝。但是，十分奇怪的是，他总是站在反叛者的一边。

这首诗是用五步抑扬素体写的，这种诗体经由马洛、莎士比亚的使用，人们是熟悉的。但是到了弥尔顿手里，这种诗体却变成雄伟的风琴乐曲。他使用的是一种由简练的英语和古典拉丁文相结合的语言——庄严、铿锵有力，但本质上是朴实的。这就是所谓的"崇高"文体。

2. **撒旦的性格**　根据弥尔顿在《失乐园》一开始时说的道理，撒旦是罪恶的化身。他是一个反叛者，搞阴谋诡计。然而，弥尔顿却不由自主地非常同情撒旦。问题是弥尔顿也是一个反叛者，曾对国王和教会同样提出过挑战，"决心不信赖他人的信仰和判断"，并且"决意要把真正的言论自由当作一个古老时代的宝藏收藏起来"。

在这首诗中，撒旦看起来并不像他应该的那样卑鄙可耻。当他被全能的上帝抛下深渊时，他喊道：

战场上虽然失利，怕什么？
这不可征服的意志，报复的决心
切齿的仇恨，和一种永不屈膝，
永不投降的意志——却都未丧失；
除此以外，还有什么不能克服的？
这种荣誉是他的愤怒或威力
所永远不能夺取的。要低头认罪
或屈膝求和……
那要比这次失败更下流，更无耻！

同时撒旦也是怀疑精神的代表。进入伊甸园后，他不懂为什么上帝不准亚当、夏娃去尝尝知识树上的果实。

知识要遭禁吗？
这事可疑，毫无理由！为什么他们的上帝
嫉妒他们这个？难道知识就是犯罪？
难道这就是死罪？难道他们只能永远
无知无识下去？难道这就是他们的幸福，
从而证明他们的服从和他们的信仰？
啊！这倒是为他们将来的失败
奠定了一块美好的基石。

好像就在述说撒旦这段经历的时候，弥尔顿记起了他自己精神上的独立，他对自由的热爱以及他超乎一切的求知欲和对革命事业的忠诚，尽管这个事业是失败了而他自己也“碰到了倒霉的日子”。

别林斯基写道："弥尔顿的诗显然是他那个时代的产物；他自己也没有想到竟把骄傲而阴沉的撒旦描绘成反对权威的叛逆之神，尽管他的本意并不是这样的。"

3．**《力士参孙》** 在弥尔顿的后期作品中，最重要的是《力士参孙》（1671年出版）。他把《旧约》（《士师记》第十三到第十六章）"力士"参孙的故事改编为诗剧：叙述以色列的大力士参孙怎样丧失了力量，后来却又恢复了力量；他如何被他的妻子非利士人大利拉出卖，并被以色列人的统治者非利士人弄瞎了双眼，又被引进到庙宇里去给非利士人"玩弄"；他怎样推倒了庙宇，与敌人同归于尽，报了仇。

显然，参孙对弥尔顿具有一种特殊的吸引力。跟弥尔顿一样，参孙也具有献身精神。

这个人生来
就有充分的力量，并受天之命
来解放我的祖国。

跟弥尔顿一样，轻率的婚姻使他怨恨。他双目失明，但又是不可战胜的。弥尔顿在写《力士参孙》时，思想上已从无可奈何的顺从转向反抗，这是因为当时他已看到辉格党这个反对派的兴起，并有推翻斯图亚特王朝的迹象。《力士参孙》是弥尔顿最反映他个人的感受并最激昂的作品。

在《力士参孙》中，几乎没有一般舞台剧中那种令人兴奋的场面。它是严格地以希腊悲剧为模式的，有合唱队，也有报幕人，并且遵守戏剧三一律。在《力士参孙》中找不到伊丽莎白时代或王政复辟时代戏剧的特点。

第六章

17 世纪后期和 18 世纪早期

一 约翰·班扬和约翰·德莱顿

1. 班扬和他的《天路历程》 约翰·班扬(1628—1688)是个补锅匠的儿子,他自己也是个穷苦的补锅匠,受教育不多,能勉强读书写字。在革命时期,他在议会军中当兵。他对一般老百姓来说是一位天才的传教士。王政复辟以后,禁止清教徒集会,但是班扬仍然继续传教。他被捕入贝德福的监狱,达十二年之久。他的杰作《天路历程》(1678)就是在狱中写成的。

《天路历程》从表面上看只是一部宗教寓言,叙述基督徒自毁灭之城出走,经过绝望的深渊、名利场、怀疑堡,途中历尽艰辛,还战胜了妖魔,终于到了欢乐山,抵达天国。但是这本书之所以有价值,还在于它提供了一幅英国城乡人民的现实主义的图画:低矮的农舍、偏僻的街巷、泥泞的道路、一排排货摊构成的名利场，场上还有流氓、轻佻的男男女女。这是一个熟悉人们是怎样生活和工作的人所说的故事。

比如说，书中描绘了英国陪审团的情况。“基督徒”和“忠实”到了名利场。由于他们除了“真理”以外拒绝购买任何东西，就挨了打，被关在笼子里，后又从笼子里放出来，用锁链捆缚着在场上游街示众，最后在地区法庭受审。法官“嫉善”召来了三名证人：“妒嫉”、“迷信”和“搬弄是非”（即传舌）。他们都作证指控“基督徒”和“忠实”二人有罪。这宗案件提交给陪审团，陪审团包括“失明先生”、“孬先生”、“恶意先生”等人。他们都认为“忠实”有罪，于是他立即被判刑。

17 世纪后期没有哪一个作家能像班扬的《天路历程》那样给我们提供一幅关于英国资产阶级的真实图画。班扬的叙事手法十分高明，因此《天路历程》成了英国文学中最受欢迎的书之一。

2. **德莱顿和资产阶级报刊** 约翰·德莱顿（1631—1700）是反动和妥协时代最典型的作家。他出身于富裕的清教徒家庭，在剑桥受教育。跟班扬一样，他在大革命时期长大成人。跟班扬不同的是，他对政治和宗教似乎从来没有打定过主意。他曾作诗恭维克伦威尔，后来又作诗赞颂皇室和英国国教，1685 年詹姆斯二世即位后，他皈依天主教。

德莱顿是一个多产的剧作家。他写过两种戏剧——一种是时髦男女打情骂俏的喜剧，另一种是大勇之士向品行端正的淑女们高声诉说衷情的“英雄剧”。现在，他的大多数剧本除专家外，很少有人去翻阅了，而专家们读德莱顿的戏剧也并不是单纯为了取乐。

德莱顿是一位讽刺大师。他是托利党人，常常撰写诗文攻击辉格党人。下面几行巧妙的英雄偶句诗是讽刺白金汉公爵的性格的：

这个人方面真多，好像不仅
是一个人，而是全人类的缩影。
生性固执，总是固执错误的意见；
什么事都干，但又干不了多少时间；
天上的月亮还只运转了一周，
而他已当过卖药的、拉提琴的、政客和小丑；
都是为了女人，他画画、喝酒、哼诗，
还有万把个主意在想象中消失，
有福的疯子，每个时刻都能得心应手，
总有新的东西可以打算或者享受。

德莱顿是桂冠诗人，但当詹姆斯二世被赶下王位时，他失去了桂冠，而不得不自谋生计。那时资产阶级的读者大众很需要在文化素养方面得到帮助，德莱顿就在这方面竭力以翻译和改写的形式介绍经典，例如维吉尔、乔叟、薄伽丘的作品。因此，随着时代的变化，宫廷诗人德莱顿变成了资产阶级社会的文人。

3. **德莱顿和近代散文** 应该记住，德莱顿是一位近代散文大家。在德莱顿之前，英语散文一般来说结构繁杂。例如弥尔顿的最好的散文具有雄伟的风格；但有时句子冗长，意义不清。除了培根、班扬和少数其他作家以外，伊丽莎白时代和詹姆斯时代的散文风格就是这样。

但是在17世纪后期发生了变化。在英国颇有影响的古典法国散文，教导人们写文章要清晰、直接、简明。同时，人们随着对科学日益增长的兴趣，也要求文章简洁。建立于1662年的皇家学会公开表明：

宁要朴素的叙述而不要"漂亮"的文章。

新散文最优秀的作家就是德莱顿,他的风格明朗、简要而平易——但绝不沉闷。这里有两段例子,一段是关于乔叟的,一段是关于莎士比亚的:

> 他[乔叟]的人物中有些是坏人,有些是好人;有些人不学无术,或者(像乔叟自己说的那样)是些卑劣的人,而有些人却是有学问的。甚至下层人物的下流话也彼此不同;管家、磨坊主和厨司,并不一样,就像装腔作势的女修道院院长,跟言语粗俗、缺牙露齿的巴斯妇人,各不相同。这样一说也就够了:在我面前有这么多人物跃然纸上,叫我不知所措,无法作出抉择。有一句谚语说得好,上帝创造万物,真是应有尽有。

> 大自然所有的形象对他[莎士比亚]来说真是俯拾皆是。他毫不费力,而是全凭运气,他描写任何事物,不但使你看得到,而且使你摸得着。有人说他没有学问,实际上这是对他更大的赞颂:他是生而有知的;他不用借助于书籍这副眼镜就可以了解自然;他深入自己的内心,就在里面找到了自然。

这种自然、简洁而辛辣、写文章跟说话一样的文风,是新社会所需的。它后来成为18世纪资产阶级社会的俱乐部和咖啡馆的最地道的语言。

二 艾迪生、斯蒂尔和蒲伯

1. **艾迪生、斯蒂尔和期刊杂文** 约瑟夫·艾迪生(1672—1719)是英国牧师的儿子,理查德·斯蒂尔(1672—1729)是爱尔兰律师的儿子。他们在查特豪斯学校,在牛津大学都是同学。艾迪生学业成绩优异,三十岁时就被选中,有当公职人员的资格。“迪克”·斯蒂尔却是另外一种人——对人亲热,和蔼可亲,但挥霍无度,有些令人无法捉摸。他没有取得学位就离开了牛津。他与人决斗过,并为剧院撰写感伤喜剧。

1709到1711年,斯蒂尔办了一份期刊,叫作《闲谈者》,每星期出版三期。艾迪生经常向该刊投稿。1711年,《闲谈者》停刊,斯蒂尔和艾迪生就发行了《旁观者》,发行数最高达到一万四千份。这份期刊每天出版,1712年停刊。

艾迪生和斯蒂尔想利用《闲谈者》和《旁观者》把新兴资产阶级(即商人、制造商和企业家)装扮成新贵绅士。资产阶级社会的罪恶和缺陷(比如:赌博、决斗、党争、势利、无聊的流行时装)都受到温和而幽默的讽刺。同时,这两份报刊对礼貌、趣味和文化提供了内行意见,使暴发户即新兴资产阶级易于接受;对戏剧和文学作品提出了易懂的评论,使人们在遇到同样题材的时候知道怎样想、怎样说才好;期刊中有日常书信,可以用作范本;也有人物素描(例如罗杰·德·柯夫雷爵士和他的朋友们),他们就像镜子,读者可以从反映出的人物身上看到自己的形象或自己喜欢的形象。这两份报刊的宗旨是教育读者,并使他们感到有趣。

这两份报刊对资产阶级文化起着微妙的影响。在整个18世纪,它们为读者反复阅读和模仿,后来成了英国传统文学的一个组成部分。他们的风格,特别是艾迪生的风格,被认为是简练、自然、口语化的典范。

2. **蒲伯和他的诗** 如果说艾迪生和斯蒂尔是资产阶级社会的代表散文家,那么亚历山大·蒲伯(1688—1744)则是当时的代表诗人。他出生于一个信奉天主教的亚麻布制品商人家庭,自幼体弱多病,身材矮小。虽然由于出身关系,他在社会上不能取得显要地位,但在文人中却获得了最高的声誉。就诗而论,他是德莱顿的真正继承人。

蒲伯是资产阶级志得意满的代言人。他说:"一条真理很清楚,凡是存在的都是正确的。"但是蒲伯是托利党人,在辉格党执政期间他为反对党写作。他谁都不怕,连不学无术、仇视诗歌的乔治二世他也不怕。跟德莱顿一样,他是社会和政治讽刺诗的大师。他的讽刺诗反映了当时首相罗伯特·渥尔波尔任内种种贪污腐化的败政。

> 兵士、教徒、爱国者、掌权之人,
> 到处都是贪婪,志气早已不存!
> ……
> 大家望着上面,瞪起敬畏的双目,
> 看那些逃避罪责、法外逍遥的家伙。
> 真理、德行和智慧天天受到斥责,
> "没有什么是圣洁的,除了罪恶。"

在我们今天看来,蒲伯最大的成就也许是他在《论批评》(1711)和《论人》(1733—1734)两首诗里常识性的警句。蒲伯是写英雄偶句的能手，有许多警句已为后人经常引用。

只有一点点知识，这是件很危险的事，
要么畅饮一番，要么别尝庇厄里亚的泉水。

真正的才智就是能把大自然打扮得格外好看，
把常常想到而从未表达的话表达得尽美尽善。

三　丹尼尔·笛福

1. **笛福和他写的政论诗文**　在整个18世纪，没有一个作家像丹尼尔·笛福（1661—1731）那样一生中有那么多的惊险经历。他父亲是一个不信奉国教的肉商，名叫詹姆斯·福（丹尼尔是在他四十多岁时才在自己的姓前面加了一个表示尊称的"笛"）。笛福婚姻美满，当了几年批发商人，生意兴隆。他支持奥伦治亲王威廉，为"光荣革命"而欢欣鼓舞。后来威廉亲王与法国作战，他的生意破产了，于是从事写作。他的全部著作差不多都是在三十五岁以后写的，他在完成他的杰作《鲁滨逊漂流记》时已经六十岁了。

1701年笛福发表了一首通俗诗《地道的英国人》，攻击那些曾经攻击国王威廉是外国人的贵族：

财富（不管怎样得来的）在英国能使
工匠变成贵族，浪子变成绅士！

这里并不需要出身和家世，
造成贵族的是有钱和无耻。

1702 年笛福写了一本通过模仿进行嘲讽的小册子，叫作《处理不信奉国教者的最简便办法》，假托一位英国国教教士主张绞死所有不信奉国教的人。他被捕入狱，并戴枷示众。他又以特有的胆识，作了一首叫《枷刑颂》的诗，把那些真正应该在那里戴枷示众的人描绘得淋漓尽致。他的朋友聚集在他的周围，对他欢呼，把他当作一位英雄。

他获释以后，开始出版《评论报》(1704—1711)，登载政治小品、社会漫谈以及对生活和风尚的一些俏皮的评论。他独力写了九期《评论报》。此外，他还为其他报刊撰稿。如果把他的期刊文章汇集成册，将是一个相当大的文库。

2. **《鲁滨逊漂流记》** 1711 年苏格兰海员亚历山大·塞尔柯克发表了他的自述。他曾经在远离智利海岸的一个孤岛上生活过五年。笛福以塞尔柯克自述为蓝本，改头换面加上自己的想象，创作了一部传记体小说——《鲁滨逊漂流记》(1719)。这部小说一出版就受到热烈赞扬，四个月内印行了四版。

故事是这样的：鲁滨逊覆舟遇险。他在水中竭力挣扎，才在一座无人居住的小岛登陆。他在岛上一住就是十八个年头。他独力修筑了一座设有防御工事的住处，种植大麦和水稻，驯养山羊，造了一艘小船，跟食人的土人作战，历尽艰辛，后来才被一艘英国船发现，把他带回英国。鲁滨逊在岛上所经历的种种，自始至终扣人心弦。

《鲁滨逊漂流记》的最大特色在于它的真实感和生动性。笛福极力使他的读者相信他叙述的是“真人真事”。

> 在我支起帐幕之前，我先在石壁的前面画了一个半圆形，它的半径，距离石壁差不多有十码，它的直径，全长有二十码。沿着这个半圆形，我插了两排很结实的木桩，把它们打进泥土里，仿佛一些木橛子，大的一头向下，高出地面约五英尺半，顶上削得尖尖的。两排之间的距离不过六英寸。然后，我又取出我从船上截下来的那些缆索，沿着半圆形，把它们一层一层地横放在两排木桩中间，一直堆到顶上，又用一些两英尺半高的木桩插在圈内，支着它们，仿佛柱子下的支柱。这样一个篱笆，真是牢固异常，不管是人是兽，都没法冲进来或爬进来。①

上面一段足以说明笛福的写作方法。坚持细节描写是笛福小说生动逼真的诀窍；上面一段文字中对木栅的大小和木栅材料的描写就是一个例子。笛福不但告诉读者鲁滨逊做了什么事，而且还告诉他这件事是怎样做的。他的散文语言是一般人民的日常语言，其特点是："清楚、流畅、明白易懂"。

3. 《鲁滨逊漂流记》的意义 《鲁滨逊漂流记》所表达的是资产阶级个人主义和个人奋斗。鲁滨逊是一个新人——他十分自信，有信心在世界任何地方开创事业。他是一个新时代的人，他毫不怀疑，毫不忧郁，而是满怀希望和信心。马克思把鲁滨逊称作是 18 世纪的个人，是"解体的封建社会和 16 世纪以来新兴生产力相结合的产物"。

鲁滨逊是他那个时代的创业者。他做好准备要征服自然，战胜敌人，在海外建立殖民地。他是商人兼冒险家，对物质利益很感兴趣。他是一个殖民者，一个帝国的建造人。《鲁滨逊漂流记》体现了正在

① 徐霞村译《鲁滨逊漂流记》，第 51 页。

兴起的资产阶级个人奋斗的精神和殖民扩张的精神。

1719 年，笛福继《鲁滨逊漂流记》之后，又出版了《鲁滨逊漂流记续编》。有趣的是，在续编中鲁滨逊和他的船员在中国海岸登陆，他的船员“既是绅士又是商人”，他们还访问了南京和北京。

《鲁滨逊漂流记》所表达的划时代的主题是：一个普普通通的人在毫无希望的环境中有能力活下去，而且还能处理自己的经济生活。在整个 18 世纪，讲授政治经济学时一直把这本书作为重要材料。

四　乔纳森·斯威夫特

1. **《桶的故事》**　乔纳森·斯威夫特（1667—1745）出身于古老的英国家族。他是一个遗腹子，出生在爱尔兰。他家境贫苦，靠伯叔资助，才得以受到早期教育并在都柏林三一学院获得了硕士学位。二十二岁那年（1689），他寄宿于母亲的远亲，辉格党人外交家威廉·坦普尔爵士家。在萨利郡，他为爵士做了十年秘书。1696 到 1697 年，他在那里写了《桶的故事》，攻击当时英国的三大教会，即英国国教、罗马天主教和不信奉国教的新教。“桶的故事”一词原系 17 世纪英国俚语，意思是玩笑、骗局或者扯淡。

斯威夫特在这本书的开头说：从前有一个人，他有三个儿子——彼得、马丁和杰克。他临终给三个儿子每人一件新上衣，告诉他们怎样穿，怎样保管。他并且在遗嘱中嘱咐他们应该和睦友爱。这里，“父亲”指的是“基督”，上衣是指基督教的信仰和教规，“遗嘱”是指《新约》，三个儿子则影射三个教会——罗马天主教（彼得）、英国国教（马丁）以及不信奉国教的新教（杰克）。

起初，三个兄弟住在一起，和睦友爱。接着他们就开始对"遗嘱"提出不同的解释。最后，"遗嘱"上说得很明白清楚的事却被曲解得面目全非。这就是说，三个教会都背离了基督所教导的朴素的宗教信仰，他们凭借朴素的基督教信仰汲汲于名利，暗施诡计，散布邪说，互相仇恨。

《桶的故事》触怒了各派权贵。安妮女王始终不能释然于怀。但是它是一部伟大的讽刺作品。据说，斯威夫特晚年重读他的这部早年著作时，把书放下，惊呼起来："天哪，我写这本书的时候，多么有才华呀！"

2. 关于爱尔兰问题的小册子 从1699年起，斯威夫特在都柏林附近的几座小教堂做牧师。1713年他被任命为都柏林圣帕特里克教堂的教长。他不喜欢爱尔兰，他形容爱尔兰是"一个肮脏破烂的狗窝"，"奴隶、恶棍、傻瓜"出没的地方。但是他跟爱尔兰人一起居住多年之后，就深深了解为什么爱兰尔变成了当时那个样子。他写了一本又一本小册子，反对英国统治者。

1724年，斯威夫特以一位麻布商的名义写了一系列的信（《麻布商书信集》），反对英国人企图使爱兰尔币贬值，即造成通货膨胀。英国政府没有跟爱尔兰人商议，就颁发了一纸特许状给一个叫威廉·伍德的人，准许他为爱尔兰发行大量铜币。斯威夫特在《麻布商书信集》里揭露了这种卑鄙的不公正的行为，并激励爱兰尔人起来维护自己的权利。1725年特许状被撤回，斯威夫特取得了胜利。爱兰尔人敬慕他，就在他生日那天举行庆祝活动。

斯威夫特愈是思量爱兰尔人民每况愈下的处境，就愈加猛烈地抨击欺压爱尔兰人民的英国人。1729年他发表了他最激烈的讽刺文章:《一个温和的建议》。斯威夫特在这本小册子中,以清晰而明确的语言一本正经地提出,应该把孩子们养肥,屠宰后送到英国市场上出售。“一周岁的健康儿童,如果喂得好,是一种最可口、最滋补、最佳的食品,无论是炖、烤、烙、煮都行……”斯威夫特还说,“屠宰以后剥皮使用,也十分经济实惠,人皮经过加工处理,可以用来给女士们制作手套,也可以用来给优雅的绅士做夏天穿的皮鞋。”

当《温和的建议》发表时,爱尔兰正发生饥荒,而不住在爱尔兰的许多地主却在英格兰或别的地方,挥霍着他们从佃农手中榨取来的地租,过着花天酒地的奢侈生活。

3.《格列佛游记》和它的重要意义 《格列佛游记》(1726)早已成为最具魅力的一部儿童故事。水手格列佛海上覆舟遇险,在小人国利立浦特登陆,那里的小人身材只有他的十二分之一,而他们的国王比他的臣民只高出一个手指甲盖。在小人中间,格列佛仿佛是一个巨人。他睡的床是用六百张小人床拼起来的,而他每天吃下肚去的饮食足够供养一千七百二十八名利立浦特人。在那里,格列佛经历了无数次奇遇。离开小人国以后,格列佛又航海遇难,这次却是在大人国布罗丁奈格登陆。他站在大人旁边十分渺小,就像利立浦特人站在他身旁一般。餐桌面“离地面三十英尺”,而盛肉的盘子直径达二十四英尺。格列佛在大人国也再次经历了无数次奇遇,其惊险不下于他在小人国的奇遇。

但是《格列佛游记》绝非一本儿童故事而已。这本书是对英国的讽刺。利立浦特是缩小了的英国;而布罗丁奈格则是放大了的英国——每件小事都可笑地大。通过讽刺的面纱可以看到斯威夫特特意选中攻击的英国政客。利立浦特的财政大臣佛林奈浦是位绳技专家。他“跳绳比全王国的任何一位大臣都要高一英寸”。这里影射的是当时的英国财政大臣罗伯特·渥尔波尔爵士。

这部讽刺作品的前两卷就是这样的。小说的第三卷是效果最弱的一部分，是嘲笑伪科学家和学究的。在第四卷慧骃国游记中，斯威夫特把讽刺范围扩大到了整个人类。

威廉·赫兹利特是这样说的：“斯威夫特通过格列佛这个人物，试图把骗人的面具从世人脸上扯下来，并把外界环境给他们的面孔上装上的一层虚荣庄重的气派剥去。只有想蒙骗别人的人才会对这本书有所不满。”

斯威夫特的正面主张很难确定。但是，《格列佛游记》表明他对当时人糟蹋人的情形确实是义愤填膺。这种愤怒来自一种勇敢的现实主义，一种敢于正视 18 世纪社会现实的能力，一种面对人生毫不畏缩的态度。斯威夫特以他独特的平易有力的文风，表达了他的感受。

第七章

18 世纪中期

一　理查森、斯摩莱特和斯特恩

1. **理查森和感伤小说**　塞缪尔·理查森（1689—1761）是德比郡一个细木工人的儿子，后在伦敦发迹，成为殷实的出版商。1740 年，他年已五旬，出版了一部书信体小说《帕梅拉》（又名《德行有报》），共四卷。

帕梅拉是一个贫穷的使女（第一个在小说中出现的使女形象），遭到雇主的浪荡儿子皮先生的无礼纠缠。她抗拒，企图逃跑，甚至想投水自尽。皮先生发现她品格端庄，无可指责，于是向她正式求婚，她接受了。于是，德行得到了酬报，即一笔数目可观的收入和较高的社会地位。整个事件由传递的一封封天真纯朴、多情善感、碎心断肠的书信表述出来，读起来令人潸然泪下。

第一部小说的成功，鼓舞理查森着手写第二部小说《克拉丽莎·哈洛》(1747—1748)，共六卷。克拉丽莎是个好人家出身的女孩，心地纯洁，品格高尚。当她在力图摆脱强迫婚姻和不愉快的家庭而出走时，落入放浪的情人洛夫莱斯的圈套。她蒙受折磨和污辱，最后伤心地含羞而死。《克拉丽莎·哈洛》是个悲剧，使读者流下了更多的眼泪。小说在欧洲大陆引起了反响，对狄德罗和卢梭等都有影响。

作为小说家，理查森有明显的弱点。他叙事重复，冗长累赘——他的作品的长度本身已成为笑柄。他总是在说教，总是在劝善，但并不总是能令人愉悦。他关于"德行有报"的见解，无论是在现世或来世，是实利主义的资产阶级道德观念，即凡是做了正当的努力就需要分享某种红利。但理查森给小说引入了一种新的东西，即感性。他小说的主题总是"德行在受难"——这是一个凄婉动人的主题。他通过对这个主题的探索，揭示了人们内心深处的感受。

2. 斯摩莱特和流浪汉小说 托拜厄斯·乔治·斯摩莱特(1721—1771)出身于苏格兰的一个地主家庭，早年受过一些医术训练。在十九岁至二十六岁期间，在西印度群岛当外科医生。他把自己早期的大部分经历写进了他的第一部小说《罗德里克·兰登历险记》[①](1748)。

像斯摩莱特本人一样，罗德里克也是苏格兰人。他经过一些外科医术训练之后，和一个理发师的儿子、老同学斯特拉普结伴南下漫游。异乎寻常的灾难与遭遇(如途遇强盗、险遭毒手等)接踵而至。在伦敦(它在书中被称为"魔鬼的客厅")，罗德里克从一个法国药剂师那里谋到一个小小的职位。他跟主人的情妇和她的女儿发生

① 又译《蓝登传》。——编注

爱情纠葛。后来，他在战舰上给外科医生当助手，随舰去了西印度群岛。航海生活中肮脏、恐怖、野蛮的内情，通过一场场非常紧张的冒险揭露了出来。小说的结尾平淡无奇，甚至粗制滥造。后来，罗德里克回到了英国，游览了伦敦和巴斯，并在绝望中遇到了他失散多年的父亲，那时他父亲已是一个大富翁了。最后，罗德里克也成了富翁，并有燕尔之喜。

《罗德里克·兰登历险记》是一部流浪汉小说，也称为恶汉小说。斯摩莱特的其他小说，像《佩里格林·皮克尔历险记》和《汉弗莱·克林克尔探险记》也都属于这一体裁。这类小说没有什么情节，而仅仅是一连串发展迅速、好恶交替、变化急剧的冒险经历的组合。斯摩莱特译过西班牙塞万提斯和法国勒萨日的作品，他继承了他们的创作传统。

斯摩莱特不是一流小说家，但他善讲故事，文笔犀利有力。他揭露了社会各阶层和各种职业中存在的罪恶和愚蠢，尤其以《罗德里克·兰登历险记》中有关航海生活的篇章最为出色。它们是英语小说中关于真实航海生活的首批图画。作为一个现实主义作家，斯摩莱特的影响在司各特、狄更斯和萨克雷的作品中都可以看到。

3. **斯特恩和“商第主义”** 和理查森一样，斯特恩也是个感伤主义作家，但情调不同。理查森的感伤主义总和道德伦理搅和在一起，帕梅拉的故事也好，克拉丽莎的故事也好，其情节的发展都显得庄重严肃。斯特恩的笔调则比较轻松，他的感伤主义富于风趣与幽默。

劳伦斯·斯特恩（1713—1768）出身于地主贵族，在剑桥上学时读过大量的奇文异书。后来在约克郡当牧师，为人机灵，但有些变化莫测。在1760到1767年间，《特里斯特拉姆·商第的生平与见解》[①]

---

① 又译《项狄传》。——编注

问世。小说的名字本身就是故作幽默。我们读到的是华尔特·商第、托比·商第、脆姆下士等的生平与见解,而不是特里斯特拉姆·商第的生平与见解。我们读完小说的一半时,才看到特里斯特拉姆的出生,而在小说远未结束之前,他早已不知去向了。

小说的写法同样是奇特的。语法和修辞全被置诸脑后,小说各章节有的很长,有的很短;有的是中间插入,有的则被删削了;有的似乎是放错了位置,只留下几页空白或一些省略小圆点。插话比比皆是,斯特恩认为,插话是“生活,阅读的灵魂”。

这本小说是一部永无休止的谈话集。特里斯特拉姆的父亲华尔特·商第在商第出生时跟商第太太、跟斯洛普医生谈话;托比叔叔,一个残疾退伍军人,跟他的仆人脆姆下士的谈话;托比叔叔和寡妇沃德曼相爱,他们谈啊,谈啊,谈了又谈。话题常在变换,谈这谈那,无论如何也不能按照主题进行。

斯特恩在《特里斯特拉姆·商第的生平与见解》里强调两点。一种是易感性,或者说是人心的柔顺,借此对时代的麻木不仁与野蛮残酷表示抗议。一头毛驴,一只苍蝇,任何一样东西,不管多么平庸卑微,都可以引起他的同情。其次是独特性(或癖性)。斯特恩在书中不断抒发自己的生活观点和奇思异想。

还必须提一提斯特恩的《法兰西和意大利的感伤旅行》(1768)。小说描述他在欧洲大陆各种意外的冒险经历——诸如:调情卖俏,微妙的处境,为了一个穷苦的修道士、为了一个老头、为了路边的一头毛驴、为了几只笼中的欧椋鸟而掉泪,等等。“我放声大笑,直笑得嚎啕大哭,而就在同样感伤的时刻,我嚎啕大哭,直哭得放声大笑。我甚至比商第还商第,”斯特恩说。

二　亨利·菲尔丁

1. **菲尔丁和他的早期小说**　亨利·菲尔丁(1707—1754)是马尔伯勒将军麾下一位将领的儿子。早年在伊顿公学受教育,18世纪30年代来到伦敦,从事谐拟剧和滑稽戏创作,剧中充满着对渥尔波尔及其内阁的攻击。1737年渥尔波尔颁布戏剧检查法,于是菲尔丁不能继续写作那类戏剧了。1740年,理查森的《帕梅拉》问世,成千上万的读者被感动得落下眼泪,而少数人则报之以大声哄笑。菲尔丁就是那少数人之一。他出版了一部谐拟小说《约瑟夫·安德鲁斯》(1742),这使那位严肃持重的出版商甚为恼怒。

约瑟夫·安德鲁斯据说是已与皮先生幸福结合的帕梅拉的弟弟,少年英俊,在帕梅拉丈夫的叔母布比·帕梅拉夫人家当侍童。他以一种庄严虔诚的态度——这里谐拟帕梅拉对皮先生的态度——拒绝了布比·帕梅拉夫人的引诱而遭到解雇。之后,约瑟夫离去,徒步寻找他的心上人,即使女范妮。一路上,他遇到了形形色色的人物——客店老板、拦路强盗、善良的牧师、邪恶的牧师、友善的旅客、自私的旅客、和蔼的绅士、傲慢的绅士。最后,真相大白,卑微的范妮原来是大名鼎鼎的帕梅拉的妹妹,而约瑟夫则是一位绅士的公子(他们在婴儿期被抱错了!)。于是他们在帕梅拉同意下结了婚。

《约瑟夫·安德鲁斯》不仅仅是一部谐拟小说,它是菲尔丁对于那可以称为人道现实主义的初次尝试。菲尔丁嘲笑理查森小说中所有在他看来不真实的、虚假的东西——伪善和假正经,同时又描写了那些虽卑微却善良的人们,诸如:马车夫、普通士兵、庄稼汉,等等。这里表现出菲尔丁和普通人民的亲密关系。

菲尔丁的第二部小说《大伟人乔纳森·怀尔德传》[①]（1743），是一部关于1725年被处以绞刑的窃贼和窃贼拘捕者的虚构传记。菲尔丁以窃贼、拦路强盗、玩牌赌徒和纽盖特监狱中贪赃枉法、野蛮残忍的官吏等作陪衬，描述了怀尔德从童年到走上绞刑架的"成功的"一生。下层社会触目惊心的画面，由于有了几个善良朴实、温厚仁爱的人物——珠宝商哈特夫利、他的妻儿和学徒弗兰德利——而显得格外醒目。菲尔丁的目的是想指出：事业的成功往往是与德行不相干的，使怀尔德成为大窃贼的那些品质，曾经同样使那些实际上并不比他强的人们发财致富，官居高位。

《大伟人乔纳森·怀尔德传》不是一部伟大的小说，书中的人物被过分写成了小说的基本思想——伟大与善良——的代言人。但小说仍不失为英语中最好的，当然也是最持久有力的讥讽作品。辉格党人和托利党人、两党制本身、官府的腐败和经济剥削等资产阶级社会的每一个方面几乎都遭到了讽刺。

2. **《汤姆·琼斯》** 菲尔丁的杰作是《汤姆·琼斯》（1749）。弃儿汤姆·琼斯是富有乡绅奥尔沃西的养子，从小和布利菲尔一起被抚养长大。布利菲尔是奥尔沃西的妹妹布里奇特的儿子，也是奥尔沃西的法定继承人。他们两人恰好形成了对比。汤姆乐天不羁，但一旦被人激怒，也会起而反抗；布利菲尔则是伪善的化身。他俩都常与邻近乡绅之女苏菲亚·韦斯顿结伴嬉戏，苏菲亚钟情于汤姆，但她的家庭却催逼她与讨厌的布利菲尔结合。

由于布利菲尔的挑唆，汤姆被逐出乡绅奥尔沃西的家门。他于是离乡去伦敦应募。苏菲亚不顾习俗，随后赶路去伦敦寻找汤姆。在途

① 又译《大伟人江奈生·魏尔德传》。——编注

中，他们曾多次近在咫尺，可能相遇，但始终未遇。这对情侣究竟会不会相遇并言归于好呢？菲尔丁让人迷惑不解。一路上，他们遇见了各种各样的人，诸如：乐善好施的绅士、利嘴薄舌的泼妇和老处女、两面三刀的恶棍，等等。后来，他们抵达伦敦，都市生活及其风流艳事和淫乱放荡在小说中得到了反映。小说中插曲很多，题外议论也不计其数，直到最后，才真相大白，原来汤姆是奥尔沃西之妹的私生子，布利菲尔是一切纠纷的罪魁祸首。最终，汤姆被确认为他舅父的继承人。故事以汤姆和苏菲亚结成伴侣而结束。

《汤姆·琼斯》是卡尔·马克思最喜爱的读物之一。弗朗茨·梅林写道："马克思高度评价18世纪的英国小说，尤其推崇菲尔丁的《汤姆·琼斯》。就其特有的方式而言，这部小说也是它那个时代的一面镜子。"

菲尔丁的目的就是使这部小说成为"那个时代的一面镜子"。菲尔丁坚持称《汤姆·琼斯》为"历史"。他说："我们的任务就是履行一个忠实历史家的职责，按照人性的本来面目来描写人性，而不是按照我们希望它是什么样子来描写它。"

3.《阿米莉亚》——菲尔丁的最后一部小说 菲尔丁管他的小说叫"散文滑稽史诗"。这是说，它是这样一种艺术形式，它对于18世纪社会的作用就像史诗在远古社会里的作用一样。它是一面真实的镜子，同时又是当代生活中一种批判性的想法。

他的最后一部小说《阿米莉亚》(1751)也是如此。这部小说开门见山的第一句话是："底下要讲的那段历史是叙述一对非常善良的男女在结成良缘之后所遭遇到的种种事件。"早在1749年，菲尔丁就被任命为中塞克斯(即伦敦)的治安法官。因此他有条件描写当时他所见所闻的伦敦生活，并抒发对这种生活的感受。跟《汤姆·琼斯》不同，《阿米莉亚》描述了一幅阴暗的图画。这对“非常善良的男女”，男的叫布斯上尉，犯过错误，女的（即阿米莉亚）却是个忠实而有勇气的贤妻良母。布斯想改邪归正，老老实实地过活。然而，他在社会上仍不断地遭受到种种凌辱。书中描写的有妓女、老鸨、男女流氓、戏弄和欺诈弱者和不幸者的骗子。纽盖特监狱则是外界社会的缩影，只不过是更耸人听闻一点罢了。在这社会里，身居高位者享受着特权，而美德则一文不值。这部小说提出的问题，即社会不公平的问题，始终没有得到解决。读者看完这本书时，一定会跟阿米莉亚一起慨叹：“老天哪！我们的大人物是些什么东西做成的啊？难道他们确实属于另一类型而跟别人不同吗？难道他们生来就没有心肝的吗？”小说的结局是不自然的。布斯成了虔诚的基督徒。至于阿米莉亚，她继承了一笔遗产，于是这对夫妇就可以太太平平地到乡间去过活了。然而，尽管有这些局限性，这部小说仍可认为是狄德罗的问题戏剧和戈德温的问题小说之先驱。

三　约翰逊和约翰逊的游从

1. **辞典学家、批评家约翰逊**　塞缪尔·约翰逊（1709—1784）是利奇菲尔德的一个书商的儿子，在他父亲的书店里度过了自己的童年，“曾在那里涉猎过许多当时大学里也不常见的书籍”。后来他在牛津大学修业了几个学期，但未获得学位。1737 年他抵达伦敦时，几乎是身无半文，于是开始了雇佣文人的生涯。

1747年，约翰逊接受一批书商的雇用，打算编写一部英语辞典。他指望得到切斯特菲尔德勋爵的资助，但勋爵大人不予理睬，直到1754年辞典编成时才有所表示。这时，约翰逊给切斯特菲尔德写了一封信，此信闻名遐迩，这是理所当然的。

> 老爷，当初我在尊府外客厅恭候求见，也可说遭到拒绝，现在算起来，七个年头已经过去了。七年来，我吃过种种苦头，但始终没有中断我的编写工作，这是不用抱怨的，因为抱怨是无济于事的。现在，我终于使它接近于出版，虽然我没有得到一点帮助的行动，没有听到一句勉励的话语，也没有看到一次赞许的微笑。这样的待遇，我未敢妄想，因为我从来没有一位恩主……

这封信意义深远。它标志着作家隶属于贵族恩主的时代，已逐渐地过渡到作家成为资本主义制度下生产者的时代。著书立说已成为一种职业，文学作品已成为一种商品。约翰逊写的文学作品复杂多样，计有两首诗、一个剧本、一部小说、一部莎士比亚戏剧校订集、《英国诗人传》和大量报刊文章。1755年出版的《辞典》确立了他的声誉，但并没有增加他的收入。在1762年他开始领取政府退休金之前，他始终没有停止过为生活而挣扎。"只有傻瓜不为金钱而写作，"约翰逊说。

约翰逊是托利党人，是保守派。他的著作，包括《辞典》，都暴露出他那托利党人的偏见。他在晚年写的《英国诗人传》里，曾对自己不能十分理解的斯威夫特和弥尔顿有所贬抑。他不同情当时的社会和政治运动。他反对美国革命，如果他多活几年的话，同样会反对法国大革命。

2. 鲍斯韦尔的《约翰逊传》 约翰逊之所以未被后人遗忘，与其说是因为他自己留下的著作，毋宁说是因为鲍斯韦尔替他写的传记，这部书一直被认为是英语中最伟大的一部传记。

詹姆斯·鲍斯韦尔（1740—1795）出身于苏格兰贵族，但他的行为举止很少有或根本没有贵族的那种庄重的气派。他在爱丁堡做过律师，但法律并非他的专长。他喜欢攀附社会名流，善于“交际”。二十三岁那年，他结识了年逾五旬的约翰逊，并加入了约翰逊的圈子，其中包括报章家哥尔斯密斯、画家雷诺兹、作曲家伯尼博士、演员加里克和剧作家谢里登。他观察、研究约翰逊，直到他能够惟妙惟肖地再现他老师的说话语气、习惯用语和讲话风格。1791 年，他的划时代著作《约翰逊传》问世，共两卷。

《约翰逊传》的主要成就在于它的逼真性。鲍斯韦尔写约翰逊的长处，也写他的短处，写他的随和，也写他的粗鲁，诸如：他那熊一般的形相，饭桌上的丑态，特大的胃口，惊人的茶量，喧闹的笑声，为争论而争论的癖好，“争论结束时好像鲸鱼出水吐气”，他那强烈的偏见，以及一大堆矛盾的事例。“我决不会为了讨好任何人而削去约翰逊的尖爪，”鲍斯韦尔说。但是，从《约翰逊传》里浮现出来的形象却不是一张讽刺漫画，而是一幅肢体完整的全身像。“我敢说，”鲍斯韦尔说，“人们在传记里看到的他［约翰逊］，将会比曾经活过的任何人显得更加神貌俱全。”

在这之前，传记都是些颂扬之辞。“忘掉他的种种弱点吧，他是一位非常伟大的人物”，这一直是传记作家的座右铭。鲍斯韦尔却不这样想，他刻意追求真实与逼真，他的《约翰逊传》仿佛是一部由别人执笔写的私人日记。它标志着现代传记的开端。

3. **哥尔斯密斯的诗和散文** 约翰逊俱乐部的另一个成员奥立佛·哥尔斯密斯(1730—1774)是一个爱尔兰牧师的儿子。他在卑微贫寒中总算是在都柏林三一学院获得一些教育。毕业后有几年,他在欧洲大陆流浪。1756年,他回到了伦敦,开始卖文为生,为新闻界的刻薄老板拼命写作。后来,他确立了自己的作家地位,但所得收入却因使用无度而挥霍殆尽。因此,他尽管有声誉,有朋友,但至死也未中断过卖文工作。他实际上是累死的。

在哥尔斯密斯的作品中,以下三部必须提到:《威克菲牧师传》、《荒村》、《屈身求爱》。《威克菲牧师传》(1766)一直是一部流行作品。小说的情节微不足道,甚至是荒谬的,但小说有特殊的魅力。凡是读过这部小说的人,都怎么也忘不了那个牧师。他总是在讲道劝善,他虚荣中又糅合着谦卑,他"天性善良",但由于那难以应付的家庭,他总是面临着种种麻烦。小说描绘的封建资产阶级社会被浸没在田园牧歌般的幻象之中。

同样,《荒村》(1770)也充满着田园牧歌般的幻象。该诗是用英雄联韵体写成的。诗中有一些重要章节,描述圈地运动和农民被逐出家园的残酷场面,但他描绘农村中那种怡然自得的情景——舞蹈、黄昏时刻户内外的活动、酒店、教师、老牧师——却是理想化了的。"哪里有这般可爱的人儿,这般迷人的事物呢?"人们相互询问着,他们跑遍了英格兰和爱尔兰也没有找到它们的原型。

《屈身求爱》(1773)首次上演就获得成功。这出戏也一直是最流行的五六部喜剧之一。年轻腼腆的马洛去向哈德卡斯尔小姐求爱,他把她家错认为客店,把她的乡绅父亲哈德卡斯尔错认为客店老板,把小姐本人错认为侍女。哈德卡斯尔小姐将错就错，以侍女身份来争取她那位腼腆爱恋者的欢心。剧本里有许多滑稽可笑的场面和恶作剧，还有迷人的歌曲。产生喜剧气氛的根源是封建资产阶级社会人与人之间不自然的关系。但是，这里同样有着田园牧歌般的魅力。

哥尔斯密斯不是一个深刻的社会评论家，他仅仅触及事物的表面，而从来没有深入内部。

4. 谢里登和他的《造谣学校》 和哥尔斯密斯一样，理查德·布林斯利·谢里登（1751—1816）也出生于爱尔兰。父亲曾当过演员、戏院经理和朗诵家，母亲写过一部小说和两个剧本。谢里登年轻时在哈罗公学和自己家里受教育。大约二十岁时，他写过一首精巧的讽刺诗，其中包括下面常被引用的英雄联韵句：

你提笔疾书以示教养，
但轻易成章读者遭殃。

二十四岁时，他接替加里克，先当德鲁瑞戏院经理，后又连续多年当该戏院的老板。

谢里登的代表作《造谣学校》于1777年上演。剧本里实际上有两条线：第一条线写一伙造谣者；第二条线写彼得爵士那伙人的故事。造谣者以斯尼惠尔夫人为首，给剧本创造了气氛。彼得爵士那伙人包括：一个年老的丈夫和一个年轻活泼的妻子；两个兄弟，一个是伪君子，另一个是挥金如土的浪子；一个长期在外、刚从印度归来的叔叔；一个受他监护的年轻的女继承人。谢里登不善于安排情节，但善于创作成功的场景（如：造谣者俱乐部、大拍卖、屏风布景等场面）。

谢里登是18世纪社会的大评论家。他讽刺的对象有：年轻的纨绔子弟、讲究时髦的贵妇人、多愁善感的少女、愚蠢笨拙的丈夫、表里不一的伪君子、蹩脚的评论家，以及谣言散布者，等等。他的讽刺机智俏皮、巧妙善辩。

谢里登不到三十岁就誉满剧坛。此后，他进入政界，当上了议会议员，并在辉格党短暂的执政期间担任过好几个政府职务。他反对对美战争，苦心弹劾沃伦·黑斯廷斯，主张合理分配议会代表席位和新闻自由。

四　诗歌：从新古典主义到浪漫主义

1. **变化中的诗歌模式**　约在半个世纪之中，蒲伯的英雄联韵诗给英诗定下了模式。蒲伯和蒲伯派的诗，是理性的，而不是感性或感受的诗；是关于城市的，而不是关于乡村的诗；是对古典诗歌的模仿，而不是自然流露之作。这类诗歌被称为新古典主义诗歌。

但到了该世纪的第二个二十五年，诗歌模式的改变已初露端倪。《四季歌》的作者詹姆斯·汤姆逊（1700—1748），从“烟雾弥漫的城市喧嚣”转向“怡人心脾的乡村景色”，从抽象的人性转向农民大众的简朴生活和日常工作。该世纪中期，威廉·柯林斯富于感情地描绘了黄昏时辰（《黄昏颂》），而剑桥大学学者托马斯·格雷则以无懈可击的韵律哀悼了那些默默无闻的死者（《墓园哀歌》）：

别让“野心”嘲笑他们有益的劳动，

平凡的欢乐和默默无闻的结局；
“宏伟”也别露出轻蔑的笑容，
倾听穷苦人又短又简的生活记录。

与此同时，詹姆斯·麦克弗森出版了《奥西恩》(1762)，一首据称出于一位古代凯尔特诗人手笔的长篇叙事诗。托马斯·珀西复兴了古老的英式民谣和民歌。悠久古老的题材被用来促进诗歌的发展。诗人表达了他们对时代的动荡不安的厌恶，热切地向往“自然简朴的安排”。在该世纪的最后二十五年，哥尔斯密斯、库珀和克雷布吐露了他们各自对现实中存在着的种种困难都有所感受的心境。正是库珀宣称：“上帝创造了乡村，凡人建立了城市。”

就这样，诗歌离开了客厅，转而描述纯朴平凡的人们。它摆脱了蒲伯派的束缚，摆脱了他那“挺胸直背，昂首阔步”的韵律。理性的优势地位给感性或感受所代替。这种诗歌，由于缺乏更好的术语，被称为浪漫主义诗歌。

2. 彭斯和他的抒情诗 罗伯特·彭斯(1759—1796)是18世纪最伟大的抒情诗人，他出生于苏格兰西南地区离埃尔郡不远的杜恩河畔。诗人的父亲是一个穷苦的“佃农”。彭斯年轻时经历过耕作和收获的许多困乏日子，但他仍然腾出时间完成一个苏格兰农民的普通教育。他曾听他母亲讲过种种歌谣，后来又熟读了一本流行歌曲集。“我熟记这些歌曲，”他说，“赶车时记，下地时记，一首首地记，一行行地记。”

1784年，彭斯家迁往莫斯基尔的一个小农场定居，一家人住在一所两间屋带一间阁楼的房子里。彭斯一边耕作，一边恋爱，一边作歌。

每天收工回家，他通常都回到自己的阁楼里，写下他在田间构思好的诗歌。1786 年，《苏格兰方言诗歌集》问世，使这位农民诗人开始闻名于英格兰和苏格兰的文学界。后来他被任命为邓弗里斯的一个税务员，从事他所说的“计量老婆子的酒瓶”的工作。由于有了可以糊口的工资和较多的空闲时间，他继续进行诗歌写作。1796 年，诗人逝世，年仅三十七岁。

彭斯的抒情诗植根于苏格兰的丰富民歌，朴实无华，但并不缺乏艺术，而且因为它们是当时心情的极其自然、极其自由的流露，所以听起来就像鸟儿的歌唱那样自然生动：

啊，我爱人像一朵红红的玫瑰，
　它在六月里初开：
啊，我爱人像一支乐曲，
　它美妙地演奏起来。
你是那么漂亮，我美丽的姑娘，
　我爱你是那么深切：
我会一直爱你，亲爱的，
　一直到四海枯竭……[①]

《友谊地久天长》、《约翰·安德森，我爱》，《你们啊，河岸、山坡和溪水》、《高原玛丽》、《苏格兰人之歌》、《如果你站在冷风里》等，都属于彭斯的不朽之作。

3. 彭斯的讽刺诗和叙事诗　作为诗人，彭斯知道自己的身份与职责。他一方面反对人有贵贱或等级高低之分，如《不管那一套》；另

① 袁可嘉译《彭斯诗钞》，第 152 页。

一方面又在自己的不朽之作《佃农的周末之夜》里描绘了“善良的平民大众”的感情与仪表（诗中那个“劳累困乏的佃农”就是他那个“佃农”父亲的画像）。彭斯蔑视学院式的知识，认为真正的灵感应当在“自然之火的火花”中找到。

在“旧光派”的眼里，彭斯是个叛逆者。他是写讽刺诗的大师，矛头直指口是心非、矫揉造作、腐化堕落，特别是那大谈地狱和罚进地狱的神学。他的《神圣市集》充满着戏谑和笑声。三个女人正走在通往布道帐篷——彭斯称为“神圣市集”——的路上：

我的名字叫开心——你的亲亲，
　你最亲近的友人；
这位姑娘名叫迷信，
　那个名叫假正经。

圣集上，牧师开始布道，正讲到地狱就是那个“魔鬼居住的地方”：

一个无底无边的地洞，
　装满了燃烧的硫磺；
火焰熊熊、灼热的空气，
　能融化最坚硬的花岗石。
那些半寐者一惊而醒，
　地狱的怒吼仿佛听见；
他们马上发现原来是邻人，
　呼呼的鼾声响成一片，

他睡着了，那一天。[1]

彭斯强烈同情法国大革命，这使得他与当地的社团发生尖锐冲突。他虽享有诗人的盛名，但几乎被排斥在各社团之外。

① 袁可嘉译《彭斯诗钞》，第68页。

第八章

浪漫主义时期（上）

一　激进主义和浪漫主义

1. **普赖斯、伯克和汤姆·潘恩**　1789年，巴士底狱被攻陷后，不信奉国教的牧师理查德·普赖斯博士在伦敦给激进人士做了一次布道。布道的要点是：人民有权选举治理者并有权“撤除渎职的治理者”。对于这次的布道，议会议员埃德蒙·伯克写了《对法国革命的感想》（1790）作为回应。伯克看到的只是法国大革命的残酷，而睁眼不见旧政权所造成的悲惨、苦难和不公平。《感想》激起了众人的反驳，其中最值得注意的是汤姆·潘恩的《人权论》。用汤姆·潘恩的不朽名言来说，伯克是“哀怜鸟的羽毛，却忘了那奄奄待毙的鸟”。

“人类思想和心灵的解放者”汤姆·潘恩（1737—1809）先后当过船舶支索修理工、水手和税务官。1774年，他三十七岁时，赴美当了新闻记者，主张废除黑奴制和公正对待妇女。美国独立战争爆发后，当各殖民地领袖仍然希望和平解决时，潘恩发表了一本流传极广的小册子《常识》，建议成立“自由独立的美利坚合众国”。他对北美殖民地的独立事业作出了无法估量的贡献。

潘恩的《人权论》于1791年问世，其主题是“自由”。潘恩从洛克和卢梭那里吸取了政治自由主义中的各种主张，并把他对于不平等与压迫的愤怒，对于各种特权的鄙视和对于最下层人民的深切尊重等情绪注入了这些主张。正是在他的影响下，苏格兰制鞋匠托马斯·哈代创建了伦敦争取议会改革的通讯协会。协会有三万名成员，其中有汤姆·潘恩、威廉·布莱克和威廉·戈德温。1794年，革命浪潮在英国达到高峰，在一次周年庆祝会上，“人权”和“自由”成了主要的祝酒辞。

2. 哲学家和小说家戈德温 上面略述的关于法国大革命的论争，最终由《政治正义论》(1793)的作者威廉·戈德温提高到哲学的高度。

威廉·戈德温(1756—1820)原是一位基督教长老会的牧师。在法国唯物主义者的影响下，他放弃了原来的信仰，逐渐形成了自己的革命思想。他在《政治正义论》中指出，迄今为止的历史是战争、专制、欺诈、抢劫、非正义以及人与人之间不平等种种罪行的记录。他认为，这一切是由不健全的社会政治制度造成的，因为人必然受他的环境制约。但如果环境得到改变并能适应人的健康发展，那么人本身是可臻完善的。戈德温坚持主张建立以理性为基础的一切人间的平等关系，他认为理性是生活的唯一指南，同时坚决主张废除各种形式的人为等级差别。这些主张包含着大量的空想主义成分，但在当时却具有巨大的革命意义。

戈德温还写了几部小说，其中以《凯莱布·威廉斯》（1794）为最有趣味。青年仆人凯莱布掌握着主人、乡绅福克兰德曾经杀过人的秘密，但福克兰德的社会威望却使他能够保持优势地位，并继续揪住他的牺牲品不放，残酷无情地对他进行迫害。小说一方面暴露了特权阶级所拥有的权力，另一方面又揭示了下层人民所处的孤弱无援的地位。小说作为对现存社会的总控诉，补充了哲学著作《政治正义论》。

戈德温对年轻一代有非常大的影响。威廉·黑兹利特写道："人们谈论得最多的、最怀有敬意的、最常求教的，莫过于他［戈德温］了。每当谈论到自由、真理或正义时，他的名字总要被提到。"又说："在我们的时代里，还没有一部作品能像《政治正义论》那样给我国的哲学思想以如此沉重的打击。"

3. 威廉·布莱克——浪漫主义的先驱 一个多世纪以来，威廉·布莱克之所以被人记得，是因为他写下了一些短小的抒情诗（如《虎》）和一些可供人们引用的诗句，如：

在一粒沙里看到一个大地，
　在一朵野花里看到一个太空，
要把那"无限"放在你的手里，
　并掌握"无穷"在一个小时之中。

威廉·布莱克是在过去的五十年中，才被公认为英国浪漫主义的先驱的。

诗人和画家威廉·布莱克（1757—1827）生在伦敦，他以雕版为业。从青少年时期起，他就是个幻想家和梦想家。但他从未脱离当时的革命运动，如美国的独立宣言、法国的大革命和英国的激进主义运动。他的创作力在法国大革命时期最为旺盛，而在拿破仑战争时期以及随之而来的反动时期，他也从未丧失过他的活力。他为民族独立和民主革命而继续写作，并憧憬着一个较好的社会秩序。他的作品有：《诗歌素描》(1783)、《天真之歌》(1789)、《经验之歌》(1794)、《天堂与地狱的结合》(1793)，以及统称为《先知书》的许多其他诗歌。

威廉·布莱克的早期诗歌新颖、直白、易懂，后期作品却比较晦涩。在内容和形式上，他是最具有独创性的诗人之一。他有自己的神话，既非希腊的也非希伯来的。他按自己的方式进行写作，有时写格律诗，有时则写像华尔特·惠特曼那样的散文诗。

他的《先知书》始终充满了在新与旧、自由与奴役，或用他自己的语言来说，犹立生和福松或罗杰的宇宙斗争的幻景。例如，他的《四个巨人》(1797—1802)包含了九个关于从各种束缚中解放出来的幻景。后来，雪莱写《解放了的普罗米修斯》以及济慈写《海庇里安》就是用他的这种写作方法。

然而，浪漫主义绝不是一个统一的运动。一些著名的评论家已经提出：不要用“浪漫主义”(Romanticism)一语，而用“多种浪漫主义”(Romanticisms)这个词。

二　华滋华斯和柯勒律治

1. **华滋华斯及其早期诗歌**　威廉·华滋华斯(1770—1850)是

在易受影响的青年时期受到法国大革命影响的诗人之一。他出生于湖区的一个小村庄，是一个律师的儿子，曾在剑桥大学受过教育。1790年，他徒步游历欧洲大陆，那时法国大革命正在进行，他仿佛觉得当时的法国是“站立在黄金时期的顶点”，并指示着人性新生的前程。在完成于1798到1805年的《序曲》中，华滋华斯写道：

> 活在那个黎明更新时期真是幸福，
> 而年轻少壮则有如登天！啊！时代啊，
> 那些贫乏的、陈旧的、可怕的
> 习俗、法律和法令，立即引起了人们的注意，
> 好像它们是传奇中的国家的事物一样！
> ……消沉者
> 已经奋起，活跃者欣喜若狂！
> 在梦想中度过童年的人们，
> ……
> 被召唤来发挥他们的才能！
> 不在乌托邦，不在地下什么场所，
> 也不在某个隐蔽的岛屿，天知道在哪里！
> 而就在这个世界，这个属于
> 我们大家的世界，就在这里，最后
> 我们将找到幸福，或者什么都没有！

华滋华斯是戈德温的追随者。“扔下你的化学书，”他对一个法学院的青年学生说，“读一读戈德温论必然性的著作吧！”有一个时

期，法国大革命是他的唯一目标，而革命时期发生的重大事件则是他主要关注的事。他的诗《罪恶与伤悲》（1793—1794）就是在《凯莱布·威廉斯》的影响下写成的。这篇诗揭露了战争的苦难、刑法的不公正，以及特权阶级对毫无防卫能力的穷苦人的种种迫害。

2. 华滋华斯作为大自然的诗人 华滋华斯的革命热情没有维持多久。到1795年，他就已经从“人的世界”转向“大自然的世界”了，并逐步倒向英国保守主义的一边。

1798年，华滋华斯和他的朋友塞缪尔·泰勒·柯勒律治合作出版了一本题为《抒情歌谣》的小诗集，其中大部分诗作出自华滋华斯手笔，用简朴的语言描写简朴的生活，如：一个年龄太小还不懂得生死之别的小姑娘、一个双腿瘦削干瘪的老猎手、一个爱着她的弱智子女而忧心忡忡的母亲，等等。

1799年，华滋华斯隐退回到他的故乡，即湖区山地。他就在那里写诗，并度过了他漫长而平静的大半生。

华滋华斯最优秀的诗歌，大部分作于1797至1807年之间，表达了大自然以及与大自然朝夕相处的男男女女的客观真实状况（如露西组诗、《孤独的收割者》等）；他的政治性的十四行诗则表达了他的爱国情绪。但在他的大多数诗作中都有使大自然神秘化，并让自己沉溺于泛神主义幻想之中的倾向。他给大自然加上它并不具有的美德，而且常以田园牧歌式的朦胧不清的眼光，来看待他所选择的退隐地区的人们。湖区成了他的象牙之塔。

华滋华斯对农民阶级传统的和陈旧不变的特征写得很多，他颂扬逆来顺受，颂扬它的贫困、无知和偏狭，而且欣赏人们智力上的落后。在他生命的最后二十年里，力图维护过去的和过时的东西，他反对议会改革，反对天主教徒的解放。因此，在年轻一代的心目中，他是一个“落荒而逃的首领”。

3. 柯勒律治和遁世浪漫主义 像华滋华斯一样，塞缪尔·泰勒·柯勒律治（1772—1834）也一度对法国大革命怀有很高的热情。他是德文郡一个牧师的儿子，曾在基督公学和剑桥大学受过教育。1789年，他写了《巴士底狱的陷落》，流露了激进情绪。在戈德温的《政治正义论》影响下，他和友人罗伯特·骚塞曾打算移居美国，建立一个没有偏见，没有传统，而以“个人财产一体化”为基础的“乌托邦式的”社会。然而，他们对能否改造自己已被错误教育引入歧途的思想表示怀疑！他们二人在布里斯托尔演讲——骚塞讲历史，柯勒律治讲政治和宗教——借以筹措赴美旅费。他们的乌托邦计划始终未能实现。不久，他们两人都脱离了进步运动。

柯勒律治是一个梦想家，是浪漫主义的一个流派——遁世派——的代表。他的代表诗作《古舟子咏》、《克里斯托贝尔》和《忽必烈汗》都是些诗的梦幻，而那首残缺不全的《忽必烈汗》确实是在一次睡梦中诌成的，如果我们相信作者自述的话。柯勒律治的这些诗都是逃避现实的——逃往遥远和过去，躲进中世纪的传奇世界。《忽必烈汗》描绘了那个东方征服者的一座迷人的宫廷；《克里斯托贝尔》描写了一个幽灵出没的城堡；而《古舟子咏》则把我们引向魔鬼成灾的海域，至于那海域在哪里，没有人知道。

在这些诗中，各种人和人物形象都不是真实的，而是神秘的、超自然的。它们不是生活的映象，而是想象的影子。这些东西，他要求读者“能心甘情愿，不加怀疑地读下去”。

三　华尔特·司各特爵士

1. 华尔特·司各特的文学生涯　华尔特·司各特（1771—1832）出生于爱丁堡，是一个律师的儿子。他虽然在爱丁堡读过“中学”，但他主要靠自学完成自己的教育。他攻读法律，并取得律师资格。他担任过各种职务——二十八岁时在塞尔扣克郡当警长，三十五岁时出任爱丁堡刑事法庭秘书。他是诗人、小说家，也是政务活动家。

作为诗人，司各特成熟较晚。他最初从事苏格兰边区民谣的搜集和编辑。1805 年，他作为中世纪传奇的现代临摹作家，一举成名。他的《最后一个行吟诗人之歌》风靡一时。随后发表的诗作有：以亨利八世时期为背景的《马密恩》和描述苏格兰高地氏族战争的《湖上夫人》等。诗作展示了如画的景色、超自然的事物，以及骑士的服饰，节奏明快，激动人心。

司各特四十岁后才开始小说家的生涯。他身负公私职责，健康状况不好，但他以狂热的速度写了一大书架的小说。在十七年里，他创作了二十六部历史小说，其中有十六部描写各个时期的苏格兰历史，六部描写英格兰历史，四部描写英伦三岛以外地区的历史。在他之前，似乎还没有一位作家有过这么丰富多产的一生。

司各特不仅对历史感兴趣，而且还具有卓越的历史感。他的传奇诗和小说，尤其是那些描写中世纪的作品，常常含有某种逃避现实的因素。但他的最佳作品，如《中洛锡安之心》，对真实人的生活作了生动的描写，尽管这类描写往往带有浪漫主义幻想的色彩。

2. 传奇诗、民谣和歌　司各特的传奇诗，现在很少有人去诵读了，但其中的某些片断和许多抒情诗则是例外，如：《洛青瓦》（见《马密恩》)、《北方的竖琴》、《战士们,休息吧,战争结束了!》(见《湖上夫人》)、《布里格纳尔两岸》(见《罗克毕》)等。下面一节选自《最后一个行吟诗人之歌》,这节短小而有代表性的诗,显示了司各特的爱国主义精神:

有没有人,灵魂完全僵死,
他从来没有对自己诉说:
　“这是我的,我自己的故乡!”
他心里好像从未感到在发烧
当他倦游异国,拔脚回来,回到
　他的,他自己的故乡?
如果真有其人,那么你得留意,
　行吟诗人决不为他纵情献艺,
虽然他头衔很多,家世尊荣,
还有,财富可以无尽无穷,
不管他那些头衔、权力和财富,
这个集一切于己身的家伙,
活着时,应该取消他的名目,
死去时,人死心死,跌入
他所来自的污秽的尘冢,
没人哭泣,没人致敬,没人歌诵。

司各特还写过一些曲调优美的歌曲,散见在他的传奇诗和小说中。《中洛锡安之心》中那个不幸的疯姑娘临终前唱的“骄傲的梅西”之歌,颇有古代民谣中那种言简意赅、阴森可怖的味道:

骄傲的梅西大清早
  在树林里游荡；
可爱的知更雀美妙地
  在灌木上歌唱。

“告诉我，你快活的小鸟，
  什么时候我才团圆？”
“当六个盛装的绅士
  把你抬往教堂的墓园。”

“谁来为新娘铺床，
  鸟儿啊，你倒说说？”
“头发斑白的掘墓人，
  会及时为你挖好墓穴。”

“坟头墓石上的萤火虫
  将不停地为你照明；
教堂顶上的鸱鸺将歌唱：
  ‘欢迎你，骄傲的夫人。’”

3.《**中洛锡安之心**》 小说一开始，描述了1736年由波蒂厄斯引起的暴动。沉郁、坚定、愤怒的人们冲进爱丁堡监狱托尔布斯（通称“中洛锡安之心”），揪出了没有充分的理由就开枪扫射人群的波蒂厄斯上尉，并把他绞死。小说以此为背景，展开了主要情节——农家姑娘珍妮·迪恩斯的故事。珍妮的同父异母妹妹埃菲因犯杀婴罪而被监禁在托尔布斯。埃菲拒绝越狱逃跑(司各特告诉我们为什么),后被提审。在一个令人肠断的场面中,珍妮拒绝做伪证(司各特再一次告诉我们为什么),虽然这样做本可使她妹妹无罪获释。但珍妮离开家乡,徒步前往伦敦,向卡罗琳王后激昂陈情,最终为她妹妹求得赦免。司各特不仅给我们展示了一幅广阔多姿的生活画面,而且还让我们看到酿成这种局面并导致书中人物所作所为的那些社会和历史力量。

小说的中心部分是对埃菲的审讯(第二十二章)及其前因与后果。司各特作了认真的尝试,如实地反映苏格兰人民经历中的遭遇和忧虑。我们看到的审讯不仅仅是一个轰动一时的事件,而且是一个包含着对立的文化和不同的社会准则之间的具有重大意义的冲突事件,诸如:仁慈对世故、农民对城镇、苏格兰对英格兰,等等。

司各特是个守旧派,他崇尚地位,乐于使自己成为一个阿勃茨福特庄园的慈善地主。但由于他具有历史感,他对苏格兰低地的农民的可怜处境表示同情,与他们关系密切。

四 简·奥斯丁

1. **奥斯丁和她的世界** 简·奥斯丁(1775—1817)并不是一位浪漫主义作家,虽然她生活和工作在通常所谓的浪漫主义时期。她一生很少与外界接触。她出身于离温切斯特不远的斯蒂文顿的一个孩子众多而富有生气的牧师家庭。大约在二十岁左右,她开始写小说。她的小说每一部都经过修改,没有一部是一写完就出版的。她一共写了八部小说，只有四部是在她有生之年出版的，其中包括《傲慢与偏见》(1813) 和《埃玛》(1815—1816)。

简·奥斯丁在斯蒂文顿和肯特的乡间教区度过她的大半生，没有跟伟人与杰出人物往来的经历。她明智地把自己的工作局限于描写她那个由乡村绅士、淑女、势利眼、讨厌者和社会上的"向上爬者"等组成的小世界。她说："一个乡村中的三四户人家是合适的写作对象。"她十分谦虚地称自己的作品为"方方的二英寸大小的象牙小品"。她总是写她熟悉的和理解的，即教区生活，包括互访、漫步、野餐、叙谈、聚会、舞会、婚姻等活动。经常有一种说法，认为奥斯丁从来不写没有妇女参加的场景。

在奥斯丁的小世界里，当时的各种重大事件都被排除在外。拿破仑战争席卷而过，在她的书中几乎没有留下痕迹，而工业革命甚至连提也没有提到。她晚年还收到一封皇室发来的信，请她写写科堡皇族。但她没有动心。她颇有自知之明，始终不离开"自己那个富有想象的灵感的范围"。

2.《傲慢与偏见》和《埃玛》 在奥斯丁的各部小说中，最流行的是《傲慢与偏见》，而结构最完美的则是《埃玛》。

《傲慢与偏见》是以一句讽刺而饶有风趣的话开头的："一个举世公认的真理是，一个富有的单身汉必定需要一个妻子。"它描写朗伯恩的贝内特家里有五个女儿待嫁，而这时恰好有富有的单身汉来到朗伯恩和附近的地方。宾利和贝内特的长女简相爱，宾利的朋友达西则看上了简的妹妹伊丽莎白，但达西在一次舞会上因态度傲慢而伤害了伊丽莎白的自尊心，使她产生反感。由于一个人的傲慢，另一个人有偏见，彼此反感愈来愈深，但达西仍身不由主地迷恋着伊丽莎白。过了一段时间，伊丽莎白去英格兰北部旅行，碰巧与达西相遇，傲慢克服了，偏见消除了。故事最后以简和伊丽莎白结婚而结束。

《埃玛》也是写婚姻的。海伯里的埃玛姑娘，聪明自负，爱做媒人。她为本地的一个牧师挑选了哈利特姑娘。哈利特和埃玛不同，她温柔可爱，但不聪明，而且出身不好。后来，埃玛发现她的牵线活动却鼓励了埃尔顿来追求她自己，于是计划成为泡影。接着，她自己挑选了佛兰克·丘吉尔，而给哈利特挑了奈特利先生。但事实是，丘吉尔已与埃玛的情敌简·弗尔法克斯私下相许，而年龄不小的奈特利先生却已爱上了她自己。……就这样，她犯了一个又一个错误。但埃玛有个优点：她能进行自我检讨，并善于吸取经验教训。小说的基本思想是幻想与现实的对立。

两部小说中都有刻画得很出色的次要人物。在《傲慢与偏见》中，有古里古怪的贝内特先生、他那位愚蠢可笑的太太、笨拙乏味的柯林斯牧师和势利的凯瑟琳夫人等；在《埃玛》中，有吉诃德式的伍德豪斯先生、饶舌的贝茨小姐和“向上爬”的埃尔顿先生。

3. **小说家奥斯丁** 前面已经说过，奥斯丁的世界是一个小世界——朗伯恩世界或哈特菲尔德世界。她曾因没有写滑铁卢战役、法国大革命和工业革命而受到指责。这种指责是不中肯的。她写她所熟悉的和理解的，谁也不能指望一个小说家做比这更多的事。

不过，奥斯丁的世界不仅小，而且窄。她对阶级社会——少数人以牺牲多数人的利益而生活的社会——所持的全盘接受的态度限制了她的视野。诚然，谄上傲下、沾沾自喜、屈尊相待、漠不关心、形形色色的不仁慈的行为都遭到嘲讪，但阶级社会的根本基础未受到触动。奥斯丁判断标准的阶级基础大大地限制了她的小说的价值。

奥斯丁的长处在于她的现实主义创作方法，在于她展示了一个真实而具体的社会中实际存在着的各种有关行为和感情的问题。朗伯恩是什么样子，她就给它写成什么样子；哈特菲尔德是什么样子，她就给它写成什么样子。她让读者深切地了解到，小说中的男男女女在各个特定的情境中是如何解决各自的生活，特别是婚姻问题的。她专心致志地关注着人们的感情，并能热情而又客观地描绘他们的感情。

华尔特·司各特爵士很赞赏奥斯丁的写作艺术，他在日记中写道："那位小姐在描绘日常生活中的各种人物、各种感情和各种错综复杂的纠葛等方面，有独到的才能，这种才能真是奇特，我从来也没有见过。写些汪、汪、汪式的文章，像任何人一样，我也能动动笔，但用那样精巧细致的笔触，把日常生活中平凡的人和事写得饶有趣味……那是我办不到的。这样一位有才能的作家竟会死得那么早，真可惜啊！"奥斯丁于 1817 年逝世，年仅四十一岁。她的创作规模是无法与司各特那种史诗式的宏伟、民族性的广阔相比较的，但她是小说技巧的大师之一。

第九章

浪漫主义时期（下）

一 乔治·戈登·拜伦

1. **拜伦勋爵的早期经历** 乔治·戈登·拜伦（1788—1824）出身于一个古老的贵族家庭。他在伦敦出生，在苏格兰长大。他十岁时，叔祖父去世，他承袭了纽斯特德（诺丁汉郡）拜伦勋爵的封号。他是在哈罗公学和剑桥大学受的教育。1807年，他发表了《闲暇的时光》，遭到《爱丁堡评论》抨击。拜伦以《英国诗人与苏格兰评论家》（1809）作为回应，辛辣地讽刺了那些脱离当时进步运动的浪漫派诗人：杰弗里、骚塞、华滋华斯和柯勒律治。

1809年，他前往地中海各国游历，关于这些国家，他已读过了不少书籍。他取道葡萄牙和西班牙，航行至阿尔巴尼亚，最后到达雅典。1811年，他回到了英国，带回了几篇诗稿。1812年3月10日，当《恰尔德·哈罗德游记》的前两章发表时，他［用他自己的话来说］“一觉醒来，成了大名”。

拜伦达到法定年龄后，就进入了上议院。1812年，他在上议院发表演说，为诺丁汉的纺织机破坏者辩护，并替爱尔兰天主教徒讲话。作为一个演说家，他以谈锋犀利著称。他指出，黑人已经从压迫中解救出来了，但爱尔兰人还没有。他说道："我怜悯天主教农民，因为他们连生而为黑人的幸运都没有。"

有好几年，拜伦享有非凡的声誉。1815年，他同安娜·伊莎贝拉·密尔班克结了婚。夫妇之间不融洽，他们在第二年就分居了。但舆论反对拜伦，这使这位骄傲者中最骄傲的人饱尝了毁誉无常的滋味。1816年，他怀着鄙夷的情绪离开了英国，再也没有回来。

2. 拜伦勋爵在欧洲大陆 拜伦以后的岁月大部分是在瑞士和意大利度过的。在意大利，他写下了《恰尔德·哈罗德》的最后两章（1816），以及大部分诗剧和他的代表作《堂·璜》。他和叫作烧炭党的革命组织发生了联系，这个组织当时正在争取意大利的解放。1821年，希腊爆发了反对土耳其统治的战争。一直关注着希腊人事业的拜伦，雇佣了一队士兵，于1823年航向希腊的西海岸。他的威望很高，调解了革命领导人之间的分歧。1824年，他在梅索朗吉昂死于一场寒热病。

在去世前三个月，即在他三十六岁生日的那天的早晨，拜伦写下了他最后一首诗，其结尾两节如下：

如果你懊悔虚度了青春，
　为什么还要贪生？

光荣的葬身之地
就在这里，走上沙场，赶快出征，
在沙场上终止你的呼吸！

战士的坟墓，是你最好的归宿，
寻觅吧——人们总不爱寻觅；
看看你的周围，选好你的墓穴，
然后静静地安息。

拜伦是很少几个在欧洲享有崇高声誉的近代英国诗人之一。伟大的德国诗人歌德说，拜伦“毫无疑问被视为本世纪最伟大的天才”。拜伦的“才气大、力气大和口气大”给他以深刻的印象。他说：“英国人想怎样看待拜伦，就怎样去看待他吧。但有一点是肯定的，他们指不出一个和拜伦相似的诗人来。拜伦不同于其他所有的诗人，而总的来说，他更伟大。”

3.《恰尔德·哈罗德游记》《恰尔德·哈罗德》共有四章，是用斯宾塞章节体写就的一部诗。“恰尔德”这一词是采用该词的中世纪意义，表示一类骑士。诗在开始时似乎是要叙述哈罗德的冒险故事，但很快就转为对一系列风景秀丽和具有历史意义的地方的描绘，这些地方是他游历南欧时经过的。诗人在描述时，往往情不自禁地以抒情的笔触讴歌与这些地方有关的重大事件和伟人。

在前两章中，拜伦描述了在拿破仑战争时期的葡萄牙、西班牙、意大利、希腊和阿尔巴尼亚。他谴责专制统治并赞扬争取自由的人民：西班牙的游击队、阿尔巴尼亚的战士和希腊的爱国者。在第三和第四章中，拜伦歌颂了欧洲大自然的壮丽——莱茵河、阿尔卑斯山和地中海；歌颂了欧洲历史上的伟大人物，如卢梭和伏尔泰等；歌颂了欧洲的建筑和雕刻。诗中著名的片段有：阿尔卑斯山中的雷暴雨，对滑铁卢、莱蒙湖、罗马、威尼斯的描写，以及对海洋的诉说情怀。

这部长诗展现了拜伦式的英雄恰尔德·哈罗德的形象——他孤独无友，意志坚强，始终与传统世界势不两立，无时无刻不在支持人民实现其渴求自由的愿望。当时的社会使他深感憎恶，于是在孤寂中转向大自然，如在第四章第一百七十八节，他写道：

那荒无人迹的森林有一种乐趣，
那寂寥的海岸边另有一种欢欣，
茫茫的海中有一个社会，没有谁
能侵扰，在海啸中有一种乐声：
我不是不爱人类，但我更爱自然。[①]

4. **《堂·璜》：一部讽刺史诗** 《堂·璜》是拜伦的代表作，共分十六章，作于1818至1823年之间。前五章发表于1819至1821年之间，较后的一些发表于1823至1824年之间。诗中英雄的名字取自一个西班牙传说，但他的性格是拜伦自己的创造。

《堂·璜》比《恰尔德·哈罗德》故事性强一些。它叙述堂·璜所受的教育；他在海上的遇难以及他与希腊某一岛屿上一个海盗的女儿海黛的田园牧歌式的恋爱；它还讲述了他在君士坦丁堡土耳其王后处的逗留；他在俄罗斯战争中的英勇事迹；他作为女沙皇凯瑟琳

---

① 梁真译《拜伦抒情诗选》，新文艺出版社，1959年，第138页。

的宠臣，在彼得堡的淹留；他如何卧病而被送回英国去休养；以及他所目睹的英国。"所有的这些以及其他几件事"就是拜伦笔下的主题，是史诗般的宏伟主题。

堂·璜的历险以1780至1790年这段时间为背景(他参加了1790年苏沃洛夫所指挥的讨伐土耳其人的伊兹梅尔战役)，但诗中对欧洲社会所作的描绘，都是滑铁卢战役后那个反动专制时期的写照。拜伦的攻击锋芒直指暴君、战争、反动政客(如卡斯累利和惠灵顿)、不革命的诗人(如骚塞、华滋华斯和柯勒律治)，以及英国的各个方面。拜伦是欧洲所有国家的政治自由和民族解放的信使，他说："如果可能，我一定向顽石说法，要它们起来反抗暴君。"(第八章，第一百三十五节)。他在第九章第二十八节又写道：

只消挥动一只手臂，就会把它们的蛛网拂掉！
  如果没有蛛网，它们的毒汁和爪子
就起不了作用。善良的人们(应该说是各国的人民)，
  记住我的话吧，前进，不要停止！

此诗是用"八行诗体"写的，这原是一种意大利格律，拜伦把它改成为自己的诗体。诗的体裁是谈话式的，具有拜伦谈论时那种自然流畅，犹如"一条溪流，时而平稳，时而湍急，时而又飞流直下而形成瀑布—— 一首交织着哲学和俚语的诗—— 一首无所不具的诗"。

5. 较短的诗和抒情诗　除《恰尔德·哈罗德》、《堂·璜》和八部诗剧外，拜伦还写了许多较短的诗，《普罗米修斯》和《锡隆的囚徒》即其中两首。这两首诗都写于1816年。他念念不忘希腊神话中送火

者普罗米修斯的形象，并经常在他的诗歌中提到他。对拜伦来说，正如对其他像雪莱之类的革命浪漫主义作家一样，普罗米修斯是一个叛逆者，他因替人类效劳而受苦难。

你那百折不挠的灵魂——
　天上和人间的暴风雨
怎能摧毁你的果敢和坚忍！
　你给了我们巨大的教训：
你是一个标记，一个象征，
　标帜着人的命运和力量；
和你相同，人也有神的一半，
　是浊流来自圣洁的源泉；[①]

一个受苦者的形象，一个既仁慈而又敢于向强权挑战的人的形象，激起了拜伦的激情和信念，唤起了他的热情。弗朗索瓦·庞尼瓦尔（1493—1570）就是这样一个受苦者。他原是瑞士一个小修道院的院长，后来参加了那些要把日内瓦变成一个共和国的爱国者的行列。他在锡隆城堡中被囚了六年。这就是拜伦戏剧式的独白诗《锡隆的囚徒》和他的《关于锡隆的十四行诗》的主题。

锡隆！你的监狱成了一隅圣地，
　你阴郁的地面变成了神坛，
因为庞尼瓦尔在那里走来走去
　印下深痕，仿佛你冰冷的石板

① 梁真译《拜伦抒情诗选》，新文艺出版社，1957 年，第 101 页。

是生草的泥土！别涂去那些足迹！

因为它们在暴政下向上帝求援。[①]

在拜伦的抒情诗中，《她走在美的光彩中》、《那么，我们就再别去流浪了》、《献给音乐》和《今天我满了三十六岁》这几首诗几乎在所有的英文诗歌选集中都可以找到。

二 珀西·比希·雪莱

1. **雪莱的生平** 珀西·比希·雪莱（1792—1822）出生于一个富有的思想保守的家庭。从十岁到十八岁，他主要是在伊顿公学求学，在专制的制度管理下吃了许多苦头。在牛津大学时，在戈德温的《政治正义论》影响下，他发表了一份小册子，题为《无神论的必要性》。在被学校当局传见时，他既不肯放弃他的观点，也不肯向学校认错，于是就被开除了。

离开牛津后，他流落到伦敦，写文章抨击专制暴政和顽固思想。十九岁时，他同哈丽雅特·韦斯特布鲁克结了婚，因为她也具有那些激进观点。二十岁时，他在爱尔兰，为争取爱尔兰的自由而写作和活动。二十二岁时，他抛弃了哈丽雅特，与他老师戈德温颇有才华的女儿玛丽私奔到意大利。后来又回到伦敦，生活困窘，备受屈辱，他的父亲已经拒绝接济他。他写文章抨击政府、法律、使用武力、私有财产和婚姻等制度和习俗。1818年，他离开英国，前往意大利，从此再也没

① 梁真译《拜伦抒情诗选》，新文艺出版社，1957年，第147页。

有回来。

有一段时间，雪莱与拜伦经常见面。跟拜伦一样，雪莱也有一个叛逆的灵魂。他总是紧跟当时的进步运动，如意大利烧炭党的活动、英国争取改革的运动和希腊争取独立的斗争等。在意大利，他写下了许多诗篇，包括他的代表作《解放了的普罗米修斯》（1820）。

雪莱一直酷爱划船消遣。1822 年 7 月初，他驾船从莱里奇到里窝那去迎接他那位从英国来的意大利朋友利·亨特。返航途中，他遇上了风暴，落水溺死。火化之后，他的骨灰被葬在罗马的新教公墓里。在他的墓碑上写着他所喜爱的几句莎士比亚的诗句：

他消失的全身没有一处不曾
受到海水神奇的变幻，
化成瑰宝，富丽而珍怪。①

2.《麦布女王》和《伊斯兰的起义》 《麦布女王》（1813）是雪莱早期作品中最重要的。这是一首哲理诗，他在其中表达了他对当代社会和正统基督教的激进的看法。诗中的中心人物伊昂珊入睡后，梦见她被带到麦布女王的宫廷里，在那里她看到两种景象：一种景象是战争、迷信和商业给人类造成的苦难，另一种是人类通过理智、科学和纯洁的心灵而重获新生。

这首诗表明，他受到潘恩、戈德温和法国唯物主义者的影响。雪莱否认上帝的存在和基督的神性。他揭露基督教会是偏执和压迫这两者的同盟。他攻击国王们和政客们的专制暴政、教士们更加恶劣的

① 朱生豪译《莎士比亚全集》第 1 册，人民文学出版社，第 22 页。

专横跋扈和商人们的自私贪婪。只要废除宗教、恢复理智，人类将会很快摆脱政府、法律、使用武力、私有财产和婚姻之类人为的制度和习俗，而跨入一个自由、互爱和幸福的时代。

《伊斯兰的起义》(1818) 原名为《莱翁和西丝娜》，即诗中的男女主人公——他们是兄妹又是情侣。这是出版商所不能接受的，因此诗中两位主人公的关系以及诗的标题都被作了改变。诗中的主要人物是：一个献身于自由和正义事业的慷慨青年；他的同伴，一个慷慨、热情的女子；一个富有智慧的老人，他的年龄和阅历使他完全摆脱了自私的动机。这首诗以寓言的方式阐述了如何通过心灵高尚的男女的爱和献身精神，使世界从专制统治下解放出来。

这两首诗都遭到反对，而《麦布女王》更是一再受到禁止。但它们还是被非法地翻印出来，并在当时的激进分子中广泛传阅。

3. 《解放了的普罗米修斯》 雪莱最伟大的作品《解放了的普罗米修斯》是一部抒情诗剧。剧情以希腊神话为依据。在希腊戏剧家埃斯库勒斯的笔下，普罗米修斯是一个因把火种带给人类而触犯宙斯(朱庇特)的人。宙斯用铁链把他拴在一块岩石上加以惩罚，但普罗米修斯最终与宙斯和解了，因为他向宙斯透露了那个威胁着宙斯帝国的一项暗藏的危险。雪莱宣称，他对“使这个斗士与人类的压迫者和解这样一种软弱无力的戏剧结尾感到厌恶”。

雪莱的诗剧在开场的时候，普罗米修斯已经被折磨了许多个世纪，但他也获得了智慧和洞察力。朱庇特要求普罗米修斯透露那个秘密，但普罗米修斯拒绝屈从于这个暴虐无道的统治者，因此受了更多的折磨。远在印度的一个山谷里，居住着亚细亚，她是普罗米修斯的爱人，是爱之神灵。她请求永恒的命运之神德摩戈根向她透露普罗米修斯的命运，德摩戈根给她看了他们未来的景象。继之而来的是朱庇特的倒台，他因与忒提斯结婚而招致了那个暗藏的危险。他们所生的孩子大力神赫克里斯推翻了他，解放了普罗米修斯。于是，宇宙中所有的神灵都唱起了战胜专制的暴政、宽恕、友爱和不可征服的抗暴力量的凯歌。

诗中朱庇特代表着专制和独裁以及在他的权势之下所产生的那些东西，即那些使人类深感厌恶的制度和习俗。

那些粗俗的形状，人神共弃的形状，
它们采取了多种名称和多种方式，
奇怪、粗野、可怕、黑暗、可恶的东西
全是朱庇特，就是世界上的暴君。

普罗米修斯代表着人类的解放者和救星。

要忍受苦难，那“希望”所认为的无限的苦难；
要饶恕不义之行，那比死和夜更黑暗的冤案；
　要反抗权势，看来好像是万能的权势；
要爱，要忍受，要希望，直等到“希望”之神
在废墟上把它所想做的东西做成；
　既不变卦，也不动摇，也不泄气；
这个，像你的光荣一样，泰坦啊，就在这里
有安好、伟大和愉快，有自由和美丽；
只有这样才是生命、快乐、王国和胜利。

至于命运之神德摩戈根，他不仅仅是一场众神之战中的胜利者。他的胜利还表明：虽然“时间”可能站在人类的压迫者一边，但“永恒”终将是把胜利带给他们的救星。

《解放了的普罗米修斯》跟《伊斯兰的起义》一样，它呼吁年轻而慷慨的知识分子在滑铁卢之后的反动时期里，不要陷于绝望和变得玩世不恭：一场变革就要来临，雪莱就是这样想的。

4. 较短的诗和抒情诗　1819年的“曼彻斯特大屠杀”引起了雪莱“强烈的愤慨和同情”。他写下了《暴政的假面游行》。在这首诗中，他描述了那威胁着要粉碎“希望”的骷髅——专制暴君——的游行队伍及战车，劝告英国的劳工大众去抵抗剥削。他以同样的调子，写下了《致英国人之歌》：

> 英国人民啊，何必为地主而耕？
> 他们一直把你们当作贱种！[①]

除这两首外，还应提一下《颂歌，写于西班牙人重获自由之前》，这或许是这几首中最美的一首。

雪莱写了一些歌颂大自然的十分精美的抒情诗，但是这些诗决不只限于单纯的描写。由于诗人通过各种方式表现了表象世界与实在世界、现在与未来之间的对比，这就使得这些诗歌充满了活力。

沉重地压在他心上的是那个表象世界——我们不得不忍受的充满忧患的生活，以及在专制之下的种种不幸和极度的痛苦。但是忧郁的情绪常常让位于对那隐现在薄纱后面的理想的实在和未来的前

---

① 梁真译《雪莱抒情诗选》，人民文学出版社，1958年。

途的认识。西风,这严冬和死亡的先兆将会来到;但同样可以肯定的是:春天也不会很远了(《西风颂》)。我们是束缚在土地上的,我们最甜蜜的歌儿也是悲伤的;但云雀的曲子表现了爱情和欢乐的实在性(《云雀颂》)。如果说雪莱不时对现在感到悲观,他却从未丧失对未来的信心。他的诗歌对他来说有着这样一个目的:“唤起公众的希望,启发和改善人类”。

恩格斯在他的《英国工人阶级状况》(1844)中写道:“雪莱,天才的预言家,雪莱和拜伦,满腔热情的、辛辣地讽刺现今社会,他们的读者大多数是工人;资产者所读的只是经过阉割并使之适合于今天的伪善道德的版本。”①

三　约翰·济慈

1. 济慈的生平和性格　在那些伟大的浪漫主义作家中,没有比约翰·济慈(1795—1821)出身更为寒微的了。他的父亲是伦敦一个马厩的马夫长。他只受过五年的正式学校教育。十六岁时,在他的双亲去世后,他给一个兼做药剂师的外科医生当学徒。他在医院里学医,并于1815年获得外科开业许可证。但是真正使他感兴趣的不是外科,而是诗歌。

在学校的最后一年和学徒期中,他阅读了斯宾塞、弥尔顿和其他英国诗人的作品,对于古典艺术和文学也略有涉猎。他结识了进步的报纸撰稿人利·亨特,通过亨特又结识了雪莱和艺术家海登。1816年,

① 恩格斯:《英国工人阶级状况》,人民出版社,1956年,第291页。

他写下了著名的十四行诗《初读查普曼所译荷马史诗》——这是他受到公众注意的第一首诗。

济慈开始以写诗为职业。他一遍又一遍地阅读莎士比亚的作品，他对弥尔顿也非常关注，并进行认真的思考。1818年，他发表了《恩底弥翁》，此诗受到了反动批评家的疯狂的攻击。但他并不因此而气馁。他说："道路是通过应用、学习和思索而开辟出来的。"

济慈最好的诗，几乎都是在他人生最后两年半的时间里写成的，如《圣阿格尼斯节前夕》、重要的颂诗和十四行诗，以及《海庇里安》的两种稿本。他的健康日趋恶化，经济也越来越困难。在医生的劝告之下，他于1820年乘船到意大利，希望在气候比较暖和的地方能够恢复健康。1821年，他死于肺结核，遗体葬于罗马的新教徒公墓。雪莱在比萨听到噩耗之后，写了《阿多尼斯》一诗，这是一个天才献给另一个天才的颂诗。

济慈在政治上是一个热情的自由主义者。他十分关注当时的社会和政治问题。他反对已成为一种制度的基督教，并拒绝接受它的神学理论。他以毕生的精力寻求生活和艺术中的美和爱。

2. 《恩底弥翁》和《圣阿格尼斯节前夕》 《恩底弥翁》是一首叙事长诗，也是济慈最长的一篇作品。它叙述了希腊神话中牧人恩底弥翁和月神辛锡厄的恋爱，这是民间流传的凡人和神之间爱情的一个古老传说。诗的主题是探索美和爱的理想。诗的开头几行表达了济慈最深刻的信念之一：

美的事物给人以永恒的欢乐；
它的魅力与日俱增；还有呢，

它决不会化为乌有；

济慈在《恩底弥翁》中对爱情和激情的讴歌，正如在他早期一般诗歌中那样，乃是他对英国资产阶级清教主义的顽固和虚伪所作的一首抗议的抒情诗。济慈渴望一种不为少数几个幸运者所独享，而是为人人所共享的幸福。他用感官方面的细节来描绘美的欢乐和享受，认为这种欢乐和享受是人人都可得到的，是普通人同神所共有的。诗人的这种自由思想，以及诗中追求欢乐者的形象，在托利党的刊物——《布莱克伍德》和《季刊》杂志中受到非难。

《圣阿格尼斯节前夕》是一篇诗体故事，一首以反封建为背景的对美和爱的赞歌。按照天主教的传统说法，如果姑娘们在圣阿格尼斯节（1 月 21 日）前夕，举行了某些她们喜爱的仪式，那么在夜里她们就会像在幻觉之中那样看见她们未来的丈夫。很久以前，就在这样一个夜里——一个酷寒的冬夜，一个名叫马德琳的姑娘确实这样做起梦来，醒来时却发现她的幻觉变成了现实。在她身边，她的情人波菲罗在俯视着她，但他的家族与她的家族有不共戴天的世仇。于是他们俩便私奔了：

他们俩不见了；啊，很久很久以前
一对情人在风暴之中逃走了。

在波菲罗和马德琳之间，青春爱情的热烈与冬夜的严寒和封建习俗的冷酷形成了对比。在英诗中，这个故事给人们的美感印象是无与伦比的。它令人想到莎士比亚的《罗密欧与朱丽叶》。

3.《海庇里安》的两种稿本 济慈的最大抱负是写一部史诗，他认为最伟大的诗歌是戏剧性的或史诗性的。他最初的计划是把《海庇里安》(1819)扩展成一部约十卷的长诗，但最后只完成了两卷半。诗的主题是神话里叫作泰坦的巨人们被真正的神所推翻的事，这些神乃是济慈在查普曼所译的"荷马"和希腊神话中读到的。他打算把宇宙原始统治者的垮台解释为一种历史的必然。当由阿波罗来体现的更高贵的权力出现时，泰坦是注定要垮台的，因为阿波罗是这样的一个神：他的力量寓意于美、明智和诗歌之中。《海庇里安》在其所涉及的无限的广度上，在其所包含的哲学寓意和所刻画的泰坦形象上，都类似拜伦和雪莱的诗歌，例如雪莱的《解放了的普罗米修斯》。对于济慈，正如对于雪莱一样，诸神的垮台就意味着存在着的一切必然要进行改变：它象征着生命的发展，象征着一种前进的运动。

《海庇里安》有两种稿本。第一稿题为《海庇里安：一个片断》。从艺术上来看，这个稿子比较匀称和一致。但是，题为《海庇里安的垮台：一场梦》的第二稿则更具有意义，因为济慈对一个重大问题的看法在其中有最成熟和最充分的表述。这个在他看来无论何时都至关重要的问题是：什么是诗人的最高职责以及他对他的同胞们应持什么样的态度。在《海庇里安的垮台：一场梦》的序幕中，济慈描述了一个真正诗人发展的各个阶段。

4. 十四行诗和颂歌 在十四行诗和颂歌中，济慈找到了抒发他诗歌激情的方式。在十四行诗的创作上，莎士比亚是他的主要启蒙者和楷模；他的许多十四行诗仅次于他所师承的人的作品。评论家从他的十四行诗中选出了八首，认为它们堪与英语里最好的诗作相提并论，而且几乎是完美无瑕的。现据评论家的评价，将每首诗的第一行依次列举如下：

在黄金的国土上我曾到处旅游
当我害怕我可能不复存在的时候
可爱的姑娘们清醒地到这里来呀
四个季节谱成了一年的旋律
明亮的星星！但愿像你那样坚定不移
啊，静夜里轻轻地涂抹香膏的睡神
白昼消失了，甜蜜的东西也都消失了
当赫尔墨斯一度用他轻盈的羽翼起飞的时候

不过，在所有的抒情诗中，对济慈最适合的却是颂歌。他强烈的个人感情和爱好——他对秋天的可爱和对夜莺歌声所感到的喜悦、他对美的事物瞬息即逝所感到的忧伤，以及他对所有这一切在艺术和文学中获得新的不朽生命所抱的热情——都在他的颂歌（《秋颂》、《夜莺颂》、《忧郁颂》和《希腊古瓮颂》）中直接，而不是通过寓言的方式得到了抒发。不拘形式的颂歌，要比十四行诗的篇幅宽阔一些，在音调上更加庄严、更加崇高，在音律和诗行上也更富有变化，因此颂歌这种形式最适合济慈表达他的性情——他的严肃、他的沉思，他在探讨一个思想时从容不迫的态度，以及他爱用大量的具体形象来发挥和丰富这个思想的特点。

第十章

维多利亚时期（上）

一 “残酷的30年代和饥饿的40年代”

1. **通俗的社会抗议诗歌** 第一次议会改革法案（1832）之后的三四十年是工业资本主义时代。资产阶级利用新的工商业条件成长兴旺起来，并变得富有而重要。另一方面，贫穷的劳苦大众却在雇主的剥削之下过着悲惨的生活，因而历史上的19世纪30年代和40年代被称为“残酷的30年代和饥饿的40年代”。

这种“英国的状况”产生了许多描写社会抗议的诗歌。在30年代，被称为“谷物法诗人”的埃比尼泽·埃利奥特写下了两首关于失业和劳资之间斗争的诗歌（《歌》和《战歌》）。在40年代，伊丽莎白·巴雷特的《孩子们的哭喊声》和托马斯·胡德的《衬衫之歌》、《劳工之歌》及《悲叹之桥》都发表于1843年，流传甚广。

《衬衫之歌》在法国和德国也很流行。人们把它印在棉布手帕上，在街头巷尾传颂：

指痛无人知，目肿难为哭。
贫女手中线，身上无完服。
一针复一针，将以救饥腹。
穷愁难自聊，姑唱缝衣曲。[①]

恩格斯评述道："这首诗使资产阶级女郎们流下了不少怜悯的但毫无用处的眼泪。"[②]

2. **宪章派诗歌** 30年代和40年代是宪章运动的年代，列宁把这个运动称为第一次广泛的、真正群众性和政治性的无产阶级革命运动。[③]在这一运动中，产生了很多刚健有力的散文和一些诗歌。当时的通俗诗歌是多种多样的，其中有许多都已经散佚。在盖斯凯尔夫人的《玛丽·巴顿》中，我们还能看到几首。在恩格斯的著作中，也保存了一首：

不列颠的儿女，虽说你身为奴隶，
但这不是造物主上帝的本意。
他赋予我们大家以生命和自由，
但决不，决不让任何人去当奴隶。

① 刘半农译文。
② 恩格斯：《英国工人阶级状况》，人民出版社，1956年，第261页。
③ 列宁：《第三国际及其在历史上的地位》，《列宁全集》卷29，第276页。

在宪章派诗人中，有爱德华·米德、埃比尼泽·琼斯和欧内斯特·琼斯。欧内斯特·琼斯（1819—1869）是其中最杰出的一个，他因发表革命演说而被监禁两年。有一段时间，他曾是马克思和恩格斯的追随者。他是《民主之歌》组诗的作者，在这组诗中，以《下层阶级之歌》最为有力、最为成功：

我们耕地播种——十分低贱，
　我们用手挖肮脏的泥沼，
直到金色的麦子长满了平原，
　山谷里长满芬芳的干草。
我们的地位——十分十分低贱，
　就在地主双脚下边，
我们虽低贱——还配种种庄稼，
　我们太低贱，不配吃面包。[①]

《雇佣劳动者之歌》[②]是用同样的调子写成的一首诗，它号召人们起来行动，其所用叠句如下：

未来的日子，降临的希望，
　不义终将在公理前折腰；
鼓起一点点勇气，弟兄！
　把那个明天变成——今朝。[③]

---

① 袁可嘉译《英国宪章派诗选》，第118页。
② 又译《雇农之歌》。——编注
③ 袁可嘉译《英国宪章派诗选》，第121页。

3. **批判现实主义的兴起** “英国的状况”在19世纪最流行的文学形式——小说——中得到了更充分的反映。

在英国，和其他资本主义国家一样，也存在着两个阶级和两种文化：即一方为落后的、反动的有钱阶级；另一方为进步的、革命的无产阶级。这个时代最好的小说，不是在资产阶级时髦趣味的土壤上繁荣起来的，而是在反对这些趣味的过程中兴盛起来的。它向整个文明世界披露了资产阶级见不得人的精神世界，因而做出了具有历史意义的贡献。马克思在1854年写道：

> 现代英国的一派出色的小说家，以他们那明白晓畅和令人感动的描写，向世界揭示了政治和社会的真理，比起政治家、政论家和道德家合起来所做的还多。他们描写了资产阶级的各个阶层：从那把各种“事务”轻蔑地看作某种庸俗事情的“极可尊敬的”食利者和公债持有者，一直到小铺老板和诉讼代理人。如同狄更斯、萨克雷、夏洛特·勃朗蒂和盖斯凯尔夫人所描写的那样，他们都自命不凡、拘于小节、欺压弱者、不学无术。文明世界证实了那以痛斥的警句形式对这一阶级所下的判决，这个警句是：“对上谄媚，对下欺压。”①

以下各节所要谈的是这一时期的伟大现实主义作家狄更斯、萨克雷、勃朗蒂姊妹和盖斯凯尔夫人。

① 《马克思恩格斯论艺术》卷2，人民文学出版社，1963年，第402页。

二 查尔斯·狄更斯

1. **狄更斯的生平和著作** 查尔斯·狄更斯(1812—1870)的童年是很不幸的。他的父亲是海军部门的一名小职员,为人和蔼可亲,但不会节俭度日,有好些年因债务被关在监狱里。狄更斯在十一岁时,就得在伦敦一家黑鞋油作坊里,从早到晚地从事令人烦闷的劳动。很久以后,甚至在成名之后,他也无法忘记这些艰苦的岁月。

狄更斯只连续上过两年学,但他在父亲家里读了所能找到的一切书籍,就这样补足了他应受的大部分教育。十五岁离开学校后,他先做了一个律师的书记员,然后又当了一家报社的记者。从早年起,他就养成了徒步漫游伦敦的习惯,往往一天要走十几英里的路,他更喜爱在夜间漫步,观察那些贫困受压迫的人的生活。他深知受苦是怎么一回事。自始至终,他都保持着对穷人的同情。

二十四岁时,狄更斯以“连载”的形式发表了《匹克威克外传》(1836—1837),这是一系列幽默和讽刺小品,获得了全国性的成功。随后他发表了《奥列佛·特维斯特》[①](1837—1838)和《尼古拉斯·尼克贝》[②](1838—1839)等成熟的小说,前者揭露了济贫院的黑暗,后者抨击了恃强欺弱的小学校长。三十岁时,狄更斯在美国游历了五个月。他在《美国札记》和《马丁·朱述尔维特》两本书中,对美国资产阶级的庸俗和虚伪进行了严厉的批判。

狄更斯到处目睹资产阶级社会的罪恶,他在连续发表的一些小说中揭露并痛斥了这些罪恶。这些小说有:《董贝父子》(1846—

---

① 又译《雾都孤儿》。——编注

② 又译《少爷返乡》。——编注

1848)、《大卫·科波菲尔》(1849—1850)、《荒凉山庄》(1852—1853)、《艰难时世》(1854)、《小杜丽》(1855—1857)、《双城记》(1859)和《远大前程》(1860—1861)。在二十九年里,他一共发表了二十二部小说,其中有十四部可列为他的主要小说。同时,他还编辑期刊、积极从事慈善事业、参加业余的戏剧演出,并把他作品中的片段作朗读表演。他劳累而死,终年五十八岁,留下了最后一部小说《埃德温·德鲁德的秘密》尚未完成。

2. 《奥列佛·特维斯特》 1834年通过了新的济贫法。按照该法令,建立了新的贫民收容所,即济贫院。贫而无告者已不再是慈善事业的对象了,他们被集中在监狱一般的建筑物内,即所谓"济贫法的巴士底狱"里,由一些官员来管理。那些官员毫无教养,对他们看管下的贫民往往毫无同情之心。《奥列佛·特维斯特》揭露了这些按济贫法履行其职责的各级官员和当局的残忍和卑鄙。

小说是以奥列佛在一所济贫院里的诞生和他母亲的死亡开始的。他母亲原先是在马路上被人发现的。奥列佛在那里被养大,十岁时在一所济贫院棺材店里当学徒,后来逃走,流落到伦敦,落入一个肮脏的贼窝头子老费金的魔掌中。这个贼窝是伦敦无家可归的流浪儿和凶残的盗贼的聚集之地。奥列佛不是被迫去帮助费金一伙扒窃,便是被迫从窗口爬进一所乡间住宅,把门打开,放进盗贼。下层社会的黑暗生活被生动而真实地描绘出来。奥列佛是一个具有象征意义的人物:他代表着所有济贫院里的孤儿,而他的境遇充满着戏剧性的象征力量。

跟狄更斯的其他许多小说一样,《奥列佛·特维斯特》中也包含了一些不大可能的事。奥列佛运气好,能被正派人收养——先是被那个仁慈的老绅士收养，而老绅士原来是他父亲的亲密朋友；后来又被那个仁慈的夫人收养，而她呢，原来是他的姨母！这些天意般的巧合，再加上不真实的情感和肤浅的感伤成分，构成了这部小说中最薄弱的部分。

3. **《大卫·科波菲尔》** 《大卫·科波菲尔》是狄更斯心爱的一部小说。它通过对一个人的生活经历的描述，展现了一幅真实生活的多方面的画面，狄更斯在描绘中把自己的生活线索也编了进去。

大卫在他继父莫德斯通先生的摆布之下，过着不幸的家庭生活，后来又在冷酷无情的克里克尔粗暴的管理之下，过着同样不幸的学校生活。母亲一去世，他便被送到一家黑鞋油作坊里当童工。他结识了那位独特的米考伯先生，这位先生使我们联想到狄更斯自己的父亲。大卫前往多佛，请求他仅仅听说过的贝特西·特罗特伍德姨婆的帮助。姨婆决定收养他；从此以后，他便开始了新的生活。书中主要的自传性的线索在这里开始分叉，引出了一连串次要的情节。贯穿小说的主题乃是大卫的奇遇。他爱上了朵拉，同她结了婚。朵拉死后，他娶了姨婆的律师代理人的女儿，“从此以后幸福地”生活着。

次要情节之一是关于小埃米莉的故事。她是亚茅斯一个迷人的渔家孤儿。她被大卫以前的一个名叫斯蒂尔福斯的英俊贵族同学所诱骗，后来又遭到抛弃。另一个次要情节是关于一个律师的书记员尤赖亚·希普的故事。他是世界上最低贱的、最卑鄙的家伙。小说里的每一个次要情节，如同主要情节一样，由于有许多附属的枝节而进一步复杂化了。随着插曲和人物的增多，这部小说也就成为人类生活潮流本身的象征了。

《大卫·科波菲尔》中的阶级倾向性是值得重视的。半贵族式的人物——斯蒂尔福斯一家和另外几个人物——被明确地划入"坏的"一类人物之中。富有的资产阶级人物,除了贝特西·特罗特伍德和迪克先生之外,要不是恶棍(如莫德斯通)、说谎者(如斯彭洛先生),就是道德上的懦弱者(如威克菲尔德先生)。占据舞台中心和赢得我们同情的,却是中等偏下层阶级的人物(如米考伯先生)和无产阶级人物(如佩格蒂一家)。把斯蒂尔福斯和佩格蒂两家摆在一起,表现出某种非常接近于天然的阶级对立的情况。

4. **狄更斯的后期小说** 狄更斯在后期小说里,触及了资产阶级社会中,基本结构所产生的越来越大的问题。这表明他与资产阶级社会分歧越来越大。

《荒凉山庄》是对司法机构的拖沓进行的抨击。狄更斯写道:"英国司法界的一大原则就是为它自己做生意。在那狭窄的曲折的司法程序中,并没有一条独特的、明确的、始终坚持的原则可言。"作者介绍了一群司法界的代表人物,其中有大法官,他的邪恶行为决定着整个司法事务。

《艰难时世》是狄更斯根据他自己对曼彻斯特工业状况的观察写成的。小说中的反面人物是工厂主兼银行家又兼雇主的庞得贝。小说抨击了由曼彻斯特学派所代表的整个资本主义伦理,如自由放任主义、经济学和伦理学。

《双城记》是狄更斯所有小说中最成功的富有戏剧性的小说。它的基本情节是曼奈特医生被囚禁及其后果。小说对圣安托万郊区、对攻打巴士底狱前的准备、对巴士底狱之占领、对九月"大屠杀",以及对革命法庭都作了生动的描写。他以历史的真实性描绘了群众的反抗,把它写成一次正义的、必不可少的人民起义,因为人民的苦难和贫困已经恶化到再也无法容忍的程度。狄更斯为法国大革命所作的辩护，按照当时英国舆论的标准来衡量，是很偏激的。但是，狄更斯附和了当时的看法，认为监狱中被清洗的“受害者”主要是无辜的贵族，他们之所以有罪仅仅是因为他们属于贵族阶级。

《双城记》明确地显示了狄更斯对起义人民的同情，对起义本身的同情，甚至在一定的限度内对人民打击压迫者的愤怒复仇行为的同情。

5. 狄更斯作为一个小说家 拉尔夫·福克斯在其《小说与人民》中评述道：“在狄更斯身上，他们[维多利亚时代的人]找到了一个天才，他使小说恢复了它的整个史诗的性质。他那丰满的心灵所创造的故事、诗歌和人物已永远进入了世界上所有英语国家和地区人们的生活之中。他的有些人物几乎无人不知，他们已经成为我们近代民间文学艺术的一个部分。这确实是作家们所能达到的最高成就。他只有凭借他的天才、博爱和一种对生活诗意的感受，才能达到这种成就。”

狄更斯热爱生活，但他憎恨他生活于其中的社会制度。他揭露济贫院、债务监狱、私立学校、工厂制度和法庭。他抨击了那些伪善者、因循守旧的虔诚者以及他们的“慈善”。他尽量利用他的天赋的观察能力——即洞察事物所有细节的能力，并尽量发挥他的讽刺和谴责的才能。邦布尔、莫德斯通、尤赖亚·希普、佩克斯尼夫以及其他一些恶棍，不仅仅是遭到了揭露，而且也可以说是在读者面前受到了肉体上的鞭笞。

狄更斯也有他的局限性。他相信普通人民。在他去世前不到一年所作的一篇讲演中，他明确表示他对统治英国的人们的信心是“无穷的小”，而对被统治的人们的信心却是“无限的”。但不知何故，他认为对如此严重的罪恶，唯一可行的医治办法——即进行彻底的社会革命，在当时似乎是完全不可能实现的。他受到宪章运动的影响，但他既不相信它的政治纲领，也不相信它的鼓动方法。

作为一个小说家，狄更斯受到他那个时代的局限，那个时代所要求表达的是感伤情绪、保持沉默和维持体面。他不得不在道德上和语言上接受资产阶级社会的习俗。许多生动有力的场面因受感伤主义的浸染而变得暗淡了，许多出色的篇页由于情节奇异、追求惩恶扬善的结局而被破坏了。

三　威廉·梅克庇斯·萨克雷

1. **萨克雷的生平和著作**　萨克雷（1811—1863）和查尔斯·狄更斯常常被人们放在一起来加以比较。在某些方面，他们两人是很相似的：他们都是从当新闻记者开始其文学生涯的，两人都揭露资产阶级社会的罪恶。但萨克雷主要致力于揭露上层社会的风俗习惯和中产阶级的傲慢自负。他一向不如狄更斯那样为人们所喜爱，虽然在40年代后期和50年代，他与狄更斯在小说方面分享着最高的荣誉。

萨克雷出生在加尔各答，是东印度公司一个官员的儿子。他曾就读于查特公学和剑桥大学。剑桥毕业后，他在德国闲游了一段时间，会见了年迈的歌德。之后他就从事新闻工作。他以各种笔名对上层社会作了许多速写，即对恶棍、无赖和盗贼们所作的速写。1844年，他不再写流氓无赖，而是开始写势利者之流。那个时代是势利者甚为得逞的时期，萨克雷仔细观察了形形色色的势利者和他们的各个方面，揭露了他们装腔作势和虚伪的特性。

1847年，萨克雷三十六岁时，发表了《名利场》，确立了他作为一个小说家的声誉。这本书是对上层社会生活的一种愤世嫉俗的讽刺。他说："我不能不接受我所观察到的真理，并且描述我所看到的事物。"几年后，当他经过伦敦青年街他曾住过的小屋时，他对一位朋友说："跪下来吧，你这个无赖，因为《名利场》是在这里写的；而我呢，要和你一道跪下，因为我自己就很看重这部小说。"

高尔基把萨克雷列入西欧最卓越的作家行列里。他写道："斯威夫特、拉伯雷、伏尔泰、勒萨日、拜伦、萨克雷、海涅、维尔哈伦、阿纳托尔·法朗士以及其他许多作家，是对统治阶级罪恶的极其真实而又有力的揭露者。"

1848年以后，萨克雷作品中的现实主义有所削弱。1848年的革命运动——伦敦的宪章派请愿和巴黎工人的七月起义使他感到惊恐。他越来越甚地从当时的社会转向过去的历史。他对18世纪的兴趣，在他的《英国幽默作家》和《四位乔治》的讲稿中表现了出来，也在他的历史小说《亨利·艾斯芒德》和《弗吉尼亚人》里也表现了出来。

2. 《名利场》的故事梗概 《名利场》虽然是以滑铁卢战役时期为背景，但实质上是一部关于当代生活的小说。小说的中心人物是蓓基·夏普，一个出身比较低微而又身无分文的孤女。摆在她面前的只有两条路：一条是屈从于永远为人奴仆的消极道路，另一条是独自进行反抗的积极道路。蓓基选了第二条道路。

离开平克顿学校后，蓓基到她的同学温柔娴静的阿米莉亚·赛特笠家里去作客。这是一个很有钱的人家。在这里,她遇到了阿米莉亚的哥哥乔斯,他未婚,是一个肥胖、笨拙而又腼腆的人。她立即对他采取行动,然而没有达到目的。之后她在毕脱·克劳莱爵士家中获得了一个家庭教师的职位。克劳莱是一个男爵,肮脏邋遢、满嘴脏话、整日酗酒,并且毫无礼貌。在这里,她迷住了毕脱爵士的儿子罗登·克劳莱上尉,一个赌徒。

随后传来了要军队开到滑铁卢的号令。克劳莱上尉和阿米莉亚的新婚丈夫奥斯本上尉,同成千上万的英国军人都走上了战场。蓓基前往布鲁塞尔,与她在那里遇到的人搅在一起。萨克雷对滑铁卢所作的描绘并不是对那场战争的直接写照,而是那些等待战争结局的平民所想象的一种情景。这是一篇非凡的文学杰作。

奥斯本上尉在滑铁卢战役中阵亡。赛特笠家族衰败了,阿米莉亚也陷于贫困之中。她最后接受了举止笨拙但心地善良的都宾上尉的求婚——都宾是一个杂货商的儿子,多年来为她效劳并倾心于她。与此同时,蓓基继续向上爬。她与罗登摆设门面,过着不稳定却时髦的生活。她接受了上流社会中地位最高的斯丹恩勋爵的礼物和所献的殷勤。这种关系后来被发现,醒悟了的罗登把斯丹恩勋爵打倒在地,并把他赶了出去。蓓基躲了起来,把她所能拿到的钱财统统带走了。数年后她又和乔斯建立了联系,乔斯尽其所能地满足她:为了她,他在保险公司给自己投保,而后很快就去世了。蓓基利用这笔钱在巴斯的体面社会中站稳了脚根,在她的周围聚集了一群很有势力的优秀人士,他们认为她是一位备受伤害的女子。

3. **社会讽刺小说《名利场》** 《名利场》展现了资产阶级社会以及该社会所产生的人与人之间的关系。萨克雷戳穿了名利场中的虚伪，揭示了在名利场优雅炫目的表面之下令人作呕的、残暴的、卑鄙的丑恶本质。

在《名利场》中，萨克雷主要描写的是这样一些人：正如他所说的，"除了荣华富贵什么也不崇拜，除了功名利禄什么也看不见"。他反对贵族制度。他的"温良的"读者们曾提出抗议，说他把毕脱爵士"描写得过火"了，又说在他那个社会阶层中不可能有这么样的粗鄙。萨克雷回答说："在整部书中，那个人物几乎是唯一的一幅精确无误的肖像。"老奥斯本对乔治死亡的反应、巴里亚克里斯夫人在布鲁塞尔坐在她那无马可驾的马车里的情景、对斯丹恩勋爵的住宅和家庭的描写——所有的这些插曲都是极其成功的。

至于蓓基·夏普，她是所有小说中塑造得最成功的人物之一。她具有活力和魅力。人们随着她游历了名利场。她是人们决不会错认的一个人，而且（和奥列佛·特维斯特一样）她具有一种典型的象征品质：她代表着具有反抗精神的每一位女性，对某些社会习俗强加在她们身上的屈辱进行抗争。

然而萨克雷也有他的局限性。他对上层社会的讽刺总是被他那种松散而笼统的冷嘲热讽的评论所冲淡。萨克雷曾面对这个世界进行了观察，但不想继续观察下去了。这部小说的结尾最软弱无力：

> 唉，浮名浮利，一切虚空！我们这些人里面谁是真正快活的？谁是称心如意的？就算当时遂了心愿，过后还不是照样不满意？——来吧，孩子们，收拾起戏台，藏起木偶人，咱们的戏已经演完了。[1]

① 杨必译《名利场》卷2，第374页。

4.《亨利·艾斯芒德》 当我们从《名利场》转到《亨利·艾斯芒德》(1852)时,我们即是从滑铁卢战役时期转到了布莱宁战役时期。这个故事是由亨利·艾斯芒德以回忆自己的童年和青年时代的形式来讲述的。艾斯芒德是老卡斯乌德勋爵的一个私生儿子,而在新卡斯乌德勋爵的家中长大。他忠于年轻的卡斯乌德夫人,同她的儿子佛兰克结为好友,并喜爱她的漂亮的女儿比阿特丽克斯。他上了大学,投入了政治运动,参加了对法战争,还从事过其他活动。

故事中有一部分是叙述比阿特丽克斯的生平的。正如《名利场》中蓓基·夏普一样,比阿特丽克斯是一个“向上爬”的人。像蓓基一样,比阿特丽克斯也是一个很会打算盘的人,自私自利,一心只想嫁入一个高贵家庭。终于,她抓住了汉密尔顿公爵。但是就在举行婚礼的前夕,比阿特丽克斯的美梦破灭了,因为公爵在一场决斗中突然死于莫恩勋爵之手。

卡斯乌德一家都是斯图亚特王朝的同情者,正在进行阴谋活动,想把詹姆斯二世的儿子詹姆斯·斯图亚特拥上王位。亨利·艾斯芒德前往法国,秘密地把斯图亚特王子带回英国。这时当朝的君主安妮女王正在弥留之际,王子被带去晋谒了她,她似乎也赞成他继承王位。于是便确定了日子来正式宣布他为女王的继承人。到了那天,斯图亚特王朝的同情者都前来集合,王子却不见了。因为比阿特丽克斯已把王子勾引到卡斯乌德城堡去了。当王子回到伦敦时,为时已晚。女王已逝,而乔治一世已当了国王!故事以亨利·艾斯芒德结婚为结尾,但与他结婚的并不是比阿特丽克斯本人,而是她的母亲。为此作者受到许多读者的谴责。

小说生动地刻画了安妮女王时代的英国社会里的人和习俗，同时也描绘了战争、决斗、党派政治、社会上的罪恶和官员的腐败。艾迪生、斯蒂尔、斯威夫特、愚蠢而堕落的王位觊觎者、莫恩和汉密尔顿，以及马尔巴勒公爵，在作者笔下无不栩栩如生。对比阿特丽克斯这个"向上爬者"的性格的刻画极为卓越。萨克雷的弱点在于他缺乏完整的历史感。萨克雷虽然批判了腐败的贵族、政府体制以及根据1689年的人权法案所制定的宪法，但他没有把历史写成是人民起着决定性作用的一个过程。萨克雷很同情地谈到了人民以及他们困厄的命运，但是他没能在人民身上看到一种决定历史发展的动力。

四　勃朗蒂姊妹和盖斯凯尔夫人

1. 勃朗蒂姊妹　勃朗蒂姊妹——夏洛特（1816—1855）、爱米丽（1818—1848）和安妮（1820—1849）——是在一所名为霍沃思的牧师住宅里长大的，它位于约克郡沼泽地上一座荒凉的、风吹雨打的村庄附近。住在那一带的人，一类是农民、手织机织工和机械化制造厂里的雇工；另一类是新兴的工业资产阶级暴发户。勃朗蒂姊妹在西赖丁一所牧师女子学校里度过了一段不愉快的岁月，西赖丁曾是勒德派骚动的地方。

大约有十年（1835—1845）之久，勃朗蒂姊妹勤奋努力，以教书谋生。夏洛特曾有两次，安妮也有两次在私人家里做家庭女教师，而爱米丽则在一所女子学校教了六个月的书，备感痛苦。为了争取更好的教书资格，夏洛特和爱米丽于1842年前往布鲁塞尔，师从艾格夫妇学习法语和德语。她们曾打算自己开办一所学校，但这项计划从来没有实行。

勃朗蒂姊妹“很小的时候就怀着有朝一日成为作家的梦想”。1846 年，她们以柯勒·埃利斯和阿克顿·贝尔的笔名出版了一本诗集。在她们那个时代，一个女人需要有极大的勇气才敢发表作品。“女性”作家不可能指望有什么读者，因此她必须在人们知道她是一个女子之前赢得读者。至于那卷诗集，仅仅卖出了两本。与此同时，她们已经开始写小说。1847 年，夏洛特的《简·爱》、爱米丽的《呼啸山庄》和安妮的《安格尼斯·格雷》出版了。《简·爱》一出版，立即轰动一时，取得了巨大成功。1848 年，爱米丽去世，翌年，安妮也去世了，两人都是肺结核的受害者。夏洛特是三姊妹中最多产的一个，1848 年出版《雪莉》，1853 年出版《维莱特》。1854 年，她与尼科尔斯结婚，一年之后便去世了。

2. 夏洛特的《简·爱》 小说是以描写小简开始的。孤女小简被寄养在孀居的舅妈家里，受到歧视。由于不服管教，她被送进一所“慈善”寄宿学校，这所学校以非常严厉的纪律进行管理。简认真学习，获得了担任教师的资格。她登出广告，谋求职位，而后受雇于罗切斯特，在他的乡间宅第桑菲尔德为他的法国私生女儿做家庭教师。简和罗切斯特之间产生了爱情关系。简的果敢自由的精神、激情似火的灵魂，使得惯于居高临下的罗切斯特向她求婚。但就在圣坛前，婚礼仪式被打断了，因为简发现罗切斯特是一个有妇之夫，他的妻子是疯子，就在桑菲尔德。

简离开了桑菲尔德，漫无目的地远走。里弗斯一家搭救了她，并要她和严肃冷淡的圣约翰·里弗斯结婚，以便她能在圣约翰身边协助传教。她几乎同意了，但就在她沉思的时候，耳边响起罗切斯特呼喊她的名字的声音。她回到桑菲尔德，但庄园已被罗切斯特的疯女人焚毁了。在附近一座僻静的村舍里，她找到了罗切斯特，他孤零零一个人，双目已经失明。后来，他们结了婚，一起找到了幸福。

作者以极其强烈的情感来讲述这个故事。简的极度痛苦被表现得如此强烈，而用以表现的语言又极其简朴、生动，所以人们在读到这些部分时不能不受到感动。这部书并不是一部传奇。像夏洛特·勃朗蒂的其他小说一样，《简·爱》的特点是：对日常现实作了毫不留情的真实的描述。小说里的情节即使是在最令人激动的时候，它的细节都严格地忠实于现实生活。

《简·爱》在维多利亚时代的小说中独树一帜；它是英国第一部小说，或许甚至可以说是迄今最有影响力、最受欢迎的一部描述追求自由、具有反抗精神的妇女的一部小说，这种妇女要求自由地去感受、自由地去讲她所感受到的一切。简虽然贫穷，却是独立的。她能自谋生路，而"不需要出卖她的灵魂去获取幸福"。她并不怕直率地告诉罗切斯特：她爱他，但鄙视他，因为他想娶一个富有、漂亮，但在精神上低劣的女子为妻。在《简·爱》一书中，女人变得有发言权了，可以在平等的条件下面对男人。

3. **爱米丽的《呼啸山庄》** "Wuthering"是约克郡的方言词，意为"weathering"（风吹雨打）。正如爱米丽用讽刺的口吻所说的：这是"一个很有意味的地方性的形容词，它描绘了山庄在狂风暴雨中所受到的大气层动乱的袭击"。

这是一个描写压迫与反抗、狂风暴雨的天气和狂风暴雨般的激情的故事。恩肖先生是呼啸山庄上一个富有的约克郡人。他从利物浦的贫民窟里带回了一个肤色灰黄、衣服褴褛的小男孩，把他叫作希斯克利夫。这个小男孩同恩肖的儿子兴德利和女儿凯瑟琳一同长大。凯瑟琳爱希斯克利夫，但兴德利则因妒忌其父对他的钟爱而仇恨他。父母一去世，兴德利便把希斯克利夫降到一个农奴的地位。凯瑟琳主张人与人之间的博爱，在兴德利的暴虐的压制下，成了希斯克利夫的反叛伙伴。但是凯瑟琳抵挡不住舒适的社会生活对她的诱惑。她背弃了希斯克利夫，嫁给了邻村画眉山庄有钱的地主家庭出身的埃德加·林顿。这件事发生以后，希斯克利夫便消失了。

几年之后，希斯克利夫回来了，富有、亨通，一派绅士风度。凯瑟琳处于希斯克利夫和埃德加·林顿之间，感到尴尬，终于精神失常了。她给埃德加生下女儿凯西之后，便去世了。希斯克利夫于是开始进行报复，他要把两个家庭一齐毁掉。他用他们自己的武器——金钱和包办婚姻——来对付他们。他买下了兴德利的全部财产，使他变成了一个酒鬼和赌徒，这样兴德利的儿子黑尔顿也就沦为希斯克利夫家里的一个乞食者。希斯克利夫娶了埃德加·林顿的妹妹伊莎贝拉，并在她死后，安排了他有病的儿子与凯西·林顿的婚事。他使他的宿敌兴德利的儿子黑尔顿对他产生了强烈的依恋感，从而取得至高无上的统治阶级的胜利。但是，他整个的报复都归于失败，因为凯西忠于黑尔顿，而这两个年轻的情侣将会对他们的压迫者进行反抗。

在小说中任何问题也没有解决，但许多东西被揭示出来。蒙在资产阶级个人本来面目上的那块面纱被拉掉了。《呼啸山庄》是对19世纪资本主义社会中人在肉体上和精神上所受到的压力、紧张和冲突的一种富有想象力或象征性的表述。《呼啸山庄》中的男女并不是想象世界中的人，而是爱米丽·勃朗蒂所知道的那个世界中的人，他们反抗压迫的斗争象征着阶级社会中永远不会停息的斗争。

小说的结构很好，激动人心的力量一直持续到小说结束。爱米丽·勃朗蒂的写作风格简朴无饰，但很有力。她对景色的描绘在英国小说中是极为卓越、无与伦比的。

4. 盖斯凯尔夫人的小说 盖斯凯尔夫人（1810—1865），娘家姓斯蒂文森，是一个唯一神派牧师的女儿，她也嫁给了一个唯一神派的牧师。她一生的大部分时间是在曼彻斯特度过的。1848年，即宪章运动高涨的那一年，她发表了她的第一部小说《玛丽·巴顿》，这部小说赢得了狄更斯和一般民众的赞许。

《玛丽·巴顿》是第一部劳工小说，它描写了有产者和无产者的冲突。它讲述了一个朴实、诚恳的人怎样被人诬告犯有谋杀罪，他的女儿怎样从绞刑架下把他救了下来，以及这个女儿在一个富有的工厂主的儿子卑怯地使用诡计把她诱骗而几至把她毁灭之后，又怎样争取独立并嫁给一个强壮有为的劳工。盖斯凯尔夫人勇敢地处理了“饥饿的40年代”的迫切的工业问题：低工资、悲惨处境、罢工、雇主及政府的冷漠无情。小说出版后引起了一场赞扬和责难的双重风暴。

继《玛丽·巴顿》之后，盖斯凯尔夫人发表了《克兰福镇》（1853），这本书是盖斯凯尔夫人对她早年在纳茨福德认识的一些地方上的纯朴而卑微的人们所作的一系列的素描。1855年，盖斯凯尔夫人再次转而描写那个时代的严重的工业状况。《北与南》是一部关于劳资之间斗争的小说。书中对英格兰南部古老的农业乡绅阶级与北部有钱的新工业家作了对比。书中有一些典型人物，如那个因无法使良心得到安宁而放弃了薪俸的教士和那个把社会激进主义与无神论结合起来的工联主义的职员。本书与狄更斯的《艰难时世》和夏洛特·勃朗蒂的《雪莉》有着明显的联系。

《玛丽·巴顿》和《北与南》是两本带有启发性的书，就是在今天也仍有其启发性。盖斯凯尔夫人是第一个把“职工”作为小说人物来塑造的人。她所提出的补救方法是在主人和仆人之间建立良好的理解——这是她和她那个时代许多批判现实主义作家所共有的一种资产阶级局限性。

盖斯凯尔夫人也是一部传记杰作《夏洛特·勃朗蒂传》(1857)的作者。

第十一章

维多利亚时期（下）

一　丁尼生、勃朗宁以及诗歌创作思想上的后退

1. 丁尼生及其传奇世界　艾尔弗雷德·丁尼生勋爵（1809—1892）是一个牧师的儿子，生长在一个乡间教区长的家庭里，受业于剑桥大学。19 世纪 40 年代，他确立了诗人的声誉。他听觉灵敏，写作精益求精。但是，他从当时丑恶的工业主义转向传奇世界，即古典的、中世纪的和英国的传奇故事。特别使他着迷的是关于亚瑟王及其宫廷中骑士和贵妇人的传说。丁尼生的《国王叙事诗》（1859、1869、1872）的背景既不是古代的不列颠，也不是中世纪的骑士制度，而是诗人想象的传奇世界，也就是诗人在其中躲避的世界。在他的手中，诗歌成了一种由魔法控制的遥远幻境。

1850 年，丁尼生被封为桂冠诗人，以接替威廉·华滋华斯，于是

就成了“官方”诗人。他痛恨不抵抗主义，并时刻准备在不列颠帝国受到威胁时发出拿起武器的号召。他赋诗支持克里米亚战争（《轻骑旅的冲锋》等），反对印度兵变（《保卫勒克瑙》）。丁尼生写诗时始终着眼于他的那些资产阶级读者。而作为桂冠诗人，他更着眼于维多利亚女王。

维多利亚女王时代的世界是广大人民群众受苦受难的世界。丁尼生对此并非无动于衷。他早年读过进化论，又和达尔文相识。但是，像达尔文及其当时的追随者一样，丁尼生以个体生存竞争的理论来解释人类社会。他将资本主义的残酷归结于大自然的残酷。到了晚年，他听到个人生活中那些痛苦的哭喊声，于是作为他诗歌特征的那种平静悦耳的和声便开始充满了一种较为深沉、较为骚动的音调。但他坚持自己的信念，而且愈加退避到他那个传奇世界中去了。

2. **勃朗宁和意大利文艺复兴** 罗伯特·勃朗宁（1812—1889）是一个英格兰银行职员的儿子，从私人教师学习并受业于伦敦大学。他年轻时曾想有所作为，写了一首题为《迷失的领袖》的诗歌，针对愈来愈退缩的华滋华斯：

莎士比亚是我们的，弥尔顿是为我们的，
　彭斯、雪莱则
　和我们一道——他们从坟墓中
　往外注视！
他却独自脱离队伍的前列和自由人——
　独自掉在队伍的后面，和奴隶在一起！

1846年，勃朗宁和《孩子们的哭声》的作者伊丽莎白·巴雷特秘密结婚，并带她到佛罗伦萨居住。1848年，他们在佛罗伦萨感受到了那股席卷整个欧洲的革命热情。勃朗宁夫人和她丈夫比起来，对政治自由和那些影响社会团体的运动更加感兴趣。勃朗宁也重视人身自由，但主要是把它作为一种达到个人发展的工具。他错误地认为，只有个人自由才能带来社会进步。

正当丁尼生躲避在他那传奇世界里的时候，勃朗宁离开阴沉枯燥的现实世界，转向意大利历史及16世纪的传奇故事。他开始对意大利文艺复兴时期的人物——如贵族、教士、炼金术士、画家、音乐家和江湖庸医感兴趣。勃朗宁的写作方法是：先将这些人物置于他们所处的时代环境中，然后以丰富的想象力去再现他们；他不是平铺直叙，而是戏剧性地去再现他们，即将他们置于他们生命中某些最能揭示问题的时刻，然后再将他们展现在我们面前，让他们自己来替自己说话。他写了若干篇"戏剧独白"，其中有一些仍然值得阅读，例如，《我已故的公爵夫人》、《主教吩咐后事》（全名是《圣普拉西德教堂的主教吩咐后事》），等等。

和丁尼生比较起来，勃朗宁则更加脱离维多利亚的悲惨世界。他不太知道邪恶，坚信社会是在进步的，而进步是解决人类蒙受的种种罪恶的唯一方法，如在《比芭经过》中他写道：

上帝在天国——
世间万事顺利。

3．唯美主义和颓废派 唯美主义是维多利亚时代的一种创作思想上的倒退。他的鼓吹者是但丁·迦百列·罗塞蒂(1828—1882)。罗塞蒂是一群被称为拉斐尔前派的唯美主义者的领袖。他将维多利亚时代大量文学作品所谈论的社会和政治问题统统排斥于他的作品之外。对他来说,生活只是为了提供艺术形象而存在的,他渴望的是一个由符号、风、幽暗月光照耀的水面、半明半暗中看到的瑰丽异彩所构成的世界,这完全不是现实的世界而是空间的一瞬息。爱和美是他写作的主题。在写这两个主题时,他将神秘主义和肉欲这两个主题奇怪地结合在一起。在罗塞蒂及其追随者(例如他妹妹克里斯蒂娜·罗塞蒂、在成为社会主义者之前的威廉·莫里斯、批评家华尔特·佩特、奥斯卡·王尔德)的作品中,艺术世界和现实世界是完全脱离的。

唯美主义或"为艺术而艺术"是马克思所说的资本主义社会"商品——拜物主义"的一种形式。恩格斯在《反杜林论》中非常清晰地解释了这种社会特征:

> [这种社会]都有一个特点:这里的生产者丧失了对他们自己的社会关系的支配权。每个人都用自己偶然拥有的生产资料并为自己的特殊的交换需要而各自进行生产。谁也不知道,他的那种商品出现在市场上的会有多少,究竟需要多少;谁也不知道,他的个人产品是否真正为人所需要,是否能收回它的成本,或者是否能卖出去。社会生产的无政府状态占统治地位。但是,商品生产同任何其他生产形式一样,有其……规律。……这些规律是作为他们的生产形式的盲目起作用的自然规律为自己开辟道路的。产品支配着生产者。[①]

① 恩格斯:《反杜林论》,人民出版社,1970年,第269页。

"生产者丧失了对他们自己的社会关系的支配权。"资产阶级的诗人亦复如此。他脱离了现实社会,因此也脱离了艺术的源泉——他是与社会背道而驰的。"产品支配着生产者",一首诗或一件艺术品亦复如此。技巧和"传统"被认为高于一切。唯美主义、形式主义、象征主义等只不过是颓废派在诗歌创作上的不同类型而已。

二 卡莱尔、罗斯金和赫胥黎

1. **卡莱尔及其英雄崇拜** 托马斯·卡莱尔(1795—1882)出身于一个苏格兰农民家庭,受业于爱丁堡大学。他是19世纪初研究德语的少数几个人之一。他通过介绍歌德和席勒,对英国文学作出了很大的贡献。1837年,他发表了《法国大革命》一书,确立了他的作家声誉。萨克雷给《泰晤士报》撰写了一篇热情洋溢的书评。据说,狄更斯不论走到哪里,随身都带着一本《法国大革命》。

卡莱尔并非没有察觉到"英国的状况"——事实上,创造这个短语的也正是他,这个短语日后成为许多书籍的主题。他反对经济上的自由放任、政治上的资产阶级民主以及哲学上的机械唯物主义。他的心一直向着受苦受难的人民。在宪章运动的那些岁月里,他在许多书籍和小册子中都写到这些穷苦人民,如《宪章运动》(1840)、《过去和现在》(1843)。但是,他对他们是否有能力管理自己缺乏信心。他错误地断言:"世界史只不过是伟人的传记。"他在《英雄与英雄崇拜》一书中,发展了关于英雄的神秘理论。

马克思和恩格斯在一篇论及卡莱尔著作的长文中写道：

> 当资产阶级的态度、趣味和思想在整个英国正统文学中居于绝对统治地位的时候，他在文学方面反对了资产阶级，而且他的言论有时甚至具有革命性。例如他的法国革命史、他为克伦威尔的辩护、他的论宪章主义的小册子以及他的《过去和现在》都是这样。但是在所有这些著作里，对现代的批判是和颂扬中世纪这种完全违反历史的做法紧密地联系着的，其实这种做法在英国的革命者，如科贝特和一部分宪章主义者中也经常可以看到。过去至少社会发展的某一阶段的兴盛时代使他欢欣鼓舞，现代却使他悲观失望，未来则使他心惊胆战。[①]

卡莱尔暴露了工业资本主义和卑鄙的商业主义的罪恶，但他除了要人们相信他所认为的那种卓越的个人即英雄之外，没有提出任何的补救措施。

2. 罗斯金和对中世纪的爱好 约翰·罗斯金（1819—1900）是个富裕酒商的儿子，受业于伦敦大学和牛津大学，学习素描和油画。他写了大量关于绘画和建筑的著作。他观察颜色和形式精确无误，他的词汇极为丰富。他写下了在英语散文中关于大自然和艺术的一些最华丽的篇章。

罗斯金在《给那后来的》（1862）中抨击了他那个时代的工业主义和商业主义。他给工人写了一系列的信件，题为《福尔斯·克莱维格拉》（1871—1887）。他说，人类的一切工作都依赖工人的幸福生活。而工人只有像手工艺时代的人那样生活时，才能获得幸福。那时，人

① 《马克思恩格斯论艺术》卷2，人民文学出版社，1963年，第299页。

们用自己的双手制作所需要的一切，对自己的工作感到自豪，并满足人对美的那种自然的本能追求。

罗斯金想竭力改变英国生活中的整个社会和经济体制。他想废除机器和机器所制造的商品，从而使生活再次变得简朴和自然，同时，每个人在认清了他所制作的东西和干活的一切意义和目的之后，会对制作和干活感到快乐。每个人将按劳取酬，而国家将防止任何人牺牲他人利益来积累财富。

为了将他的理论付诸实践，他花了十分之一的财产建立了圣乔治同业公会——一个农业和手工业的合作组织。在本质上，这是试图回复到一种无可挽回的过去时代，试图在工业中建立起一种新封建主义。他原来打算使大家分享收益，但事实上没有收益可供分享。同时，组织中存在着分歧和失望。整个计划正像它必然会崩溃那样，迅速地崩溃了。

3. **赫胥黎和科学普及** 托马斯·亨利·赫胥黎(1825—1895)是维多利亚时期最杰出的散文作家之一，他也是一个科学家。赫胥黎是个失意的中学校长助理的儿子。他在伦敦大学攻读理科时，成绩卓越。毕业后，他进入海军部门当助理外科医生，并参加了前往新几内亚的科学探险队。至于他如何为建立科学家的声誉而奋斗，他在《自传》(1889—1890)中作了深刻的描述。

当《物种起源》于1859年出版时，赫胥黎成了它的积极捍卫者和传播者。接着发生了一场激烈的论战。1860年，牛津大学举行英国协会会议。会上，塞缪尔·威尔伯福斯主教对着拥挤的演讲厅里的听众发表演说，他嘲讽达尔文，并猛烈抨击赫胥黎。在演讲快结束时，他“微笑的脸上带着傲慢的神气”，对赫胥黎说，他“想请教赫胥黎，他是通过他祖父还是他祖母而从猴子变来的？”赫胥黎应听众的要求进行讨论。他只作了一个简单但戏剧性的回答，他说：“他并不因为祖先是猴子而感到羞愧，却因为跟一个利用伟大才能来掩盖真理的人有关联而感到羞耻。”他的第一部科普性著作《人在自然界中的位置》极受欢迎，销售如同小说，并传到美国和德国。

赫胥黎撰文抨击宗教教条和反动教士。他还撰文抨击美国黑奴制度。跟卡莱尔不同，他把英雄崇拜看成是一种偶像崇拜。他将实验制度引入自然科学教程。他是19世纪为科学摇旗呐喊的伟大辩护士。他说：“为了做正确的事而学习真实的东西这句话，对于所有那些无法以权威的东风来满足精神上的饥饿的人们来说，总结了人所担负的全部责任。”

跟达尔文一样，甚至超过了达尔文的另外一些追随者（如赫伯特·斯宾塞），赫胥黎错误地运用进化论来解释人类社会（《人类社会中的生存竞争》，1888）。他没能摆脱唯心主义，他称自己不是一个唯物主义者，而是一个不可知论者。

三　乔治·艾略特和塞缪尔·勃特勒

1. 现实主义作家乔治·艾略特　乔治·艾略特（玛丽·安·艾文斯，1819—1880）的童年是在沃里克郡一个大庄园的一间农舍里度过的。她父亲是该庄园的代理人。她在私人教师的教育下，获得了大量关于语言、文学和音乐的知识。她在二十二岁时离开农庄，之后由于和“进步”人士接触，而跟正统的基督教决裂。她在三十三岁时，前往伦敦当新闻记者，结识了像赫伯特·斯宾塞、托马斯·亨利·赫胥黎和乔治·亨利·路易斯那样的“进步”思想家。后来，她嫁给了路易斯。她翻译了费尔巴哈的《基督教的本质》(1854)。

乔治·艾略特从中年起开始由撰写哲学论文转向小说写作。她早期的文章使用“乔治·艾略特”这个随意采用的名字。狄更斯、萨克雷和盖斯凯尔夫人都对她非常钦佩。她的声誉是在《亚当·比德》(1859)出版之后确立的，之后，她又相继出版了《弗洛斯河上的磨坊》(1860)、《织工马南传》(1861)、《米德尔马契》(1871—1872)。

作为小说家，乔治·艾略特力求做到逼真。她在《亚当·比德》中说：

> 我主要的意图只是将男女人物和所发生的事情，按照他们反映在我头脑这面镜子里的情况，老老实实地写出来。一面镜子当然不是没有缺点的，所以反映出来的形象往往会有点歪曲和模糊。可是我仍然觉得我应该力求精确地把反映在我头脑中的一切告诉你们，如同我在见证席上发誓讲述我亲眼所见的事物一样。

但乔治·艾略特所做的还不止于此。她既是一个创作家，又是个研究哲学和心理学的学者。她的大脑受过分析、解释和探求事物原由的训练。她写小说时，把精力集中于如下的事情上：解释她所描绘的人物会采取的每一个步骤，他们的全部感情以及导致他们采取某一特定行动和由此而产生结果的一切内心斗争。她是一个所谓心理小说的作家。

2.《织工马南传》和《米德尔马契》 赛拉斯·马南是个织工，生活贫困、身体畸形，家住北部工业区某地，由于遭人诬告犯有盗窃罪而被迫背井离乡。他躲在拉瓦诺这个村庄里，继续做织布营生，很少与乡邻来往。他的生活除省钱、积钱和数钱之外，别无其他目标。一天晚上，他的积蓄失窃了，他的快乐也随之化为乌有。接着，在一个除夕的夜晚，一个遭人遗弃的金发女孩悄悄地爬进了他的小屋。赛拉斯收养了她，叫她埃比，像对亲生女儿那样爱护她。埃比让赛拉斯找回了由于丢失黄金而失去的快乐。

是谁偷了赛拉斯的黄金？埃比又是从何而来？这两个问题在以后的许多岁月里始终是个谜。后来，把赛拉斯家门附近的池塘抽干了，才发现窃贼的尸体，尸体手中仍紧紧攥着金子。窃贼是乡绅卡斯那个放荡堕落的儿子邓斯坦。这事被揭露后感动了邓斯坦的哥哥戈弗雷，他立即承认自己是埃比的父亲。原来戈弗雷曾遗弃过一个女人，那女人是抱着婴儿企图强入卡斯的宅第时死在雪地里的……这部小说大量地揭露了资产阶级制度下人们隐藏在背后的动机和冲动。

《米德尔马契》是部巨著，其写作规模在维多利亚时代的小说中是绝无仅有的。书中，对失去理想这个问题作了论述。多萝西亚·布鲁克出身于英国地主阶级，但她所渴望的超出了她那个阶级的那种“温文尔雅”的自私自利。她拒绝当地一个贵族的求婚，却接受了迂腐得令人讨厌的卡索邦的求婚，从而酿成了灾祸。卡索邦甚至在度蜜月时仍在探究他的那个《一切神话的说明》，并由于缺乏同情心而疏远了多萝西亚。与此同时，雄心勃勃的年轻医生特梯厄斯·李德盖特一心想在科学上有所发现并在医学上进行改革，但他犯了一个巨大的错误，娶了漂亮却平庸的罗莎蒙德·文西，文西的实利主义终究使李德盖特的希望成为泡影。

但是，这些不是孤立的片断。多萝西亚和李德盖特的生活跟米德尔马契这个地方许多人的生活是休戚相关的。乔治·艾略特说："没有一种不为广泛的公众生活所决定的私生活。"我们对作者关于社会生活是相互关联的这种坚定不移的思想，具有深刻的印象。作者是通过细心累积细节并深入分析动机和行为而把这种相互关系揭示出来的。

乔治·艾略特的弱点在于她的唯心主义哲学。在孔德及其实证主义的影响下（艾略特的丈夫乔治·亨利·路易斯是孔德在英国的代表），她相信"人类的宗教"，并错误地认为这种宗教能够解决社会生活中的一切矛盾。她借着对一个孩子的爱来说明这种爱可对赛拉斯孤独、痛苦的性格产生影响。她还表达了这样的观点，即米德尔马契这个地方的社会，可以通过人道的原则而重新变得生气蓬勃。正是这种唯心主义，减弱了乔治·艾略特所有作品的社会意义。

3. 塞缪尔·勃特勒及其《埃瑞璜》 塞缪尔·勃特勒（1835—1902）的祖父和父亲都是牧师。少年时代，他由于家教过于严厉并要求循规蹈矩，而感到很大的痛苦。父亲要他当牧师，但他从剑桥大学毕业后，由于自己没有这种信念，拒绝接受圣职。1850 年，他移居新西兰，在那里经营牧羊业，攒了一小笔财产，后来这笔财产因朋友失慎而丧失。1864 年回到英国，他开始学画，并撰文讨论诸如宗教、进化论、绘画和音乐、荷马和莎士比亚等问题。勃特勒是当时最有才艺、最具独创性的人物之一。他最杰出的文学作品是《埃瑞璜》和《众生之道》。

《埃瑞璜》出版于 1872 年。它使勃特勒在他同时代的人中建立起了声誉。故事的主人公希格斯先生在新西兰跋山涉水，来到了一个迄今未被发现的国度，那里居住着稀奇古怪的人民——这个国度又像英国，又不像英国。其中一个显著的差别是那里没有机器。

书中辩解说，机器对人类是个威胁。起初机器卑躬屈膝地做人类的奴仆，现在却正在迅速地成为人类的主人，以致可能最终不再需要人类。勃特勒在这里表达了维多利亚时代许多知识分子普遍对资本主义机器生产的结果所抱有的恐惧。勃特勒确实承认，机器如果加以适当管理，可以使人类加强对其周围环境的控制。但他似乎又觉得，埃瑞璜人没有机器，生活反而要好一些。

埃瑞璜 (乌有之乡) 决不是一个理想国，虽然它有一些美好的东西——舒适的习俗和制度。埃瑞璜人把不健康看作犯罪。他们崇拜伊特格隆 (格兰迪女士，即过于讲究礼节的人)，伊特格隆的信条是按惯例办事。他们到非理性院校听课，每所院校都设有讲授人情世故的讲座。

《埃瑞璜》是部讽刺小说。它揭露了维多利亚社会那种浅薄的自相矛盾和可疑的价值观，以及由此而产生的自以为是的行为。勃特勒想象出来的东西与《格列佛游记》有相似之处，并且同样引人入胜。书中对资产阶级制度提出了有价值的批判。

4. **《众生之道》** 这部小说写于 1873 至 1885 年之间，但直到 1903 年才出版。它对维多利亚时代的习俗和尊严进行了最有力的抨击。勃特勒借主人公之口，在第八十四章发表了如下的议论：

> 有许多东西需要说出来而人们不敢说出来，有许多虚假的东西需要加以抨击，却没有人加以抨击。我觉得，我能够说全英国除我本人之外没有另外一个人敢于说出的东西，但那些东西迫切地要求

人们说出来。

小说的主人公叫欧内斯特·庞铁弗克斯，他是满嘴仁义道德的教区牧师西奥博尔德·庞铁弗克斯的儿子，他祖父叫乔治·庞铁弗克斯，是个专出宗教书籍的出版商，曾祖父约翰·庞铁弗克斯是个乡下木匠。欧内斯特童年时代经常遭到他父亲最不讲理的惩罚。（“当一个人爱钱如命时，要他在任何时候同样疼爱他的孩子是不容易的。”）他在一个从不理解自己的学生而又自命不凡的教师那里接受教育，然后被送往剑桥大学读神学。压制酿成了飞来横祸。离开剑桥大学时，欧内斯特竟然去侮辱一位年轻女人，他把她当成了妓女，结果被判处六个月监禁。他瞻前顾后。他恨他的父母，想跟他们脱离关系。……最后，他靠姑妈的意外遗产被赎了出来，获得了自由和独立。

小说内容中有好多是自传性的。勃特勒本人以双重角色即以主人公以及主人公的律师和朋友的身份出现。他把他的父母和他所认识的其他一些人放进了小说。小说中有些信件就是他父亲和他本人的原信。乔治·萧伯纳把此书说成是“对父母亲的长时间的慢性杀害”。然而，小说并非仅仅是一部自传：这是众生之道。小说所描绘的那些维多利亚中期英国家庭生活的真实画面，不仅是一种控诉，而且是一部文献。像《呼啸山庄》一样，《众生之道》表明：在资本主义社会中，完美的人生是无法实现的。

勃特勒有非凡的笔调。他怎么感觉就怎么写，而且不能容忍冗长夸张的文风。和斯威夫特教长一样，他具有诚挚宽厚、直截了当、才智过人、文体优美、痛恨假话等美德。在《埃瑞璜》和《众生之道》里，他在某种程度上再现了斯威夫特的精神。

四　莫里斯及社会主义浪漫文学

1. **莫里斯的生活进程**　威廉·莫里斯（1834—1896）是伦敦一个富裕经纪人的儿子，就读于马尔堡公学和牛津大学。在他十四五岁时就已经对中世纪的事物发生了兴趣，喜爱出自中世纪工匠之手的精美制品。他二十四岁时出版了关于亚瑟王的传奇故事：《捍卫桂尼维尔王后及其他诗歌》（1858）。之后，他又去从事装饰艺术。他筹建了一所生产家具、玻璃制品、棉织品的工场，使这些产品富有一种新的美感，来替代这些产品中所常见的丑陋式样。他设计了一种简朴而又舒适的椅子，这种椅子至今仍以他的名字命名。

与此同时，莫里斯又以乔叟的笔法写了一些关于希腊和中世纪的传奇。正如他自己承认的那样，他是一个“空虚的日子里无病呻吟的小歌手”，仅仅为了使“那些落在黑烟熏天的尘网里干着索然无味的劳动”的人们感到快乐而歌唱。但是，作为一个有多年经验的、手艺高明的工匠，他认识到：在贪婪、不公平和外表丑陋的资本主义时代里，是不可能有真正的手艺的。他研读《资本论》，吸取了马克思主义思想，在四十四岁成了一个社会主义者。

1883 年，莫里斯加入了英国第一个社会主义政党——社会民主联盟。作为一个领导人，他热情地工作，在会场和街头发表演说，并为民主联盟的期刊《公正》撰写诗歌和散文。次年，社会民主联盟分裂，他和他的朋友们组成了社会主义同盟，并为同盟的期刊《公众福利》撰文。1896 年他逝世时，和他共事的诗人史文朋赞扬他是一位“用剑和歌”来拯救世界的“斗士和理想家”。

莫里斯为社会主义事业而写的文学作品有：《梦见约翰·保尔》

（1886）、《乌有之乡的消息》（1891）、《诗歌拾零》（1891）。《诗歌拾零》包括《那一天即将来临》和那些收在《社会主义者颂歌》中出版的诗歌。

2.《那一天即将来临》及其他诗歌 《那一天即将来临》（1884）使用的是踏步似的韵律，抑抑扬格，每行六拍，节奏不断上升，并且每行中间还有额外音节。这是莫里斯自己的创造。这首诗预言性地歌颂了无阶级社会，到那时，资本主义将被废除，自由、公平和幸福的友情将重新回到工人的生活中来，而工人将要继承一个由大自然和艺术所美化了的世界：

所有这一切将是我们和所有人的，
　当世界变得美好，
任何人都要分担生活的劳苦，
　并享受生活带来的酬报。

这首诗在结尾号召大家进行斗争。用八音节诗句写成的《劳苦之声》（1884），结尾亦复如是，它描绘了一幅资本主义制度下工人们生活的可怕画面：

在这里，我们的铁老板，
把我们制造的东西转得快些，更快些，
叫我们为了他人的奢望、他人的生活，
磨压出财富，让他们欢喜。

在这里，家是个茅棚，生活是单调，

忘记了这个世界有什么美好；

在这里，我们不想有孩子，生怕它会死掉；

在这里，欢乐是犯罪，爱情是圈套。

1887年11月13日星期日，历史上称为"血腥的星期日"。那天，伦敦的失业者为了捍卫言论自由而举行了一次声势浩大的游行。莫里斯和当时还不是很知名的乔治·萧伯纳一起参加了游行。游行者遭到警察的袭击，莫里斯的朋友阿尔弗雷德·林纳尔当场被杀。这就是莫里斯写《死亡之歌》的原委。这首歌以每册一便士的价格出售，用以资助林纳尔的孩子们。《死亡之歌》中有这样犹如号角声的叠句：

他们不该杀一个，不该杀一个，也不该杀几千，

如果想蒙蔽天下，他们应该把所有的人一齐杀光。

3. 莫里斯的社会主义传奇故事 《梦见约翰·保尔》是个梦想曲。叙述者在梦境中回到了14世纪的英国，发现自己处于农民革命之中。他听约翰·保尔作了一次慷慨激昂的演说，过后又跟一位农民领袖作了认真的长谈。叙述者对乡村一端所发生的战斗作了生动的描写……叙述者醒来，听到现代工业主义的工厂的汽笛声在呼唤人们去工作。这样就从14世纪一下子跃入了19世纪。这是一篇具有永久价值和美的作品。

但是，莫里斯为歌颂社会主义事业而写的最好的作品是《乌有之乡的消息》。这部作品在1890年的《公众福利》上以长篇连载的形式出现。书中又是一个做梦人，这次他发现自己处在一个无阶级的未来

世界。剥削已经消灭，人们幸福地工作着。城乡差别已经消失，原来一个到处是肮脏不堪的工场和一贫如洗的农场的国家，现在却变成了花园：

> 这就是我们现在的情况。英国一度是这样的国家，在森林和荒地中有许多空旷地，其中散落着一些城镇，这些城镇是封建军队的要塞、百姓的集市和工匠的聚集地。然后，英国又成为这样的国家：到处是巨大、肮脏不堪的工场和更为肮脏的赌场，周围则是些遭到工场主掠夺的农场，这些农场经营不善，一贫如洗。现在它变成了花园，在这花园里，任何东西既不浪费，也不遭受损坏，全国上下到处是那些必需的整齐、干净、漂亮的住宅、小屋和工场。倘若我们让产品制造，甚至是大规模产品制造，带着凄凉悲惨的外表，我们自己会感到实在太可耻了。

莫里斯具有非凡的视觉想象力，他在《乌有之乡的消息》中，把实现社会主义的无限可能性描写得非常形象，栩栩如生。

莫里斯的乌托邦不是另一个与现实社会脱节的、虚构出来的共和国。恰恰相反，他的乌托邦是通过斗争从现实社会中产生的，并带有斗争及其全部历史的痕迹。《乌有之乡的消息》中有一章题为《变革是怎样发生的》，其中描写了一场推翻资本主义社会建立社会主义的革命。跟费边社成员不同，莫里斯始终坚持社会主义只有通过工人阶级夺取政权来实现这一马克思的观点。莫里斯把这个变革的细节放在 1952 年，那是想象出来的。这个设想不但已经过时，也是不可能的。但他在《乌有之乡的消息》中所勾勒的革命进程——如把工人阶级组织起来，建立革命政党，推翻资本主义——表明他具有异乎寻常的见识。

虽然《乌有之乡的消息》并非没有乌托邦的元素，但这是莫里斯的最好作品，可供工人阶级作为他们日常斗争的弹药。这部作品不仅体现了个人的，而且也体现了民族的深远、不灭的希望和愿望。

第十二章

一些现代作家

一　托马斯·哈代

1. **哈代和他的世界**　托马斯·哈代（1840—1928）是一个小农场主和建造商的儿子，出生于多切斯特郡附近，在当地学校接受了私人教育。他的父亲想要他当建筑师，但他生性爱好文学。他早年写了大量诗歌，但未能获得读者的赏识，于是转入小说创作。他三十一岁时匿名发表了第一部小说《非常手段》（1871）。他在二十四年中一共写了十四部小说和四部短篇小说集。使他成名的主要小说是《还乡》（1878）、《卡斯特桥市长》（1886）、《德伯家的苔丝》（1891）和《无名的裘德》（1895）。临近19世纪末，他又重新回到了诗歌创作，发表了几卷作品。

哈代的小说和诗歌与英国西南部（其中包括萨默塞特郡、多塞特郡和德文郡）这一特定地区的人民有着密切的联系。在哈代写小说的那个年代，他称为威塞克斯的这个地方具有丰富的传统和民间传说以及浓厚的迷信思想。哈代对民间习俗具有强烈的感受：农民的歌曲、舞蹈和古老的宗教音乐都使他着迷。他正是在那里，也就是在他自己的人（农民和下层乡绅）中间，度过了一生中大部分的岁月，也正是这些人的朴素生活给他的小说和诗歌提供了素材。

然而，这个农村并不是一个不受外部世界影响的孤立地区。甚至在哈代的青年时期，铁路和资本主义机械化生活已经开始影响多切斯特郡的乡镇。同时，农民阶级已经显露出衰败的迹象。整个社会结构充满了发生悲剧的可能性。哈代对农民和他们的宗法制度深表同情。但是，由于他无法理解他那个时代所发生的社会变化的性质和意义，他常常会像宿命论者那样看待人，把人看作是被其身外力量所左右而无能为力的玩物。他的批判现实主义小说由于这种“对生活抱有的黄昏思想”即悲观主义而受到损害。

2.《还乡》 小说开始时对一个叫作爱格敦荒原的荒凉高地进行了出色的描写。居住在那块高地上的人过着简朴的生活，他们仍然保持着远古以来的传统，如五朔节的花柱舞、11 月 5 日的篝火、圣诞节的化装剧。哈代把农民的生活和生产戏剧化了，描绘出了一幅非常完整的画面。

克林姆·姚伯曾在巴黎待过，现在已经回到他寡居的母亲和温柔的表妹托马逊的身边。他被尤斯塔莎·斐伊的魅力所吸引。尤斯塔莎·斐伊是从一个时髦世界来到这里的，她不喜欢这块荒原，讨厌那种简朴、平凡的刻板生活。克林姆对于钻石商这个行业的虚荣和无用感到厌恶，他计划开办一所农民学校。他认为尤斯塔莎是个合意的助手，而尤斯塔莎却向往着“时髦的巴黎”，认为她可以诱使克林姆把她带往国外。他们就这样结婚了，但这门亲事使得姚伯老夫人非常不愉快。

不幸的事情纷至沓来。克林姆视力衰退，只能去干割荆兰的活计，尤斯塔莎则由于倦怠而意志消沉。在一个闷热的日子，姚伯夫人突然来访，想和儿子和好。但由于种种不幸的情况凑在一起，尤斯塔莎未能让姚伯夫人进门。姚伯夫人只得离去，由于过度悲伤而死在路上。克林姆和尤斯塔莎发生了争吵，随后分居。尤斯塔莎与她的旧日情人，即已和克林姆表妹托马逊结婚的收税员韦狄恢复了暧昧关系。在一个暴风雨的夜晚，尤斯塔莎和韦狄企图私奔，但在路上两人都被淹死了。

这就是在资本主义条件下，哈代所描写的那个威塞克斯农村崩溃时期普通人民生活中所发生的悲剧。这部小说说明了：在一个以利己主义为基础的社会中，壮志宏图是怎样遭到破灭的，对幸福的向往又是怎样遭到挫折的。

然而，哈代却有他自己的解释。他认为，克林姆、姚伯夫人和尤斯塔莎在为获得幸福而进行的斗争中，同样面临着不幸的命运。命运出于纯粹的任性摆布，使他们的努力白费！

3. **《德伯家的苔丝》** 哈代说，《德伯家的苔丝》的主题是关于一个“纯洁女子”的命运。事实上，它的主题是英国农民阶级的瓦解——这个过程在哈代那个时代已经达到了最后的悲剧阶段。《苔丝》讲的是一个农村瓦解的故事，也是一个农村瓦解的象征。和维多利亚时代任何其他小说相比，《苔丝》是一本有价值的社会纪实小说。

苔丝·德伯菲尔德是个农村姑娘，其父母的地位略高于农场工人。小说开头，德伯菲尔德一家的日子已经很不好过。为了解决家庭经济问题，琼·德伯菲尔德劝说她女儿苔丝去看望特兰里奇镇的德贝维尔一家，好跟族中较富有的那一支"攀上亲戚关系"。然而，这一家根本不是真正的德贝维尔，而是一个暴发户，是挤进乡绅阶级的那些资本家的后代。由于统治阶级的怜悯，苔丝在那里成了一名工人。尽管她力图保住自尊，她还是被艾力克·德贝维尔诱奸了，还生下了一个孩子。

孩子夭折之后，苔丝在泰波塞斯的奶牛场当雇佣工人。在那里，她遇到并爱上了有才识的安琪尔·克莱尔，想通过婚姻逃脱她的命运。结果，克莱尔是一个道学先生、伪君子、势利小人，甚至比艾力克·德贝维尔更残酷。他得知苔丝的经历后，大发雷霆，并离开英国，去了巴西。苔丝的处境更糟糕了，她沦为在最艰苦条件下工作的雇佣工人。打谷的那幕（第四十七章）象征着资本主义新型农场上那种丧失人性的关系。

不幸纷至沓来。苔丝的父亲去世后，她家被赶出了他们的小屋。为了维持一家人的生计，苔丝被迫回到艾力克·德贝维尔那里。此时，安琪尔·克莱尔出现了，他已反思忏悔。最后，苔丝为了维护尊严，杀死了艾力克·德贝维尔。她触犯了刑律，被捕受审，并被处以绞刑。

哈代把小说中发生的大量事情归结于大自然，归结于残酷的命运。他在这部小说的前言中引用了格洛斯特对李尔王所说的话：

> 我们之于神灵正如苍蝇之于顽童，
> 神灵杀死我们只是为了开心。

哈代虽然由于他那种悲观、宿命论的世界观而对整个故事作了曲解，但他所描绘的那幅关于在资本主义条件下农民阶级崩溃的画面还是很真实的。

哈代以“一个纯洁女子的真实故事”来作为这部小说的副标题，这是对维多利亚时代习俗的挑战。当哈代写这本书时，有三家出版商与他接洽，但其中两家以所谓“体面”关系为理由，拒绝接受写就的手稿。为了生计，哈代被迫删去冒犯“体面”的段落，然后才在《书画》杂志上连载。后来，小说照原稿刊印出版时曾引起轩然大波。

二　约翰·高尔斯华绥

1. **高尔斯华绥的文学生涯**　约翰·高尔斯华绥（1867—1933）出身于德文郡的一个古老家族，受业于哈罗公学和牛津大学。他在一度尝试了律师业务并广泛地旅游之后，就作为一个乡绅安居下来从事写作。他的书读起来饶有趣味。1932 年他获得了诺贝尔文学奖。

1904 年他发表了《岛国的法利赛人》，这部小说使高尔斯华绥成为了一个批判现实主义的作家。高尔斯华绥心目中的“岛国的法利赛人”是指自以为是和虚伪的英国资产阶级。主人公理查德·谢尔顿起初是个传统的资产阶级分子，但在经历了一个时期的失望之后，他开始对现实抱批判态度。他游历了全英国，并对自己同胞的缺点，如说假话、心胸狭隘、自觉与不自觉的虚伪以及愚蠢，感到厌恶。他开始去寻求美、热情、正义和智慧，但一样东西也没有找到。只是徒然地渴望在英国社会中过上好的生活——这是贯串在高尔斯华绥许多小说中的一股暗流。

1906年高尔斯华绥发表了《有产业的人》。这是一部谈论维多利亚时代后期英国中产阶级上层家庭福赛特一家生活的小说。隔了十四年（在此期间，他写了一些其他作品），高尔斯华绥重新捡起福赛特一家的故事线索，写了两部续集，这样就形成了《福赛特世家》三部曲（1922）。这是他主要的成名之作。接着他又写了另外两组三部曲：《现代喜剧》（1929）和《一章的结尾》（1934）。第一组三部曲是高尔斯华绥的代表作，而其中《有产业的人》又是他的社会批评的最高峰。

高尔斯华绥也是个多产的剧作家、短篇小说和散文作家。他最重要的戏剧是《银匣》（1909）、《斗争》（1909）、《正义》（1910）和《忠诚》（1922）。他的短篇小说如《进化》、《良心》、《迷途的狗》和《品质》已被收入各种选集。

2. **《福赛特世家》** 《福赛特世家》由以下三部小说组成：《有产业的人》（1906）、《进退两难》（1920）和《出让》（1922）。其中还有两篇插曲或短篇小说：《老福赛特的印第安之夏》[①]和《觉醒》。这些作品构成了有九百页的洋洋大作——这是一部篇幅浩翰的史诗，一部英国资产阶级大家族的史诗。

福赛特家族大得叫人摸不着头脑，而且有各种各样的人。这部小说一共叙述了三代人的事情。第一代是由六个兄弟（老乔里昂、詹姆斯、斯威辛、尼古拉斯、罗杰和蒂莫西）和四个姐妹（安妮、朱丽亚、海斯特和苏珊）为代表。小说开始时，福赛特家族中的大多数兄弟已经结婚，而且有了孩子，其中有的兄弟已经儿孙满堂。尽管福赛特兄弟在许多方面互不相同，但他们具有一个共同的家族特征，即他们都表

① 又译《晚秋佳日》。——编注

现出一种占有的本能。

> 福赛特家族的成员比起拜倒在财产下的奴隶来显然有过之而无不及。他知道一件东西的好坏，也知道一件东西是否可靠，他对财产的牢牢控制——不管它是妻子、房子、金钱，还是名誉，这都无关紧要——是他的标志。

但在福赛特家族中存在着两股力量的冲突，即以财产意识（英国的市侩气息或拜金主义）为一方和以寻求爱与美为另一方之间的冲突。第一股力量以詹姆斯·福赛特为代表。他富有，有成就，但从不摆脱这样的意识，即他占有着他所占有的一切。而这种意识甚至延伸到他的妻子艾琳身上。艾琳拼命地想从他那冷酷的掌控中挣脱出来。艾琳是高尔斯华绥小说中起来与资产阶级的“得体”或“体面”做斗争的六个美貌、神秘的女性之一。

艾琳为争取解放所做的第一次努力以她的情人——一个艺术家——的死亡而告终。在三部曲的第二部分艾琳和詹姆斯离婚了，又各自结了婚。三部曲的第三部分则集中谈论艾琳和詹姆斯再婚后各自所生的孩子，即詹姆斯的女儿和艾琳的儿子之间的爱情。小说中，艾琳自始至终站在福赛特家族成员的圈子外面，而读者只能通过这些家族成员的眼睛才看得到她。这是高尔斯华绥本人提醒读者关注的一种写作技巧。

高尔斯华绥对詹姆斯·福赛特的态度足以表明作者的性格特点。他起初憎恨詹姆斯·福赛特这个“有产业的人”，但随着他往下写，詹姆斯作为维多利亚时代社会稳定的最后残余，幸运地活到第一次世界大战后社会开始解体的那个时代时，他不知何故又开始慢慢地喜欢起詹姆斯来了。高尔斯华绥在叙述这个英国家族时是现实的，尽管他在讽刺有产阶级的自鸣得意和虚伪时非常尖锐，他还是受到了资产阶级世界观的局限。

《福赛特世家》所包括的时间是从 1886 到 1918 年停战后的那些年。这部编年史一直写到战后世界的所谓“聪明的年轻人”的时代，对这样一个时代，高尔斯华绥知道得很少，因为他只是一个持反对态度但感到迷惑不解的旁观者。这是一部篇幅浩瀚、按时间次序来撰写的小说。以后的六部小说和原来的三部曲比较起来，水平要低得多。这说明作者的现实主义在衰退。

3.《银匣》和其他剧本 由于高尔斯华绥学过法律，他的剧本内容总是和法律有关。几乎每个剧本都有一桩诉讼案件。他的第一部剧本《银匣》(1906) 表达的是这样一个思想：世上的司法制度对于穷人的惩罚要比对富人来得凶。一个富有的年轻绅士在酒醉时偷了一只钱包，接着一个穷人在酒醉时又把它偷走了。穷人被判刑坐牢，而年轻绅士却逃之夭夭，仅受了一场虚惊。《正义》(1910) 讲的是另一桩诉讼案件。威廉·福尔窦是律师的秘书，被控犯有伪造罪，对他罚过于罪，因为雇主想拿他来杀鸡儆猴。这出戏尖锐地抨击了贫富在法律面前的不平等。它演出的成功使英国的监狱管理得到了一些改革。

三幕剧《斗争》(1909) 讲的是在英国北部某工业城市已经坚持了数月的一起大罢工。这出戏真实地描写了资本家和工人之间的阶级对立。劳工领袖罗伯特的演说，从劳动者的观点出发对这个问题作了有效的论述。该剧第一、二幕获得了巨大成功。然而结尾颇有点矫揉造作。这个故事虽然充满着大吵大闹，却以妥协而告终。

高尔斯华绥的观点属于出身高贵、经济富裕的中产阶级上层世界。他所希望的是阶级调和，而不是革命。然而，他对他在戏剧和小说中所揭露和抨击的不合理制度和行贿舞弊，并非毫无察觉。他对贫穷和遭受蹂躏的人们寄予同情，并且希望对受迫害的人体现公正。尽管他有许多局限性，却仍然是英国文学中最后一批批判现实主义的代表之一。

三　赫伯特·乔治·威尔斯

1. **威尔斯和费边社会主义**　赫伯特·乔治·威尔斯（1866—1946）是个小店主的儿子。早年当过布店职员和学校教师，后来获得奖学金，才得以在伦敦皇家科学院学习生物学，二十一岁时以优异的成绩毕业。二十七岁时，他开始从事文学和新闻写作，并成为一个多产的作家。作为小说家、传记作家、散文家和小册子作者，他不仅在英国，而且在美国和欧洲都享有盛誉。

1903 年，威尔斯成为小资产阶级知识分子的组织费边社的成员。他间或把自己看作是社会主义者，但他的社会主义来自圣西门和孔德，而不是来自马克思和恩格斯。对于威尔斯来说，社会主义的原则不是革命而是爱，社会主义者的责任仅仅是“谈论、教育、讲解、写作、演讲、阅读和倾听”。他曾对理想国作过许多设想，并描写了各种各样的乌托邦，在他所写的上百本书中，大部分是乌托邦式的或带有乌托邦性质的。

恩格斯曾对费边社社员作过经典性的论述。他在 1893 年写道：

在伦敦这里，费边派是一伙野心家，他们对社会变革的必然性有足够的了解，但是他们又不肯把这一艰巨的事业仅仅付托给粗笨的无产阶级，因此他们大发慈悲地自己出来领头了。害怕革命，这是他们的基本原则。他们是道地的“有教养的人”。……

除了各种各样的废物，他们尽力出版了一些好的宣传文章，事实上这是英国人在这方面所出版的最好的东西。但是他们一旦回到他们的抹杀阶级斗争的特殊策略，那就糟糕了。他们之所以疯狂地仇恨马克思和我们大家，就是因为我们都主张阶级斗争。[①]

威尔斯并非没有察觉到资本主义的必然灭亡，但他认为可以从专家政治即由专家或少数“开明”人士统治国家的道理中获得拯救。1924 年他访问了苏联，并与斯大林进行了长时间的会晤。在那次著名的会晤中，斯大林驳斥了威尔斯的那些关于乌托邦社会的观点，并阐明了科学社会主义原则的伟大真理。

2.“科学”幻想小说和资产阶级现实主义　威尔斯具有生动活泼的想象力，爱到火星和月球上去旅行，正好像斯威夫特到小人国和大人国去旅行一样。他还喜欢猜测未来事物的形状。《时间机器》(1895) 是他比较著名的幻想小说之一。它叙述一架不是载着乘客穿越空间，而是载着乘客穿越时间的惊人机械装置。叙述者和发明者决意向前进而不是向后退，于是没过多久就发现自己已经处在公元 802,701 年了。他们发现地球上的唯一变化就是少数有闲阶级和劳苦大众之间的阶级区别。据说，其中一个阶级居住在地面上，是一种文雅悠闲、缺乏头脑的人；而另一个阶级则居住在地下，是一种像野

---

① 《马克思恩格斯书信选集》，人民出版社，1962 年，第 505 页。

兽般的吃人的人，当需要时，就从地下居住的地方爬出来，把那些贵族作为牺牲品来吞噬！

然而，威尔斯的长处并不在于他那些幻想的创作，而在于他真实地描写了资产阶级社会。他在许多小说中利用了他自己早年的经历，主要人物是布店职员、中小学校长助理和理科学生。在这类小说中，最为杰出和最受人欢迎的，也许要算《托诺—邦盖》(1909)。这部小说的主题是描写一个商业骗子的兴衰。主人公乔治·彭德里沃讲述了他和他的叔父如何从托诺—邦盖这种毫无医用价值的、假想的滋补药品，获取专利而大发横财的。他们通过广告和宣传获得成功。这部小说描绘了资产阶级社会是如何糟蹋科学，以及资本主义的广告方法又是怎样欺骗人民的。乔治·彭德里沃最后在总结整个骗局时说道："现在已经公开并弄清楚了：我和我的叔父只不过是一种现代强盗的样本而已，以那种完全随心所欲地开办起来的企业来浪费公众的积蓄。"

《托诺—邦盖》以其妙趣横生和雄辩过人而著称。但是，跟威尔斯的大多数小说一样，它"包罗万象"而缺乏艺术上的统一性。这部小说中的人物没有一个是具有生命力的，甚至连主人公亦不例外。

四　乔治·萧伯纳

1. 作为戏剧家和政论家的萧伯纳　乔治·萧伯纳(1856—1950)是个公务员的儿子，虽然出生在爱尔兰，却有出自约克郡的血统。他的童年是在都柏林度过的，青年时期在伦敦当新闻记者，在贫困中挣扎。1882 年他宣称自己是社会主义者，1884 年成为费边社成员，并替该社撰写了《宣言》。之后，他跟西德尼·韦伯和比厄特丽斯·韦伯一起写了《费边文集》(1889)。费边社的思想是萧伯纳所有作品的指导原则。恩格斯曾对费边社的思想进行过批判。

在写了五部没有成功的小说之后，萧伯纳于 1892 年转向戏剧。他在半个世纪中创作了三十多部剧本，其中有些仍然经常搬上舞台。萧伯纳才智过人，他在剧本中反对资本主义社会的贪婪、虚伪和不公正。他讽刺的范围包括宗教、政府、法律、刑罚学、医学、伪科学以及其他许许多多题目。他最重要的戏剧有《华伦夫人的职业》(1894)、《武器与武士》(1894)、《康第达》(1895)、《人与超人》(1903)、《卖花女》(1913)、《伤心之家》(1917)、《苹果车》(1930)。

萧伯纳在经济、政治、伦理、道德和艺术方面写了许多文章。他说："我每写一出剧本，就为费边社会主义作了上百篇演说，并出版了许多大部头书籍。在我的剧本背后，都有一套经过深思熟虑的社会学。"他对当时的问题总是有话可说。1914 年，他因发表了《战争的常识》而在一个时期不受欢迎。这篇文章反对英国政府为英国参加第一次世界大战所进行的辩护。第二次世界大战期间，他作为政论家采取了一种独特的立场，他坚持不懈地撰文反对法西斯主义和帝国主义。

虽然萧伯纳一直到最后都是个费边派，但在列宁和斯大林时代，他却是苏联的朋友。在伟大的十月革命之后的那些年里，他和英国政府的反苏政策进行斗争，提倡"不许干涉苏联"。1931 年，他访问莫斯科，并在那里庆祝了他的七十五岁生日。高尔基由于扁桃腺发炎未能参加他的生日庆祝，但给他写了一封祝贺信。第二次世界大战期间，萧伯纳发电报向苏联人民致敬。他在 1941 年 7 月 17 日写给法捷耶夫的信中说道："当俄国打败希特勒时，她将成为世界的精神中心。"

2.《**华伦夫人的职业**》《华伦夫人的职业》写于1893至1894年，其内容是谈资产阶级社会中的娼妓和买卖妇女的问题。华伦夫人跟富有的乔治·克劳夫茨爵士合伙开办了许多妓院，其中布鲁塞尔有两家，奥斯坦特有一家，维也纳有一家，布达佩斯有两家。华伦夫人的女儿薇薇，在一所道德气氛极浓的寄宿学院里读书，对此事一无所知。毕业后她回到家里，意外发现她母亲所干的那种令人讨厌的职业。薇薇跟克劳夫茨的一席谈话，暴露了有产阶级的那种玩世不恭的态度：

> 薇薇：我母亲原是个很穷的女人，她除了干她那个行当之外别无什么更好的办法。至于你是个有钱的绅士，而你却同样干这个行当，就是为了百分之三十五的利润。我认为你是个相当庸俗的恶棍。这就是我对你的看法。
>
> 克劳夫茨：哈！哈！哈！哈！讲下去呀，小姐，讲下去呀！我并不难过，但你倒可感到有趣。我为什么不该那样投资？我也跟其他人一样，放款收息嘛！我希望你别以为我干这一行会弄脏我的手。得啦！你总不会由于我母亲的表哥贝尔格拉维阿公爵有些房租来路不明而拒绝跟他结识吧。我想，你总不会由于教区委员会委员的租户中，有几个是客栈老板和犯过罪的人而跟坎特伯雷大主教断绝关系吧……而你想要我在所有其他人都在乖巧地、拼命地捞钱的时候放弃这百分之三十五的利润？天下没有这样的笨蛋！如果你想要根据道德原则去挑选朋友，你最好离开这个国家，除非你能跟整个体面的社会断绝关系。

这部剧是对英国资产阶级剥削和统治阶级不道德的一种强烈

抗议。剧本提出了一个严肃的社会问题，并对它进行了充分的讨论，但并没有提出任何解决的办法。该剧结束时，萧伯纳那个女主人公薇薇干脆抛弃了她的母亲，想通过诚实的工作谋生。华伦夫人被丢在那里，尖声叫道："但愿上帝保佑，如果每个人都是真的在干正当的事情！"

《华伦夫人的职业》是在萧伯纳的第一部戏剧集，即《愉快和不愉快的戏剧集》(1898)中发表的。1926年以前，此戏被认为有伤风化，因此英国检查官禁止它的演出，然而，在20世纪初期，此戏却在其他国家上演了。

3.《武器和武士》《华伦夫人的职业》是一出不愉快的戏，看了让人心里有股不好受的滋味，至于《武器和武士》，那是一出愉快的戏，令人感到有趣、发笑。

跟易卜生一样，萧伯纳是个提倡打破传统观念的人，是资产阶级社会的那种虚假理想和廉价感情的敌人。《武器和武士》本是拿来讽刺坎布里奇公爵统率下的英国军队的。19世纪末，英帝国主义的鼓吹者吉卜林在他所写的诗歌和短篇小说中，重新给"军官兼绅士"这样的民族形象涂上了新的迷人色彩。萧伯纳以深刻的幽默说明：迷人的"军官兼绅士"，即那些出身于高贵门第经过乔装打扮的武士，除了对敌人之外，对于每个人都有危险。

《武器和武士》描述了两类兵士。一类兵士如塞琪厄斯，浮夸造作，萧伯纳把他看作是资产阶级社会的摆设；另一类兵士如布伦奇利上尉，不是一个舞台上的传统角色。"他缺睡少吃，遭到三天炮击，灵魂就吓出了窍，害怕吃败仗，被敌人追击。他凭经验发现，搞几块巧克力带到战场上去吃，要比替他的左轮手枪搞些子弹更为重要。"他坦率地说："子弹在打仗时有什么用处？相反，我总是随身带着巧克力。"然而，他要胜过那个浮夸造作的军官。

在这出戏中，萧伯纳还讽刺了他所谓的那种女学生对爱情的想法，即浪漫主义的爱情——例如迷恋于"高贵的态度和动人的声音"。吃巧克力的士兵正因为不理会那位浪漫年轻小姐的"高贵的态度和动人的声音"而赢得了她的崇拜。

《武器和武士》以保加利亚为背景，人物都是保加利亚人和瑞士人。但是，人们知道作者的意图。人们对这个剧本抱有强烈的偏见，不是反对它的写作方法，而是反对它的内容。因为这个剧本取笑了英国军队，并取笑了多年来人们长期对浪漫主义爱情所怀有的理想。

4. 《苹果车》 《苹果车》的副题是《政治狂想剧》。它揭露了资产阶级民主的危机。首相普罗梯厄斯及其内阁企图迫使国王马格纳斯接受一项最后通牒，把君王降为无关紧要的人物。但国王回答说，他与其做一个区区小人物，还不如放弃王位去进行"民主"投票，自己担任首相。于是苹果车被打翻了(意即计划被破坏了)，最后通牒无效了。

正如萧伯纳在剧本前言中指出的，这并非是真正王权和民主之间的冲突，而是民主和王权的一方同财阀统治的另一方之间的冲突，因为财阀统治已经收买和并吞了民主。"金钱会讲话，金钱会出版刊物，金钱会广播，金钱会支配一切，而国王和劳工领袖同样不得不体现金钱的意志，甚至根据一种令人惊愕的悖论，他们不能不用金钱资助所办的企业，以保证金钱所应获得的利润。"

这部戏生动地描绘了资产阶级政客之间所进行的权力斗争。萧伯纳以其异乎寻常的洞察力，揭露了那些工党成员理应维护工人阶级，但实际上都是些滑头政客，他们知道如何保持舒适的工作，并尽可能从国家那盘馅饼中捞到一点东西。下面就是内阁中那个工党大臣所说的话：

就职业而说，世上没有哪个国王要比工会职员更加保险了。只有一件事情能把他解雇，这就是喝酒。但他只要不跌倒，甚至喝酒也不能把他解雇。我对这些男男女女大谈民主。我告诉他们说，他们手中有选票，又说王国、权力和荣耀都是他们的。我对他们说："你们是至高无上的，行使你们的权力吧。"他们说："对，告诉我们怎么办？"我告诉了他们。我说："你们投票选我，这就是明智地行使你们的选举权。"他们就照办了。这就是民主；并且，把适当的人安置在适当的位置上，这是件了不起的事呀。

萧伯纳在这出戏里提到了英美之间的尖锐矛盾。美国大使范奈登先生鉴于英国长期以来一直受到美国垄断资本的影响，向国王马格纳斯提出成立英美政治联盟：

哦，我们发现这里的每样东西都是我们熟悉的：我们的工业品、我们的书、我们的戏剧、我们的体育运动、我们的基督科学教堂、我们的整骨术、我们的电影和有声电影，等等。简而言之，这就是我们的东西和我们的思想。跟我们结成联盟，那只不过是对既成的事实予以官方承认罢了。你可以管它叫作心心相印。

5. 萧伯纳作为批判现实主义的作家　萧伯纳是"为艺术而艺术"流派的死敌。跟为逃避现实而写作的唯美主义者和颓废主义者不同，萧伯纳竭力抓住当时的经济、社会和政治问题。他的戏剧是问题戏剧，或像他所说的，是“进行辩论的戏剧”—— 即对经济、社会和政治问题进行讨论的戏剧。他对社会改革充满热情。他说：“在社会得到改革之前，任何人除了在那些无关紧要、鸡毛蒜皮的方面外，是无法改造自己的。”

然而，作为一个费边社成员和唯心主义者，萧伯纳具有很大的局限性。他赞成的是逐步改革而不是革命。他厌恶暴力。他曾有这样的幻想：资本主义的罪恶是可以通过许多小改革来根除的，而公有制和社会主义会逐步到来。他的戏剧和文章对资本主义制度下的许多社会弊端加以剖析，但提不出什么办法，而且他所提出的办法往往使人误入歧途。在他的错误思想中有一种他称之为“生命的力量”，据说这种生命的力量将女子比男子更强烈地引向生殖——就是说，婚姻“是以虚假的理想作为诱饵来捕捉男子的陷阱”（《人与超人》，等等）。

萧伯纳的长处在于他无情地揭露英国社会。他揭露帝国主义英国的邪恶和弊端，坚决地、不遗余力地跟那些到处可见的不公正和不人道作斗争。他最好的剧本是那些进行揭露的剧本，但就是在他较为逊色的剧本里也具有赤裸裸地进行现实主义描写的场景。“英国社会出了什么毛病？”——这是他一再提出的问题。他从许多角度，以那种在当代英国无与伦比的智慧对它进行讨论。高尔基在 1931 年 7 月 28 日给萧伯纳的信中称他为“勇敢的斗士，具有天赋的人”。高尔基又说：“你活了四分之三个世纪，你机敏的智慧给人类的保守和平庸以多少次惊人的打击。”

作为一个作家，萧伯纳有他自己的风格。他那种嘲讽和蔑视到处可以感到。他的笔调尖锐透辟，剧本中充满华丽的偶句和来源众多的实例。萧伯纳在精神上和《众生之道》的作者塞缪尔·勃特勒相似，人们也常拿他跟英国最伟大的讽刺作家乔纳森·斯威夫特作比较。

范存忠文集

英国文学史纲
A BRIEF HISTORY OF ENGLISH LITERATURE

中西文化散论
ESSAYS ON CHINESE AND WESTERN CULTURE

英美史纲
AN OUTLINE OF BRITISH AND AMERICAN HISTORY

中国文化在英国
CHINESE CULTURE IN ENGLAND

英国文学论集
ESSAYS ON ENGLISH LITERATURE